HOW TO GET ANY JOB

(OR HOW TO AVOID LIVING IN YOUR PARENTS' BASEMENT)

LIFE LAUNCH & RELAUNCH FOR EVERYONE UNDER 30

DONALD ASHER

TEN SPEED PRESS
Berkeley

For Danaelle and Nora

Published in the United States by Ten Speed Press, an imprint of the Crown Publishing Group, a division of Random House, Inc., New York.
www.crownpublishing.com
www.tenspeed.com

Ten Speed Press and the Ten Speed Press colophon are registered trademarks of Random House, Inc.

Library of Congress Cataloging-in-Publication Data
Asher, Donald.
  How to get any job: life launch & re-launch for everyone under 30,
(or how to avoid living in your parents' basement) / Donald Asher.
      p. cm.
  Rev. ed. of: How to get any job with any major : career launch &
re-launch for everyone under 30, or, how to avoid living in your
parent's basement. 2004.
  Includes bibliographical references and index.
  1. Job hunting. 2. Success in business. 3. Career development. I.
Asher, Donald. How to get any job with any major. II. Title.
  HF5382.7.A839 2009
  650.14—dc22
                              2009012096

ISBN 978–1–58008–947–0
Printed in Canada

10 9 8 7 6 5 4 3 2 1
Second Edition

Acknowledgments

I am indebted to every career center staff member who has ever advised me and shared resources and tips and techniques with me over the years, and this is literally hundreds of dedicated professionals. At the risk of omitting major contributors, and there have been so many, let me call particular attention to my debt to Dr. Robert Greenberg, NACE Fellow and former director of career services at the University of Tennessee, and founder of the Professional Development Series sponsored by the University of Tennessee and used by career centers nationwide; Russ Coughenour, current director at Tennessee, who is carrying on the fine tradition; Alan D. Ferrell, director of executive education at the Krannert School of Management, Purdue University; Midge Browning, director of academic and career advising at Principia College (and the one who first called my attention to the fact that the current generation does not identify with the word "career") and her colleague James Brandt; Tom Francis, formerly director of career services at Swarthmore College, and an early influence; renowned educational consultant Dr. Howard Figler; Julie Kern Smith with the career center at Reed College; Anne Hardin Ballard, director of the career center at Linfield College; Bob Fisher, managing director, National Education Empowerment Foundation, Inc., at www.collegecareerlifeplanning.com, who provided valuable criticism of the first edition and improved this book; Dr. Orlando Taylor, dean of the graduate school at Howard University, on general principal; and Denise Rhiner, my long-time research assistant. I also want to express my appreciation to Louise Paradis at Portland State University for material she shared with me from her excellent career development game. Veronica, Chris, Michael, Kirsty, Lorena, and Phil, you know who you are, and I want you to know I appreciate all you've done for me on this book and on all the others. And I will forever be grateful to my mother, Dr. Ruby Ausbrooks, a colleague and an inspiration; Dr. Judy Jones, my mentor for decades; and Lisa Bertschi, my astoundingly wonderful wife.

CONTENTS

PART 1
You Need to Reconsider Everything You Know about Your Employment Interests

1	Life Planning versus Getting a Job	3
2	Yes, It's All about You	20
3	What Gets You Excited? Your Top Five Issues in This World	31
4	A Little Future Visioneering	43
5	Advanced Issues in Life Planning: More than Enough Ideas	53
6	A Different Kind of Choice	74

PART 2
Finding Out about Your Interests in the Real World

7	Prepare to Learn More	85
8	Are You Ready for Networking?	93
9	Volunteer and Internship Opportunities	107
10	Summer Jobs, and "The Most Important Summer of Your Life"	119
11	More Education	134
12	How about High-Risk Choices?	143

PART 3
Now It's Time to Actually Get a Job

	CASE STUDY: How I Got My First Job	158
13	Start with a Job Target	161
14	Visualize the Job You Want	171
15	Troubleshooting Your Job Search	184
16	The Job Interview	203
	In Conclusion	227
	Index	229
	About the Author	234

You Need to Reconsider Everything You Know about Your Employment Interests

PART 1

Choose a job you love and you will

never have to work a day in your life.

—Confucius

Life Planning versus Getting a Job

Most college students want a job when what they should really want is a little life planning. What is life planning? Life planning is conducting a process of self-discovery and then matching what is discovered with the career marketplace.

Life planning is different from getting a job. Getting a job is a process of finding paid employment, whether or not there is any match whatsoever between the employee's skills, preparation, interests, or long-term goals, plus whatever is involved in performing on the job. Getting a job is a good end product to life planning, but is not an end in itself. It is, to put it simply, not the point. The point is the self-discovery and the matching.

College students have no special claim on this. A thirty-year-old, single working mother has the same opportunity to choose to get another job or choose to go through a bit of life planning. So has a fifty-year-old college professor considering leaving his tenured position. So has a sales executive with a Fortune 500 company. But college students have a unique opportunity to do this right. You have the opportunity to do this right at a juncture that can lead to a lifetime of increased happiness.

Some of the mid-career executives I work with in my career coaching practice are miserable. I am struck by what a high price poor early career decisions can have. Employment is a huge part of adult life. Between the end of college and the onset of retirement, a career takes up about 100,000 hours of our lives. That's a lot of time to be miserable. And that's not counting commuting. You will not spend that much time with your kids, should you choose to have them, or with a spouse, should you choose to have one. A job doesn't have to be the most meaningful thing in your life. Perhaps your family or your religion or your volunteer or community work will be more important to you, but nothing is likely to be bigger in terms of sheer volume of time. It is a tragedy, of Shakespearean proportion, to be miserable on the job.

On the other hand, if you find jobs you love, you'll never work a day in your life. You'll notice I wrote "jobs" in the plural. You will need to find many jobs after college.

Your Future as a Worker

According to conventional wisdom, you will need to find more than nine jobs between college and retirement. I think this is inaccurate. In fact, I believe the generation leaving college now is going to need to find some twenty to thirty jobs before retirement. The old projections were exactly that—projections of the future based on the past—assuming the future is like the past. But the future of this generation of students is different than the future of prior generations. The covenant between employers and employees has been broken. Back in the day, a white-collar worker had a job until she retired. In actual fact, that often didn't happen. But it was the operative theory. This is no longer the operative theory. A company's covenant now with its employees goes something like this: "If our needs mutually converge, great! If they don't, see ya!"

This fact changes the way *all* workers should approach their work life. You have to be ready *all the time* to find a new job.

Let me be clear about what I'm telling you: **You will be fired through no fault of your own during your work life.** You will go to work one day and find that you or your department or your office or even your entire company is no longer in business, and suddenly you need a new job. You may see it coming or you may not, but you can't say you weren't warned.

Not only will you need to find many jobs over your working lifetime, you will also pass through periods of self-employment and portfolio employment. Self-employment includes, obviously, those times when a careerist launches an entrepreneurial endeavor. But it also includes millions of workers who cannot find a job and are forced to let their services out on a contract basis, catching an assignment here, a project there, to get through a tight spot in a specific industry or local economy.

Portfolio employment is both old and new. The idea of portfolio employment goes back to the days of craftsmen's guilds, when a worker had a skill that was so valued he could set the terms of engagement with an employer or a series of simultaneous employers. The worker was like a little factory, free to trade with many buyers.

Now it means someone who has several revenue streams instead of a job. The worker becomes like a little company, with more than one customer and perhaps more than one product line. There'll be more discussion of this later in the book.

Job change may come up some twenty or thirty times for you, but other major career shifts are also on your horizon. It's one thing to find another job that you like better than the last, but it's another thing entirely to find a new career that you like better than the last. I haven't been able to find any usable research on this topic, but it seems to me that most people have at least two distinct careers, and some have five or more.

The problem with this topic is it is very hard to define a career. Does a nurse who goes to medical school and becomes a doctor have a new career, or is he just continuing with his career in health care? Does a real estate agent who becomes a developer have a new career, or is she just continuing with her interest in providing housing for families? It can be argued either way.

My observation of real people with real work lives is that most people have major shifts somewhere in their futures. I know a college professor who turned his hobby into a multimillion-dollar business. I know a soldier who became an engineer who became a real estate magnate. I know a warehouse worker who went back to college and became a high school principal. And so on.

Big Changes Are in Your Future

And you can make mistakes in your work life. In fact, feel free to make mistakes. One of things I love most about this country is that it is the land of second chances. You can fix a bad work situation anytime. In America you are not sentenced to pursue the choices that your mother or father pursued. Your family name or tribe or clan or caste does not determine your career. Your major in college does not determine what you get to do for the rest of your life. If your job or your field is no longer attractive to you, you can go in a new direction. You are in charge.

What does this have to do with life planning and getting a job? Every single time you change jobs, you have a choice: to go get another job or to do real life planning. In fact, you have a much greater chance to be happy with your work life today than in prior generations, because you have a far greater number of opportunities to change your employment situation. Every transition is an opportunity to seek employment more meaningful, more fun, more rewarding, and more to your liking.

Change Is Good

One thing should be clear: It is not acceptable to fail to learn how to do life planning. It's not something that you do once, right out of college, and then don't worry about again. It's truly a life skill, something that you need to know how to do in order to succeed in your life. Don't skip this class.

Your first task is to unlearn what you know about the relationship between college and work.

The Relationship between College and Work

This is a book about getting jobs out of college, not about choosing a major. If you want to know more about choosing a major, see *College Majors Handbook* by Neeta Fogg, Paul Harrington, and Tom Harrington, which is an outstanding study of majors and career outcomes, and *The Undecided College Student* by Virginia Gordon, which is written for advisors. Choosing a major is a big deal, but I am going to assume you've already chosen it and the only issue now is launching a successful life after college. Let's think about the link between major and employment and long-term life success.

How did you pick your major? Because you loved the subject, or because you thought it would help you get a job after college, or to please your parents, or some combination of the above?

We often go to college for the wrong reasons, and then compound the error when we try to launch a life afterward. To put it plainly, those who go to school *primarily* in order to get a job are often poorly served by doing so. They are ill-served during the college experience itself *and* ill-prepared for the employment marketplace afterward. Don't worry if you are starting to worry if this is you; it can be fixed. But let's review how this can happen.

Students may choose a major in order to have the career that they believe goes with that major. For example, they decide to become a chemical engineering major because they heard somewhere that chemical engineering majors are the highest paid upon graduation from college or university. Or they take premed classes because they think it will increase their chances of getting into medical school. Or they take engineering because their parents want them to become engineers and, their parents believe, there are always plenty of high-paying jobs for engineers. Or they pursue accounting or nursing because they think they want to be accountants or nurses.

In short, they are choosing majors because of the career outcomes of those majors, not because of any inherent desire to learn those subjects.

The problem is that these decisions are made at age eighteen or nineteen, often without any career advice at all or with advice of the very worst sort. For illustration purposes, let's examine some of the hidden biases in the above choices. For example, it is true that chemical engineering consistently draws top salary offers, but that would be irrelevant if you didn't like chemical engineering or couldn't succeed at it. It is not true that choosing a premed major makes you more likely to get into medical school; as long as you do well in the prerequisite courses, you can major in anything. It is not true that there are always plenty of jobs for engineers, either. It is true that majoring in nursing or accounting prepares you for careers in nursing or accounting, but it is equally true that majoring in nursing or accounting can lead to many other careers.

Question: What do these five college graduates have in common?

Bank officer

Stock market analyst

Music therapist

Director of a senior citizens' center

Field archaeologist

Answer: They were all French majors at the same college.[1]

Can philosophy and English majors survive on Wall Street? Of course! According to two major studies on the topic, liberal arts majors get promoted faster and tend to rise higher on the organizational charts than engineering and business majors hired at the same organization at the same time.[2]

This is not to say that your major has no impact on your earnings; it does, but other studies show that hours worked, gender, attainment of advanced degrees, being taller than average in high school, if male, and being more attractive than average—but not drop-dead gorgeous—are influences on earnings. But no one is suggesting that you change your gender or become taller in high school if that is not your nature.

All types of companies hire all types of majors. Even in high-tech companies, one quarter of the people employed do not have technical degrees. (If you want to know more about this, read William A. Schaffer's *High-Tech Careers for Low-Tech People.*) And as it turns out, music is not an uncommon major among computer programmers. Einstein studied music passionately, in addition to physics. Writing well, which is something one learns to do in an English lit program, is in such demand in all types of organizations that it is considered a key to management advancement. According to research monitored by Dr. Howard Figler, a consultant to university career centers, between 40 and 60 percent of all CEOs majored in the liberal arts as undergraduates. They would presumably have majored in such things as philosophy, music, and English literature before going on to become scions of business. These data may be influenced by issues related to class as well as choice of major, yet the inference can be made that future CEOs can start with any major.

> I am appalled, even horrified, that you have adopted Classics as a major. As a
> matter of fact, I almost puked on the way home today. I am a practical man,
> and for the life of me I cannot possibly understand why you should wish to
> speak Greek.
>
> —*From a letter from Ed Turner to his son, Ted.*[3]

There is an old saying in career counseling: Your major may help you get a job in the first place, but it is your education that helps you get promoted. I will go further and say that an undergraduate curriculum can best provide an education, while graduate school can best provide specialization. Continuing your education past the baccalaureate level is actually a much bigger influence on earnings than your choice of an undergraduate major. More than half the workers in America have been to college,[4] so it's just not that powerful a ticket, all by itself. Of course, if you are only interested in money, skip college and become a longshoreman. They earn an average of $107,000 per year in West Coast ports, and a foreman can bring in $167,000.[5]

Although it is true that all art majors earn less than all engineering majors, it is not true that you as an art major would learn less than you as an engineering major. Here's a truism for you: Individuation will always exceed group norms. One of the most successful business people I know was an art major, and his company sells products you can buy in any hardware store in the country.

Further, when students pick majors based on career outcomes, they sometimes pick majors they don't really enjoy. Sometimes this is true *even if they would have enjoyed the career associated with the major.* As just one example, a lot of premed majors would make excellent doctors, but get turned off by years of laboratory sciences that have little relevance to the curriculum or clinical training provided in medical school. Or they blow their GPAs studying subjects that aren't really required for success in medical school, and then can't get in because of a tarnished record.

However, this is not an invitation to change your major if you're on track to graduate. If you're looking down that short tunnel to commencement, don't endanger that. *Get the job done and graduate on time.* But more importantly, *don't compound a poor choice of major with a poor choice of career direction.*

Here is the biggest secret in life planning: **You can get any job with any major.**

I don't mean that all majors prepare you for all jobs equally well, but I do mean that at the juncture of college graduation, no job is inherently sealed off to you simply and solely because of your major.

For example, I don't mean to imply that it is easy to get a job in accounting if you've never taken a class in accounting, but it is not at all out of the question. It is entirely possible if you want it. I knew a college student who was a marketing major, who got a temp job with an accounting firm the summer before graduation. He helped out with some accounting and found out he liked it. He didn't change his major, but he did stay in contact with the firm during his senior year. Upon graduation they hired him, and after a few night classes, he's an accountant today.

Let me be doubly clear in my purpose of discussing the relationship between majors and possible job choices: I don't want you to abandon your major or doubt the wisdom of your choice. *I want you to abandon the limitations you have put on yourself.*

You cannot do real life planning while you are accepting a preordained conclusion. Most people receive tons of career advice and influence from family, friends, neighbors, faculty, and the media that simply don't hold up under scrutiny. Chance, inclination, and extra hard work are far more important in the long run than your major—or even your GPA or whether you were a tall male in high school.

Let's consider what employers themselves say they want in their new hires. According to a survey of corporate recruiters by the National Association of Colleges and Employers, here are the top characteristics of new hires in order of importance:

- Communication skills
- Strong work ethic
- Teamwork skills
- Initiative
- Interpersonal skills
- Problem-solving skills
- Analytical skills
- Flexibility/adaptability
- Computer skills
- Technical skills
- Detail-oriented
- Organizational skills

You'll notice that any student with any major could easily possess all of these attributes. We'll address what kind of computer skills employers want in a later section, but suffice it to say that the typical college student possesses most of them.

Some majors are obviously preparatory for a particular type of career, for example, elementary education. You can predict that a student pursuing this major plans to start her career as an elementary school teacher. In practice, however, careers change and evolve from the initial post-college job in ways that are simply not that predictable, even for those students who have a clear starting point.

By investigating real people and actual employment patterns, you will see how this works:

- Comedian Stephen Colbert was a philosophy major.

- Young MC, music mogul, was an economics major.

- Chad Hurley, founder of YouTube, was an art major.

- Basketball star Michael Jordan was a geography major.

- Alan Greenspan, former chairman of the Federal Reserve Board, started out as a music major.

- Comedian Jon Stewart was a psychology major.

- Actress Lisa Kudrow was a biology major.

- Scott Adams, creator of the *Dilbert* comic strip, was an economics major.

- Carly Fiorina, former CEO of Hewlett-Packard, was a philosophy major.

- Arnold Schwarzenegger, former Mr. Universe, film star, and now governor of California, was an economics major.

- Comedian and late night talk show host Jay Leno was a philosophy major.

- George W. Bush, former president of the United States, was a history major and is famous for saying this: "To the C students, I say, 'You, too, can be president of the United States.'"

In any case, I think you must agree by now that your major doesn't determine the first job you should seek after college.

Uncertainty Is a Good Thing

When a student is not sure of her specific job interests, that's a good sign. That's a good position to be in to start life planning work. That's a student who can have fun with the process, do self-discovery openly and honestly, and accept some of the findings without being overly cynical about them. So if you are uncertain, that's great! That's what this process is designed to resolve. You're in good company, as most students are like that, with a few interests but also a lot of divergent ideas about career direction.

There are two types of students that make career counselors really nervous: the absolutely clueless and the absolutely certain. Clueless students haven't given any thought at all to a future work life. They have willfully ignored the question. That's okay, but sooner or later it's going to come up, and then it will have to be addressed. At the other end of the spectrum, students who are absolutely certain about their career choice are equally frightening. Let's examine the second type first.

When a student tells me that she has "always wanted to be a lawyer" or "always wanted to be a doctor," alarm bells go off in my mind. This is often an ambitious student who made this decision at a very early age, perhaps as early as eight or nine years old. A parent may latch onto this early interest and reinforce it at every stage. They tell all their friends, "Jane is going to be a lawyer some day, and then a senator, and then president of the United States of America." This is not always good for Jane.

There is nothing wrong with having an employment idea at this age, but it needs to be retested and reconsidered as the young person develops and evolves.

So if you have "always wanted to be an endocrinologist," I am not asking you to abandon that goal. I am only asking you to go through the process and reaffirm that goal, using work life planning techniques, and to consider other options in case you (a) discover you're not as interested in medicine as you learn more about the profession and your personality grows and develops, or (b) discover pediatrics or radiology or audiology are more to your liking after all, or (c) discover that, by reason of your grades or your Medical College Admission Test (MCAT) scores or your recommendations or your ability to write a captivating essay in 950 words or fewer, this goal is sealed off from you.

When a student has a long-held goal, perhaps to be a novelist or a comedian or president of the United States, this is certainly useful for life planning. What is not useful is when she refuses to investigate that interest and refuses to consider other options (if for no other reason than to discard them and reaffirm the original interest).

So, if you have "always" wanted to be a research scientist, or whatever, that is when you are most in need of participating in this process with an open mind. Don't be afraid to put your interest to the test. And be careful to listen for your own voice in the process—not someone else's (your mother's or society's, just for examples).

Some of the worst career advice comes from well-meaning parents and family members. Where can you get good employment advice? From yourself. Your mother and your father and your uncle are not going to have your career. You are. So try to think about what you want out of it. We'll talk more about this later.

First, let's consider the student at the other end of the spectrum who has no idea at all about his job interests. He is the bane of career counselors everywhere. He may suffer from magical thinking: "This will all work out, somehow." He isn't particularly worried about it. Often, this type of student can just decide to address the issue and he's fine. Once he decides to consider life and employment planning, he participates in the process and recovers from his prior lack of attention to the issue.

Some students simply don't think about what is involved in planning for life after college. On every campus in the country, career counselors trade stories about students who walk in for the very first time, a month or two before graduation, or a month or two after graduation, and demand to see the "List" of jobs available for graduating seniors.

There is no such List.

Again, life planning is a process of self-discovery, followed by matching the findings from the process to the actual career marketplace.

> Give a man a fish and you feed him for a day. Teach a man to fish and you feed him for a lifetime.
>
> —*Chinese proverb*

Just as a little career counseling history: Back in the day, a career development center was called a Placement Office. Students were "placed" by a career professional. In this model, the student was a passive participant. The career professional did the assessment and the matching, and the student did as she was told. Those days are over, in large part because they did not serve the interests of the students. Students who are placed like this do not learn how to manage their own employment, and this deficiency becomes readily apparent at the first transition after placement. By the way, the tenure for college graduates in their first job is less than four years, so this comes up pretty quickly.

The placement model was abandoned; the College Placement Council, the organization that serves career center professionals, became the National Association of Colleges and Employers, and the Placement Office on most campuses became the Career Development Center or something similar.

There is some tension between parents and older administrators who themselves grew up with the placement model, and the new career professionals who employ what is called the *career education model* or the *career development model*. If your parents are mad at your college or university for not handing you a job, it is because they don't understand how a contemporary career center works. **It is your job to get a job**, and the career center is there only to help you do a good job of it.

A good friend of mine, Victoria Ball, who was at the time director of the career center at an Ivy League university, received a call from a parent in late June demanding to know why her son had not gotten a job after "that expensive Ivy League education." Ms. Ball had installed a turnstile gate to the career center that required a swipe from a student ID card to get in. She also had portable card readers for recruiting and guest speaker events. Her data capture system recorded every interaction with every student served. She was able to punch up the undergrad in question on her computer screen and ask, "Your son hasn't darkened our door in four years. Why don't you ask *him* why he doesn't have a job yet?"

Don't embarrass your parents by having them make a call like this.

Is It Possible to Be Too Open?

One of the greatest challenges in career counseling is the student who is "open to anything," as in the following exchange:

"What kind of a job would interest you?"

"I dunno. Anything."

Just for the record, it is not just undergrads who do this. I was at a top-ten MBA program recently and asked a first-year student what kind of job he was going to be seeking. He actually said, "I dunno. Anything. I guess I'll just wait to see what offers come in and then pick the one that pays the most."

Wow! This is willful ignorance on a grand scale. Guess what? The top MBA program you're enrolled in has no List either.

Again, this is not a problem if the student has just not yet considered life after graduation. In other words, if this type of student participates actively in life planning, then "No harm, no foul." He can recover, learn how this works, and succeed.

However, there is a final subcategory of student who is more dangerously clueless, and this is the one who insists on remaining clueless. He is in a slightly bigger pickle. He refuses to rise to his own assistance. If a student has no job goals and insists on hanging on to his position, then there is a train wreck in his future.

When a student is clueless and insists on embracing his cluelessness, there may be several reasons for this. One may be that he has not yet learned to live his own life—to "own" his own life. He is living his life either for or against his parents or some other authority figure. If he is living his life for this figure, he will embrace the decision he is offered and refuse to consider any evidence that it is possibly a less-than-stellar plan. This happens when someone embraces a career direction that they have no talent for, interest in, or likelihood of attaining. He is cluelessly committed to the unattainable. If he is living his life against a parental figure, then he will willfully choose to fail, secretly desiring either attention or to teach the parent a lesson for his or her over- or under-involvement. This is called disengagement. In either case, the problem is surmountable.

If you think this is you, I suggest you realize that you are in charge right now. Living your life for or against the dictates of a parental or other societal authority figure is actually a waste of your time. Seek some intervention if you cannot shake off this mindset.

Finally, those students who for any reason do not work on life goals before graduation will have ample opportunity to do so after graduation. This issue will not go away, and if you prefer, you can work on it later while living in your parents' basement.

Sometimes this is the right choice. If you're a senior overwhelmed by a heavy schoolwork load, or you have a major project due a month before graduation, or you have to work nights to pay your way through college, it is not necessarily a wrong-minded choice to put this off until the day after graduation. You are not superhuman, and there really are limits to how much you can get done during the school year.

CASE STUDY Getting a Job—Julie L.

Julie L. was described by her career center director as "a perfect candidate" who did all the right things. She had internships and appropriate volunteer experiences. She took leadership roles on campus. She studied hard to make good grades. This is her story of how she got her first full-time job after college. Note the combination of luck and hard work. Julie's experiences prove the old saying, "The harder I work, the luckier I get!" Interview with Julie:

"It all goes back to before college even started. In high school I really liked being a camp counselor, so I did that again after my freshman year. Then I realized it was important to take jobs and participate in activities that could apply to my future career. I sure didn't want to be a camp counselor after college!

"My first move was to volunteer to plan a reunion for my sorority, ZTA. Only about twenty people had been showing up for reunions, but I had bigger ideas. I made a website, recruited an advisory panel, created some 'big draw' events, a casino night, a tour of the Bush Presidential Library, and a wine tasting tour—and 350 people came! It was a lot of work, but I met 350 Zetas who were powerful and well connected. The relationships I made as a result of this event became the primary anchor of my career network.

"The other anchor was that I was an Aggie (Texas A&M University student). The A&M connection is just really strong. If you're wearing an Aggie ring, you're going to get the benefit of the doubt from any other Aggie. All students have a built-in network with alumni, I guess.

"After my success with the reunion, I decided to try to learn more about event planning. As an officer of the Liberal Arts Student Council, I was automatically on the Career Center Advisory Board. I mentioned my interest in event planning at a meeting, and a staff member wrote a woman's name on the back of his business card. It was a large trade show company out of Irving, Texas. I looked up their website. The next day I called her and left a voice mail, and I shot her an email with my resume and mentioned that I was referred by the career center, that I was secretary of my college, and threw in some details about the reunion I had planned. I found out later, she was most impressed by the fact I had done a return-on-investment analysis of our promotional expenditures. I just threw that in at the last minute, but it was what caught her eye.

"She shot me an email back saying she was going to be on campus the next week. I met her in my suit. I was a junior, and I was nervous, but I had looked up quite a bit of information on the company. I knew what they did, about their events, their clients, and I was able to relate what she did to what I had done, on a smaller scale of course. I got an internship offer. It was only $15 an hour, but it was great experience. That summer I wrote press releases and had some articles published. I met an editor at the company who was a Zeta. She let me write a special-interest piece on geeks playing music at trade shows: 'Heart of Rock 'n' Roll Beating in Tech Industry.' This became another addition to my portfolio.

"I wrote articles for them all through the following school year, and did promotions work for events on the East Coast. This added up to journalism, promotions, and marketing experience, all originating from that $15-an-hour internship. The company offered me a job after graduation, but I would have had to start in sales. That didn't seem to be a match to me, so I began to look around. Time was running out for me to come up with an option.

"Spring semester of my senior year I was taking a media writing class, and the professor referred me to the public information officer for the city of Bryan (Texas). I called the PIO and asked for an internship, or at least some assignments. He said he couldn't pay me, but he could let me write some press releases. The PIO taught me a lot by helping me build my portfolio, even though I was working for free! I also picked up a media consulting assignment in Austin during city council elections.

"Meanwhile, a Zeta connection mentioned that a man from her church was looking for a legal assistant at his law firm. I thought it sounded interesting, but she didn't remember his name. So I had to email her repeatedly to get his contact info. Finally, she forwarded his name and email address. I sent him an email and attached two writing samples. He wrote back that my Zeta contact was very well respected, so I came highly recommended. He asked me to write in two hundred words why I thought this job would be good for me. I love to write, so I did it overnight. Two hundred words exactly, in case he was counting. 'Great sample,' he said, and I was invited for an interview.

"I was offered the job during the interview. I called my parents and said, 'I got a job! I got a job!' I was so excited!

"That's how I got my first real career job."

CASE STUDY Getting the Right Job—Julie L.

"At least I thought it was a real career job. I was told I would get to do corporate communications, work on the firm newsletter, and communicate with clients. I told them I was interested in lobbying, and that I'd worked with many VIPs and big-name donors through ZTA and my term as Liberal Arts Student Council president. They seemed to be quite responsive to these interests. They told me I could work with one of their lobbyists who was working on [a special interest issue].

"But that's not what happened. I graduated, I moved to Houston, and right away I knew I was in trouble. They wanted me to sit at a front desk, look pretty, and transcribe dictation for eight hours a day. I tried to just do it, but I could feel myself losing brain cells every day. This job didn't even require a college degree! I knew I would have to start at the bottom, but I knew there had to be more to it. So I sat down with my boss and told him, 'I can do more than this.' I reminded him that I had been president of an organization serving 6,500 students, that I had been writing official communications for the city of Bryan and for a political campaign in Austin, that I had a college degree from a challenging program, and that I had served on policy-developing committees.

"He said I'd have to stick it out for a year. 'It'll take a year for you to grow into this position,' were his exact words.

"I was so mad at myself for taking that job. It was so frustrating, because you want to have faith in people, but they were clearly not going to honor their promises to me. I even had a job description with those promises on it, which they completely ignored. So disappointing. And scary. I was on my own, responsible for my own bills. It's so easy in college, because everything is temporary. If you don't like something, you don't have to worry. It's over soon enough. But in a job, that's not the case. If you need change, you have to create it. You just have to put in a leap of faith and know that you'll find something, find where you need to be. So I gave my notice. I can't believe it, but they were totally shocked. What did they think would happen?

I gave them a chance to do something to spice up the job, but they literally wanted me to do data entry for a year first. And sit out front and look pretty.

"I immediately alerted everyone on my network that I was on the market in an emergency sort of way. I was on the phone on every break and sending out emails all night. It was quite a production.

"A friend of mine back at school was very involved in College Republicans. I emailed him about my interest in lobbying and politics and explained the problem with my current job. He forwarded my email to [a friend of his], who was working on a congressional campaign. [The candidate] himself called me, and we talked politics. He wanted to know if I was conservative, what I had done in the past, what I wanted out of a job. I just told him what I thought, like he was anybody else. I guess he liked what he heard, because he set up a phone interview with his campaign manager for the next day.

"Then I met with the campaign manager and [the candidate] in Houston. The campaign was in full swing, and they needed a scheduler and press secretary to replace someone leaving right away. It was keeping track of a thousand details a day, seven days a week, and a lot of writing on the fly. It meant a huge cut in pay, but I didn't care. I thought, 'I'll learn a ton, and I agree with [the candidate's] positions. This is a risk worth taking.'

"Well, the candidate won. Now I'm in Washington, D.C., with a huge increase in pay, serving as his executive assistant and scheduler. I have more responsibility than a twenty-three-year-old could get anywhere else. Time is a politician's most important resource. Any constituent or lobbyist who wants to see the congressman must go through me first. I have to understand current legislation so I can prioritize meetings. I have to work well with constituents and maintain the trust of the congressman and his family. It is very much a public relations role. I'm using all my skills every day, while gaining new ones as fast as I can.

"Sometimes you just have to go for it to get a job you'll love."

The Role of Parental Advice

What is the purpose of a college education? This book is, in part, an answer to this question. At its beginnings in 1636, higher education in this country was designed to foster and nurture God-fearing citizens and an educated ministry. Later, post-secondary education became a training ground for primary and secondary school teachers. Recently, college has become what high school had always been until now—a springboard for a successful life.

A generation ago, it was still an elite experience. Families were happy simply to have their children in college at all. They left the structure and purpose of the college experience to the experts, namely, the faculty and the administrators.

In just one generation, however, college has become the norm. Most parents of college students have themselves been to college. Families now approach the whole college experience as consumers. They want to know about the cost versus the benefit of this college versus that university. They want to know about career outcomes, class size, and the percentage of faculty with a terminal degree. They want to know what each school's admission rate is for applicants to medical school or law school. They want to know the hours for the swimming pool and the gym.

In one sense families have become sophisticated, but in another sense they have not. In short, families are sometimes wrong.

Well-meaning parents don't always provide the most accurate advice about careers and the relationship between job choices and education. The student needs to sort through and select the advice that makes sense for her. She also needs to balance their advice with recommendations from faculty, peers, and counselors.

This is not to say that your parents' intentions are not laudable. What they want for their children is clear: for college to provide the foundation for a successful life and, most of all, to be sure their offspring "launch." Failure to launch is a big problem in America, as students with $100,000 or even $200,000 educations come home to live in the basement or over the garage, while waiting for a message from some unseen god of employment. Increasingly, young people are living at home after college, even if they have a good job.

This can be attributed in part to the disappearance of the generation gap, because parent-child values don't actually diverge much now. Part of it may be due to parental guilt at not providing you with a pre-Simpsons TV-sitcom version of home life. Heavy student debt loads combined with low starting salaries and the high cost of housing are no doubt contributing factors. But parents' most consistent fear is that their children will go to college and emerge unprepared to make their own way in the world. So behind most parental career advice is the nagging worry that their young adults will fail to become independent.

There used to be a grand tradition in this country of "fooling around" for a year or two after college. From the mid-sixties to the early eighties, it was perfectly normal to spend a year hitchhiking through Europe, backpacking in the Andes, or fishing in Alaska after college. Even spending time in the parents' basement wasn't considered all that bad. The classic movie *The Graduate* is a case study on this topic, although not a particularly happy one. A generation of career counselors advocated for the positive aspects of "floundering," as one last chance for self-discovery and to get it right before entering the working world.

I do not disagree with this theory, but parents are increasingly hard to sell on it. With oppressive debt loads and a sense that life today is hypercompetitive, parents want their young adults to leave college and hit the ground running. The old tradition of a tour, or a walkabout, or one last hurrah has pretty much died. So don't be surprised if your own parents took time off during and after college but don't want you to!

By the way, if you want your parents to accept your career choices, prove to them that you will be able to pay your own way without further support. This needs to be a major part of your rationale if you want their endorsement of any adventures or experiments.

> The most successful people are those who do all year long what they would otherwise do on their summer vacation.
>
> —*Mark Twain*

Parental involvement in itself is not a bad idea, but in practice it often suffers from two mistakes: (1) the idea that a college or a major or a career is good, better, or best in itself, rather than in relation to a particular student (you), and (2) the idea that a major determines job choices. So if parents are going to be involved, it might be useful to provide them with an updated understanding of what you'll be facing today. Share some of the data in this chapter, and above all else remember this: **It's your path, not theirs.** So choose one you're going to enjoy, that your skills and talents will make you likely to succeed in, and that complements your ideas of the life you'd like to lead. Be sure you can earn enough money to be comfortable and independent, because the alternate outcome is certainly unpleasant: to earn so little that you find yourself dependent on your parents, the government, friends, or the kindness of strangers.

Oh, and by the way, the real purpose of a college education is this: To find out what makes you happy. That's what a great deal of this book is about. College should also give you the skills you'll need to be capable of pursuing what makes you happy once you discover what it is. But if you have the skills without that knowledge, then you're all dressed up with nowhere to go; you're armed and dangerous but unsure of your target; you're a power for good but unsure of what good really is.

> The true journey of discovery does not consist in searching for new territories, but in having new eyes.
>
> —*Marcel Proust*

2

Yes, It's All about You

Your job for the remainder of part 1 of this book is to complete a series of exercises, some of which may seem to have little to do with job choices but, in fact, will help you generate many, many viable and appropriate employment ideas. Some will be reasonable and some will be, shall we say, slightly more fanciful. Your goal is to generate them all the same. Toward the end of part 1, there will be other exercises to help you narrow your list of ideas and options to a few that seem worthy of further development. This will be your real starting place. Self-discovery is the critical foundation for all good life planning. Most students skip this step and pay for it later with a difficult job search and possibly even worse, a mismatch between their personality and interests and an ill-chosen path.

In part 2, you will road test just a few carefully selected ideas. Your goal is to leave the safety and security of student life and enter the real world as a seeker of information, advice, and counsel. This will make perfect sense once you get to that stage.

In part 3, we will cover the job-seeking techniques that you'll need to find a job or an internship related to your interests. You will know much more about yourself, what you have to offer, and what employers will want, after completing parts 1 and 2.

There is one point for you to fully anticipate coming up in part 3, and that is the reintroduction of the role of chance in your development. Your goal should not be to choose a goal that you then pursue despite all obstacles or opportunities thrown in your path. Some obstacles could be fatal to your plans, and some opportunities could be so tantalizing and immediately available that following your original plan would be the height of folly.

Understanding life planning includes knowing when to be flexible and when to compromise, and embracing the powerful role that chance can play in life's outcomes. For example, a higher percentage of CEOs attribute luck as a major contributor to their success. If it's true of CEOs, it's going to be true of you, too.

So after all the work you will have done in parts 1 and 2 to plan your career, in part 3 you will be reminded that there are aspects of life that are simply beyond planning. A chance encounter on an airplane, a purely social conversation at a party, or even a new invention or a burgeoning social movement can cause you to rewrite your life plan overnight. In part 3, we'll explore how this works.

Your job now, however, is to explore yourself.

CASE STUDY More than One Way to Do It—James W.

"All through high school and college, I wanted to be a novelist. I assumed that writing fiction would be my career, so I ignored the career center. I didn't spend one minute at a career event. Wait, that's not true. I went to one because they were giving away free pizza. I think it was something about using junior year to explore career plans. It didn't matter to me, because I knew I was going to be an important American writer.

"When I graduated from college, I actually went to live in my grandmother's garret in rural Oklahoma. I thought it was very romantic, of course. My grandmother was a gracious woman. God knows what she thought, but she provided a garret, complete with a steel bed frame, a small bookshelf, and a writing table that used to be in a school library in Stillwater. It was heaven to me.

"At first I wrote to everyone I knew from college. I was mailing ten letters a day, telling people about Oklahoma, about the heat, and about my grandmother's odd habits. I always wrote actual letters on paper and sent them through the mail. I had a laptop, of course, but I typed these letters on an old Underwood typewriter that had belonged to my great-grandfather. I liked that image of myself, I think. The writer. The living antique.

"Grandma had a flock of guinea fowl, which ran loose up and down the dirt road in front of her house. She counted them every day, which was not easy because they never stood still. She had a car but no driver's license, so I took her to an auction once a week. She would sell one load of old junk and buy another. The auctions were high theatre, with all kinds of folks jammed into a suffocating steel building, every door and window thrown open, and fans blasting against one another. But most of the real action was outside, as old-timers leaned against tailgates and traded stories. I got my first chaw of tobacco outside one of these auctions. Within half an hour, I was puking up my socks.

"Weeks passed, and it was getting hotter and hotter every day. My grandmother didn't believe in air conditioning. The garret wasn't so romantic anymore. It was unbearable.

"I think I wrote fifty pages of my novel. It was about two cousins who looked just alike. Some of it was clever, but unfortunately, I realized one day that none of it was important.

"Then I ran completely out of money. I asked my grandmother if she could spot me some cash to buy stamps to send my letters. She said, 'Where did you learn that? To bum money off an old lady?' So, it was time to go.

"I called my dad, who loaned me enough to get home to Chicago. Then he had me doing yard work on some properties he owned. After a few weeks, I 'graduated' to painting and repairs. All I wanted was enough gas money to get to Seattle, where I had a friend who promised to help me get started as a freelance writer. I left September 1. I could hear my student loans ticking like a bomb. I had to get some cash flow going soon.

"I broke down in Wyoming, and I was too embarrassed to ask my dad for any more help. I had my older brother wire me $600 to get my car fixed. (The telegraph company) took 25 percent, so then I owed him $800. Once in Seattle, I basically lived on my friend's couch. I was going to learn to be a freelance writer. I was no longer a novelist. I was going to be practical. I met some editors, mooched off my friend, and worked hard on some magazine articles on spec. Then it slowly dawned on me that my friend, whom I thought was a successful freelancer, was living on something like $1,500 a month. Whoa, I thought, no way am I going to work this hard for $1,500 a month. If this is success in the freelance market, give me something else.

"So I started to look for a 'real' job. I was on every website, applying for every job I thought I could do, sometimes up to twenty in a day. For every single one, I wrote heartfelt cover letters and customized resumes. Nothing happened. Not one single interview. I think I applied for several hundred jobs this way. The one I really wanted was as a marketing assistant for a funeral home. That appealed to me, but they didn't call.

"I did pick up a side job from a friend of a friend, editing this guy's master's thesis in economics. I didn't know anything about economics, but I knew the difference between syntax and semantics, and he didn't. It was kind of interesting, actually, *The Politics of Sovereign Debt*. Very conceptual. With the money from that I made my rent.

"But I was immediately broke again. I panicked, picked up the phone and called every property management company in Seattle. I told them I knew how to paint and do repairs. I got a job within a week, painting apartments. I managed to make my rent again, but I got really depressed. Here I was, the next great American writer, painting apartments with oil-based paints, probably getting brain damage, while all the dimwits who lived in those apartments had cars that worked, could eat out in restaurants, go on vacations, and fly home for Christmas.

"One day on the bus home from my painting job, I had a chance meeting with a college friend. She said she worked for a public relations firm that was doing really cool work. She said they needed help with some projects that were behind schedule. Could I do research and writing, she asked, and did I have any better clothes? I looked at my paint-splattered overalls and reassured her that I did. So I borrowed a tie and jacket from my roommate and skipped work the next day. I took along a copy of *The Politics of Sovereign Debt*. After the interview, I got a tryout assignment, researching the legal meaning of the word *organic* and writing a white paper on it. They liked it a lot. I got another assignment. Then another. Then I told them I really needed a job. They said they could give me a temporary position. That was a year ago, so I guess it wasn't that temporary.

"I love my work. I get paid to learn every day and then write about it. I would not have accepted a job like this right out of college. Some people just need to take a winding path, even if there's a straight path that's shorter."

> Imagination is more important than knowledge.
> —*Albert Einstein*

How to Get Started

In the following chapters, I will ask you to consider and then write about your interests, your values, your known and latent strengths, and the activities that make you happy. Some of these exercises are quite difficult, and may require brutal honesty and painful soul-searching. All will require imagination. Be bold in your thinking, take risks, and don't hold back.

But do, please, take your time. Try not to rush through the exercises or skip any chapters. Work on each exercise long enough to get beyond the obvious, off-the-top-of-your-head responses. Think deeply before moving along. You're going to work for a long time. This book is designed to help you find work you'll love, that will maximize your chances of making a real difference in this world. It's not supposed to be an overnight project. As you do the exercises, respond truthfully and to the best of your knowledge in every case. Don't worry: there will be later opportunities to test your ideas against the real world of parents, bills that will come due, and the expectations of future in-laws. Your task is to be painfully honest with yourself and work on this question of what makes you tick.

Above all else: Let go of your preconceptions and enter this process with an open mind. Let the process guide you where it will.

> Learn what you are and be such.
>
> —*Pindar*

Start a life plan notebook, either on paper or in a folder in your computer. You'll see your knowledge build and evolve, and you'll get a big kick out of looking at it in ten years! But if you put this in your computer, be sure to print it all out and save the hard copies when you are done! On paper is still the best way to save important documents, since computers crash and disks fail, and technology evolves away from remembering how to run itself.

Yes, it's all about you. By now you should see that you are the focus of this book. Your needs are paramount. Your interests are valid. Your authentic self-generated thoughts are more important than anything put in your head by others or the prevailing culture.

Where You're From: The Extended Family Biography

It's always useful to start at the beginning. Begin your career notebook by recording some basic facts about yourself and the world you grew up in:

1. Date of birth:

2. Each place you've lived to date:

3. Grade school(s) you've attended:

4. Middle school(s) you've attended:

5. High school(s) you've attended:

6. Colleges or universities you've attended:

7. Your three best subjects in college:

8. All student activities:

9. All community activities:

10. Languages you speak:

11. Sports you've played:

12. Honors or awards you've received:

13. Countries you've visited:

14. Every job you've ever had:

15. Every job your mother ever had:

16. Every job your father ever had:

17. Every job any stepparents ever had:

18. Every job your grandmothers ever had:

19. Every job your grandfathers ever had:

20. Every job your aunts and uncles ever had:

21. Every job anyone else in your household ever had:

This exercise should generate many pages of notes, and may involve phone calls or emails to one or more family members to complete the information. You may discover fascinating new details about people you thought you knew well.

When working on your life plan notebook, leave plenty of extra space around each exercise, so you can add information as you think of it or learn more. Record enough of the assignment in your notebook so that you can remember what it was all about. Otherwise, you'll be really confused when you come across lists later without any identification. If you don't include "Jobs held by Uncle Charlie," you won't be able to make sense of this: "Raised rabbits, mortician, cop, tour guide." I promise you you'll be glad later if you add a few notes of context to each assignment.

As you make an effort to discover more about the careers of those in your immediate family, you may find a surprisingly wide range of choices and varying paths. Some are methodical and logical; they "make sense" and follow a pattern. Your stepmother may have begun her life as a high school teacher, then moved on to become a principal, then finally a superintendent for a school district. That makes perfect sense. While other paths in your family may seem less logical or less obviously progressive, like Uncle Charlie's: "Raised rabbits, mortician, cop, tour guide."

Oh, and don't worry that you'll have to choose employment based on your family's choices! You can be an astronaut even if nobody in your family has ever left the neighborhood. Try not to overanalyze. Just proceed with the exercises, in the order they appear in the book, and we'll consider later how to use the information.

Please resist moving forward in the book until you've completed the mini-biography above. And please don't skip anything. You may have shoveled ice cream in a mall one summer in high school and think it doesn't matter. It matters. Write it down.

Your Early Job Ideas

Assignment Part I: Can you remember your very first job idea? If you can, write it down. Dig back and remember . . . . What is the first job you saw someone doing and thought, "That looks cool; I bet it would be fun to do that."

Let me reveal my own first career fantasy. (I share this admittedly odd first employment idea with Russell Baker, the Pulitzer Prize–winning columnist for the *New York Times*, as discussed in his autobiography, *Growing Up*.)

Here's how I came by my interest: When I was about four years old, we lived on the edge of a sprawling suburb. My mother was at the time a stay-at-home mom, and my dad put on a suit and left early in the morning for a mysterious place called "the plant." I couldn't imagine a job in a plant, so that didn't generate any career ideas in my four-year-old imagination.

In my insular world of childhood, the only people with jobs that I ever saw were the electric meter readers and garbage collectors. The meter readers looked sharp in their snappy uniforms, but our neighborhood's garbage collectors used to hang discarded stuffed animals off hooks along the side of the garbage truck. They also wore big brown leather aprons. And they drove a big truck and revved the motor a lot. I distinctly remember thinking, "That looks cool; I bet it would be fun to do that." I was drawn to those big leather aprons and the opportunity to collect stuffed animals.

Now if I can reveal this to you, you can get honest with yourself and think back to your childhood. What's the first career idea you ever had?

Write it in your life plan notebook. "My very first job idea was. . . ."

Assignment Part II: What were your employment fantasies in high school? What were your daydreams from those years that might be fun to pursue today?

WAIT! I know from years of doing career development workshops that right about now some of you are going to want to start fibbing a little bit in your responses. You're going to start screening your answers for how they'll sound to others. Well, don't. It's your life plan notebook. Nobody is going to see it unless you give it to them, so please be honest and don't hold back.

I'll ask it again: What were your employment fantasies in high school? What jobs did you daydream about as a teenager? Your list should include the practical stuff you probably talked about with your friends or family, along with the stuff you secretly dreamed about.

Then, make a note about what it was that attracted you to that choice. For example, you might have dreamed of having a television show about gardening. When you consider why you had that fantasy, you realize that it was the only way you could imagine getting paid real money for gardening. So what attracted you to the fantasy show was gardening. Someone else could have the same career fantasy, but what attracted her was the opportunity to be on television.

By the way, high school career fantasies are often very honest at their roots. That direction might not seem practical or reasonable today, but there may be an aspect of it that needs to find expression in the adult you have become. If in high school you dreamed of being an actor or a comedian or a circus announcer, it doesn't necessarily mean that after college you have to be an actor, a comedian, or a circus announcer. But it does mean that you'd better be looking at job choices in which you can be "onstage," such as a motivational speaker, a litigation attorney, a rabbi or minister, a corporate trainer, a teacher or college professor. We'll look at this again later. For now, let's continue with the exercises.

Don't forget to finish each assignment before going on to the next.

Assignment Part III: What post-college jobs have you considered since you started college? I'm after an exhaustive list here, not just the latest goal or the one you may have already settled on. Write down the complete list of *every* career idea you've considered since beginning college.

At this point, you may be more influenced by such matters as prestige, income potential, and whether you have the talent or inclination to succeed. There's nothing wrong with any of these considerations per se, as long as you list everything you've ever thought about as an employment goal since starting college.

Please finish this assignment before continuing.

Some of you are going to have a very short list for all three assignments. For example, if your first goal was to be a veterinarian because you loved animals as a child, and you kept this idea throughout high school and college, then your list might look something like this: "Veterinarian. Veterinarian. Veterinarian." Except, remember what I said about recording context with each assignment? So it should read: "My earliest job idea: Veterinarian. My career fantasies while in high school: Veterinarian. My goal while in college: Veterinarian." That's fine, but if you ever thought even for a moment about being a pediatrician or a dog trainer, it could be useful for you to list those options, too.

Be probing and diligent with your memory now, and it will pay off in greater creativity and problem-solving ability later.

Industries in Your Ethos

Make a complete list of the following categories:

1. Name the industries you or anyone in your extended family has ever worked in, and

2. Name the industries that are dominant in any of the locations in which you've lived.

How are these lists useful? When we grow up within a family or in a region that is dominated by particular industries, we tend to learn about those industries almost by osmosis. Without trying at all, without reading a single book or magazine article or conducting one minute's worth of research, we automatically know a significant amount about these fields. And even more important than knowing about them, we know a surprising number of people working in these industries. Regardless of your education or work experience to date, you'll have a head start with the industries on these lists.

To facilitate this assignment, take the list of all the jobs your family members have held and extract the industry from the job. If you don't know or it's not obvious, further research may be in order. For example, you may have heard that Aunt Charlene was in sales when she was younger, but you don't know what her product line was. Or you know that Uncle Clyde used to be a design engineer, but you don't know if he was designing sporting equipment or extra fancy paper clips. You'll need to know more before you can deduce the industry.

Build a complete list of industries in which anyone in your family has worked. Make some phone calls to fill in the blanks.

As to the industries in your area, every region of the country has industries that are important to it, from New York City to, say, Northwest Arkansas. New York has Wall Street, Broadway, television, the United Nations, and tourism, among many others; and Northwest Arkansas has Wal-Mart, poultry production, trucking, and higher education, among many others.

Make a complete list of industries that predominate in the locations where you have lived.

What Are Your Friends Going to Do?

Think of your five or ten closest friends from college, or just the first five or ten that come to mind. What are they going to do after college? This is an interesting exercise because you will want to have friends when you go into the career marketplace. Assuming these people are good for you, that you enjoy them and learn things from them, it should be interesting to note what their plans are. Focus on those whom you admire, not just the ones who are most available for weekend activities.

So make a list of college peers; then write down what you know about their post-college plans.

Notice any patterns? Are they all future scientists, future teachers, future engineers? That doesn't mean you have to choose what they choose, but it might be interesting to look at career opportunities that would allow you to have friends like these in the future. So if you are a journalism major but all your friends are in the sciences, you might think about becoming a science writer. Or if you are an education major but all your friends are business majors, you might consider work as a platform trainer in a corporate staff training and development department.

Write down your friends' long-term plans, noting any patterns, and then identify jobs that might allow you to have friends like this in the future.

Obvious Choices Based on Your Major

Although I very much want you to think about your future beyond the obvious choices based on your major, there is nothing wrong with considering those as well.

There are "obvious" employment goals associated with most majors. For example, a lot of psych majors become human resources professionals, social workers, or go into advertising and marketing careers. Many economics majors work in finance or investments. Journalism majors tend to work in online or broadcast journalism, public relations, or corporate communications. And so on.

Some majors are more obvious than others. If you're an accounting major or a speech-pathology major, there will be obvious choices associated with your major. If you're an astronomer or an anthropologist, the "obvious" associated job choices will be, to put it simply, less obvious.

No matter what your major is, you're going to need help on this. See your university's career counselors. In addition to a one-on-one counseling session on what you could do with your major, there is a popular set of online handouts called "What Can I Do with This Major?" available through your career center website, or at http://career.utk.edu/students/majors/majorsindex.asp. You can also look at *The College Majors Handbook*, by Neeta P. Fogg, et al., mentioned earlier. But remember this: These are just idea generators, not roadmaps to follow!

Also, ask faculty and fellow students in your department, "What kind of jobs are recent graduates from this department getting?" You might be surprised, and you might learn about placement channels that you didn't know existed. For example, there may be a local business that hires graduates with your major, not because it is an obvious assignment, but simply because an owner or executive or department chief got her education at your university, with the same major.

So even though you can get any job with any major, build a list of the most obvious job choices associated with your major.

A Caveat: Your interests are not bound by any of the work we have done so far. Relax if you've been saying to yourself, "I don't have any interest in the careers of my family or the dustbin of Lower Southeast Nowhere where I grew up." Don't worry. We'll get to exercises that more directly involve you in the next chapter.

Do each exercise anyway. They're entertaining, and even if they don't all apply in your particular case, the fact is you can't tell without doing them which ones may strike a chord with you. Besides, your life planning notebook can become a document of enduring interest to you.

3

What Gets You Excited?
Your Top Five Issues in This World

What are the top five issues in this world that interest you? Have you thought about that? It doesn't matter whether you have any influence or power over them; at this stage that's not the point. What matters to you? What interests you? What are you concerned about?

Build a list of the Top Five Issues in This World that you care about.

They do not have to be grand issues. They could be fairly small or obscure concerns. For example, one science major saw the classic Tom Cruise movie *Top Gun* on television. In the film, one of the issues for the pilots is passing out when their bodies are subjected to too much G-force, or gravity, during accelerated diving and banking maneuvers. Needless to say, passing out while piloting a high performance jet is a problem. Our science major said to herself, "I wonder why that happens?" She pursued her interest a little further than most people would have: she got an M.D., then a Ph.D. in the new field of space physiology, and now works for NASA. The point is this: What you are interested in can be a wonderful source for career ideas. Our "space doctor" launched an exciting career by following an interest sparked by a television movie.

What fascinates you? What gets you excited? What gets you all upset and bothered?

It's amazing how many different issues we care about. It's even more amazing how divergent these issues can be on the same person's list. One student wrote on his List of Top Five Issues:

1. Damage to coral reefs

2. Global warming

3. The shelf life of a Twinkie

4. Is there a God?

5. Does providing cheap imported food ruin local agricultural and economic systems? And if so, what should be done about it?

Obviously, you should pick issues that you truly care about. The student in the example above, upon closer questioning, did actually care about each of these issues a great deal—even number three (it had to do with the shelf life of all food products). I've worked with students recently who gave the following responses to this assignment:

- Hydrogen fuel cells. Alternative energy. A post–fossil fuel energy future.

- Cars. Fast cars. All cars, really.

- The newly emerging field of adult Edu-Tainment and the revived Chautauqua movement.

- Enzyme folding and other types of chemical instruction sets.

- Obesity and the need for better understanding of nutrition science among the African-American community.

- Domestic violence.

- Practical, real-world applications for chaos theory. I would like to be a "chaos theory consultant" for government or industry, maybe even the CIA. I've never heard of this and have no idea if it's possible, but that's my interest.

- Gerontology.

- Depiction of Latinos in the media. And the whole concept that there is a single "Latino culture."

- Prosthetics. The juncture of engineering and medicine. Using mechanical engineering and industrial design to develop medically related devices.

- The decay of the public schools in urban settings.

- Military history. Strategy.

- Forensic science, especially the entomological stuff.

- Nationalism, tribalism, and the concept of "globalism." All types of group identification issues. Is it really human nature to go to war to protect the interests of an "us" against a "them"?

- Animal rights, in particular, factory farming techniques in the United States.

- Economics and the whole concept of think tanks. Some kind of policy-level economic analysis that influences corporations and governments at the highest levels.

- AmeriCorps. I think everyone should do a year or two of service or community-oriented work before focusing on their own lives.

- Poetry. Art. Poetry and art.

Build a list of the Top Five Issues in This World that you care about.

What Can You Do to Contribute to What You Care About?

Once you have your five issues, for each one make a list of jobs that would allow you to contribute to that issue. Don't worry whether or not you have the educational preparation or raw talents required to hold the job; that's a separate concern. Just make a list of jobs that would allow you to contribute to the issue in question.

Be as creative as you can when generating job ideas, and remember that some of the most interesting ways for you to contribute may not be obvious. For example, a friend of mine was interested in children, in particular, the effects of racism on minority children's career aspirations. He could have been a teacher, or a civil rights advocate, or a civil rights attorney, or an author and television pundit specializing in racism and education issues, or a research-oriented college professor, or a politician who spoke out on these concerns, or an administrator at a university. What he actually did was more interesting than all of these: he studied racism as a public health issue, and developed an epidemiological model for analysis of racism—its spread and its cost to society. In other words, he believes and teaches that racism can be thought of as an infectious disease, with predictable "infection" patterns and

symptoms in directly infected and secondarily impacted populations. He works in
the public health field as a consultant.

That's what I call thinking outside the obvious, and making a contribution to
an issue you care about!

Make a list of jobs that would allow you to address each of the issues of greatest
importance to you. Try to come up with five or more jobs for each issue. For some
issues, you may be able to imagine twenty or more jobs.

By the way, this assignment is particularly apt for group work. Show your List of
Top Five Issues to another person or a small group, and you could find yourself in a
fruitful brainstorming session. Many heads are better than one when it comes to this
type of solution thinking. Your willingness to share could result in a real breakthrough
in creativity about jobs that might interest you and allow you to contribute to issues
you really care about.

People You Admire

Whom do you admire? Who are your heroes? Make a list of twenty-five people you
admire, living or dead, who have made the world you live in a better and more interesting place, or have otherwise accomplished something that you find admirable.

Try to get beyond luminaries such as Mother Teresa and Dr. Martin Luther King,
Jr., and go on to include people in your family and other people you know.

Of course, if Hillary Clinton is a hero to you, put her down. But go on to think
about and recognize other people with less visible careers who are still worthy of
special respect. Do you have a cousin who paid her own way through college, or a
friend who beat a drug addiction, or a dad who is the kind of dad every kid should
have? These are the sorts of people who also belong on your list.

Not everyone will be a superstar, nor should they be. Some will be unsung
heroes—people who made a difference to their families, their neighborhoods, or
some smaller sphere of influence.

You don't even need to know someone's name to put him or her on your list. How
about the woman who started Teach For America? Or the priest in your neighborhood
handing out sandwiches to the homeless on Saturday mornings?

Your goal is to list twenty-five people you think represent humanity at its best—
people whom you would like to emulate or people whom you think exemplify the
human potential for good of one kind or another.

It may take some time to come up with twenty-five people. Comparing your list
to others will be useful for this exercise, or just ask people you know, "Whom do
you admire, and why?" Feel free to show them your list-in-progress.

Finish the list before going to the next part of the exercise.

Once you've completed the list, write down what each one does for a living. Sometimes, what someone does for a living is very different from what they do that causes you to admire them. Even world-famous poets, mountain climbers, and peace activists, just for example, often have some other employment that pays the bills.

So go through your list and jot down the jobs that pay the bills.

How about Yourself? Why Do You Admire You?

As you can see, many of these exercises are designed to structure introspection: to get you to think about your own desires and values and opinions in systematic ways. This is not always easy. It requires maturity, honesty, and depth of personality.

The next exercise is difficult, if not impossible, for high school students and is a challenge even in college. With that gauntlet thrown down, here is the assignment: Write down twenty-five things about yourself that you are proud of. These can be accomplishments, personality traits, special talents, or other aspects of yourself that you take pride in. It doesn't matter if others have achieved the same milestone or share the same character trait; it is important only that you find the accomplishment or the trait a source of pride.

It should be relatively easy to identify some things about you that you are proud of, but after a while you may have to reach deep into the idea bag to come up with solid reasons to admire yourself. So number one might be "I saved a life once as a lifeguard," and number twenty-three might be "I got to every class on time this week," or "I can change the oil in my car."

Some of the more interesting things students have written:

- I made a B- in organic chemistry. That's the worst grade I ever made, but it is the one I am most proud of. Organic chemistry was the hardest subject I ever took, and I even beat some of the premeds in my class.

- I escaped [my hometown], and I have never been back. If my parents want to see me, they have to visit me. As long as I live, I will never set foot in [my hometown] again.

- I have never been pregnant. Almost all of my friends have been pregnant, but not me.

- I can speak five languages, three of them fluently. There are not that many Americans who can say that. My goal is to be fluent in all five: English, Spanish, Portuguese, French, and Chinese.

- I organized a drug and alcohol convention on my campus, and nearly three thousand people participated overall.

- I stuck it out as a chemistry major. It has been really hard. I had to take three classes over, but now I'm a tutor. I think I'm a better tutor than someone who found chemistry easy from the start.

- I served on the selection committee for the new president [of the university]. And I look pretty good in a little black dress.

- I was barely able to pay for college, but I helped my parents pay for my sister's quinceañera party.

- I can make a sound like a jet engine taking off.

- I was captain of my soccer team in high school. Even though I was not a great player, I was sort of a coach and motivated everybody. I was really proud to be captain because I was elected by the team.

- I survived a personal tragedy in my family. I don't want to talk about it, but it is one of the things I am most proud of. Don't ask me about it.

- I had a letter published in the "Letters to the Editor" section of the newspaper, and a poem published in a magazine. I have written a novel, too, but I don't like it and am going to start over.

- I helped a friend break up with an abusive boyfriend. I really may have saved her life.

- I learned English only five years ago, and I am on the dean's list every semester. It is hard work, but I think it is worth it.

- I am the oldest of six children, and I helped raise my brothers and sisters. Even more important, I think, is that I didn't resent it! I love them all.

By the way, this is one of the exercises that will definitely amuse you ten years from now, so be sure to print out your entire life plan portfolio at some point.

Think hard, and identify twenty-five things about yourself that you are proud of: twenty-five accomplishments, personality traits, talents, or other aspects about yourself that you take pride in.

> To find out what one is fitted to do, and to secure an opportunity to do it, is the key to happiness.
>
> —*John Dewey*

Why Care about What You're Proud Of?

Obviously, when assessing your employment options, you'll want to ask yourself about each one: Will this choice allow me to put more items on the list of what I'm proud of? Will it create opportunities for me to accomplish things and acquire skills that I can be proud of? If you answer yes, then this should be an attractive direction to you. If you answer no, then it would be a career to avoid.

Keep in mind, there will likely be many choices that simply don't support anything on your list. Sometimes we have to work and earn money and pay our bills but not really advance in any of the areas that we care most about. Sometimes a job is just a job and becomes merely a holding pattern, something we do until we can reassess our priorities and try again to find more meaningful employment.

In a tight economy, or when for personal reasons we simply have to generate some cash flow, this is not an unwise choice. But sooner or later even the most hungry young employee has to ask: Is there something else that would be more meaningful to me? That would lead to accomplishments that would be more gratifying to me? That would lead to skills acquisition that would better allow me to advance in directions that are important to me?

I repeat: You will have many chances to do life planning and make a leap toward employment that will excite you.

By the way, the above exercise is a classic **values identification** exercise. You have identified things about yourself that you care about. The rest of this chapter is concerned with values identification and clarification.

CASE STUDY Values in the Workplace—Crystal R.

"I was originally a premed major, but my GPA soon made it clear that I would not be going to medical school. I was bummed for a while, but not too long. I'm a believer in the Serenity Prayer, you know: 'accept the things you cannot change.'

"I had been a hospital volunteer for several years, and my favorite activity was reading to sick children. I would act out all the parts in the stories, and for a few minutes I could get the kids to forget they were sick. I liked that a lot, and if you could see the looks on their parents' faces, you'd just melt. They were so appreciative of what I was doing. Maybe even more than the kids. Children are so 'in the moment,' but the folks knew I was trying to help.

"The other thing I enjoyed was sitting with patients in the post-op recovery rooms. Usually the patients were knocked out, and I would watch over them. I met several of the doctors and the hospital staff. One was a cosmetic surgeon, really talented.

Everyone respected him, but he was really nice. I asked him if I could work in his office for the summer, and he said yes.

"I loved my job. I talked to prospective patients on the phone and made appointments. I got to assist at patient-education seminars. I tried to make myself indispensable, and by the end of the summer I knew everything that went on in that office. They were asking my opinion about advertising image, how to get patients to pay who owed us money. I even observed some procedures. In three months, my experience went way beyond what a summer intern usually gets to do.

"What I liked best about working for a cosmetic surgeon was that we helped people feel good about themselves. You could see it in their eyes. And the doctor did a lot of procedures for free on kids whose families couldn't pay.

"When I graduate, I'm going into medical administration. I'm really good at working with patients, and I'm really organized. I think I can run a medical office the way it's supposed to be run."

CASE STUDY Values in the Workplace—Jessica P.

"When Crystal asked me if I wanted to work in a doctor's office, I jumped at the chance. She was going back to school, and I was just getting back from a semester abroad. I had been in France, and I just stayed for the whole summer after school let out. I learned more French goofing off around Nice than I learned in class all spring. Then it was back to reality.

"I was going to take the fall semester off anyway, and I was completely out of money, so a job sounded like a great idea. So I started on the Monday after Crystal left for [school].

"At first, I liked the job. The doctor was always running these ads, and we'd get swamped with calls. He taught us to talk to each person as though we had nothing else to do all day. So we'd answer questions, talk about the doctor's credentials, read from testimonials—that kind of thing. Our goal was to get the patients to sign up for orientation sessions. Most were one-on-one appointments. I thought they were pretty heavy-handed sales pitches, really. And the one thing we absolutely could not do was disclose prices over the phone. We knew how much each procedure cost, of course, but we were supposed to lie and say that we didn't know. It was almost an art form, and I learned to do it pretty well.

"In the end, I didn't feel good about what I was doing. Most of the patients looked fine to me when they came in. I mean, nobody's perfect, but some of these people were getting expensive and risky surgery they just didn't seem to need.

"That bothered me. So did the billing. We did some pretty shady stuff to get insurance companies to pay for procedures that weren't therapeutic at all. Billing wasn't my job, but I knew about it. Other staff people talked openly about it.

"Crystal loved this office, but I couldn't wait to get out. I know the doctor does work on kids for free, but I got the impression he did it so he could talk about it. One thing I know for sure: I am not going to work where I have to lie to people on the phone all day."

What If You Won the Lottery?

What would you do if you won $10 million in a lottery? $10 million is just about the right amount of money. If you were to win $100 million, it could ruin your life. People you couldn't remember from kindergarten would be hounding you for the rest of your days. But $10 million is just enough to free you from worrying about earning a living. Your investment returns should be somewhere between $500,000 and $1,500,000 per year. Forever.

But, what would you actually do with your time? Of course you'd take a vacation, buy a new car, and maybe select a new home right away, but what about after that?

In short, what would you do if money were no object? If making a living were simply not a concern, what would you do with your life?

Answering this question seriously is one way to discover your values. What would you do in the first three years, say, after winning a one-time payment of $10 million in the lottery? Imagine it in detail, then write it down.

What If Prestige Didn't Matter at All?

The last exercise is designed to separate your money aspirations from your job plans, at least for a moment. Suppose prestige didn't matter, either? What would you do if you didn't care what anyone else thought?

Perhaps if money and prestige didn't matter, you'd mow lawns for a living or drive a truck or fix cars in the front driveway. This is an interesting exercise. In fact, many people simply cannot think of their career ideas as separate from the money and prestige involved.

Personally, I'd be a hobo poet, seeing America from an open boxcar. Or maybe a cab driver. What would you do if prestige were not important at all to you?

What Would You Pay to Learn?

If you had unlimited resources and time, what would you pay to learn how to do? Personally, I'd finally become fluent in Spanish, and I'd travel abroad more. What do you wish you had the time and money to learn? Would you pay to learn more about film making? Would you pay to learn more about Thai cooking? Think broadly. Make a list.

Then, once you have a list of educational and experiential goals, ask yourself, "Which jobs would allow me to get paid to learn and do these things?"

In my case, for example, it would be to work in Latin America. In your case, list the jobs that would pay you to master the subjects you're interested in.

What Could You Sell with Passion?

Everybody can do sales if they really want or need to, but it depends on the match between the seller and the product. A friend of mine utterly failed at sales of radio advertising, a conceptual product he found of uncertain benefit. He later became the top producer at getting owners of older homes to agree to insulation audits provided by a government program. Though he truly believed in energy conservation, he was unmoved by blurbs for local restaurants and bars.

The key to sales is to believe in your offering. If you believe in your product, you can sell anything. What can you imagine yourself selling with passion? What would cause you to be comfortable calling up strangers and friends of friends? What product or service or societal need would cause you to want to tell the world about it?

Make a list of products, services, or ideas you think you could sell.

A Question of Values Alignment

Employers, corporations, governments, nonprofits, and other organizations have aggregate personalities. They are, in effect, like a very large person with morals, belief systems, superstitions, a personal history, mythology, folklore, and so on.

Corporate entities reveal those personalities somewhat in their official pro-nouncements, but much more so in their actions. Their actions demonstrate their true values.

People naturally identify with their employers. An employer is an extension of the self. When an employee's values align with those of the organization she serves, she will be at peace at work. She will be free to concentrate on her particular job, to contribute to the larger mission of the organization, and to operate comfortably within her sphere of influence in the context of the greater whole.

When her values do *not* align with those of the employer, she will never be at peace at work. She will suffer from what is, in effect, an internal conflict. She will hold one set of values, while another part of her (that extension of herself that is her employer) will hold another. This creates cognitive dissonance, along with coping mechanisms such as denial, compartmentalism, extreme moral relativism, and so on.

Although people do manage to work their whole lives for employers with values that conflict with their own, they are generally not happy about it. In fact, one of the primary reasons an employee will leave a job voluntarily is a mismatch between her values and the values of her employer. It's that important.

Crystal's and Jessica's stories on pages 37–39 demonstrate, not that one person's values are better than another's, only that they may be different. The crucial question is this: Do your values and the values of the organization align?

I have an acquaintance who was a stockbroker and loved working in a high-pressure, boiler-room atmosphere, where every broker lived or died by commission. As the investment advisory industry changed, and boiler rooms were less and less common, he joined a discount brokerage firm that specialized in giving group seminars to investors instead of one-on-one investment advice, and where a good deal of his income came from his base pay instead of individual sales. He hated it and quit within a year. "Biggest mistake I ever made," he said later. His competitiveness found no expression in the new company. He complained bitterly that everyone was "too nice and too slow. Going to work was like living in a movie where every scene was shot in slow motion. I thought I was slowly dying frame by frame, surrounded by morons. I could hear my own heart beat slower and slower." So he ended up finding a new industry where boiler rooms were still the norm. If your phone is ringing, that could be him now.

It is worth your while to try to identify the beliefs and values of a prospective employer before you join them. If you don't want to poison small towns in Alabama, there's at least one chemical company that you don't want to work for. And if you want to pressure customers to buy goods and services they don't need, there's at least one discount broker you don't want to work for. And if you think tobacco is a scourge upon all human societies, there is at least one recently renamed conglomerate you will want to avoid. And so on.

To discover more about an employer's values, scour their websites and all their official pronouncements, of course, but pay more attention to what recruiters and managers say privately about the company. For example, a company may publicly promote a family-friendly policy, but if you ask any manager, he'll tell you that it would be career suicide to take advantage of it. Off-the-record information reveals the real personality of a company, not its official pronouncements or paid advertisements.

And read everything in the business press about an organization's activities going back at least a year. If they've been driving widows into foreclosure with predatory lending practices or dedicating a percentage of their profits to improving urban schools near their offices, find out about it.

The Life Values Survey

What about your own work values? Have you ever systematically defined them? The Asher Career & Life Values Survey is designed to do exactly that. Go to www.donaldasher.com/careers and click on the Career Values Survey icon.

Try to respond to each survey item fairly quickly, without thinking too much. Don't worry about the implications of a question or what your answer might reveal about you. Just answer each question truthfully, in order, and move along.

Be sure to read the information at the end of the survey about how to use the survey. Then print out the survey and add it to your life planning journal.

Pay particular attention to the questions you marked "No way!" or "That's ideal!" If you think it is ideal to have a job where you can feel creative every day, or where you can work on a team, or where you can wear a suit most days, then you should be especially wary of any opportunity that does not offer those facets.

Conversely, if you marked "No way!" to a job working on commission, or working for a nonprofit, or that would require you to wear a suit most days, then you should be especially wary of any opportunity that does include those facets.

Consider which answers are most important to you. You don't want to forget these issues in the excitement of getting a job offer. The values you express here and now, with a little calm introspection, are valid. Once you start to get job offers, you'll be very tempted to compromise. This may be the right choice at the time, but do it with open eyes. Know that you're compromising, and how, and why.

Next, you will be selecting some employment directions to explore. Obviously, you want to make choices that match your values, that you can identify with, and that will help you add to your list of what you're proud of.

> Our character is what we do when we think no one is looking.
>
> —*H. Jackson Brown, Jr.*

4

A Little Future Visioneering

Certain employment environments are more conducive to rapid advancement than others. And although it is true that superstars will float to the top in every environment, what kind of environments allow *everybody* to advance rapidly?

Here are two correct answers: Those in which an entire industry is emerging for the first time, and those industries that are riding demographic trends. Let's consider emerging industries first.

Newly Emerging Industries

Getting in on the ground floor of an emerging industry will result in rapid career growth for any worker, even those with limited talent or ambition. Rising tides really do raise all boats, under these conditions. Workers with drive and ambition can achieve rapid advancement when it really matters—*early in the career*—and move themselves quickly into the executive ranks. Even workers who are not overly ambitious will experience a great deal of opportunity and a chance to move around within a company (or companies). They can use this mobility to find the niche where they will really thrive and be most happy.

Getting in on the ground floor of a rapid-growth company or a rapid-growth industry is almost always a great career booster.

However, you have to get in early in the boom cycle, and at the time it's not always easy to tell where that is. After an initial boom in a new industry, there is often a correction, followed by a return to more sane and orderly, yet still strong, growth. According to economists, society tends to overestimate the early returns from a new technology and underestimate the long-term impact.[6] A stable, more mature industry will grow in a straight line, usually tracking population growth. A new industry hits like a shockwave, which often looks like the solid line in the graph below.

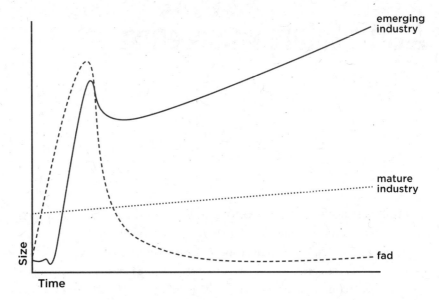

With hindsight, it is always easy to see which industries were emerging industries and which were mature. But in real time it is not always so clear.

Compare the growth pattern for emerging markets after the shockwave correction with the growth potential in a stable, mature industry. Yes, the ride can be rocky with both fads and more useful new technologies, but the long-term benefits of working in emerging industries are just too large to ignore. Some possibilities for our times are biomedical engineering, biotechnology, nanotechnology, and emerging energy alternatives.

While no one knows for sure, computer technology and the Internet seem likely to continue to grow, although perhaps at a reduced frenzy. In case you're interested, the advent of automobiles and railroads created exactly these same economic explosions with the same shockwave and correction cycles, before continuing to impact society in a big way.

Sometimes just one company is responsible for an emerging industry's really taking off, such as when Wal-Mart went from a single store to the largest employer in the world in just one generation. There are true stories of secretaries and clerical workers who bought Wal-Mart stock in the early years and later retired as millionaires. The same thing happened at Genentech, a biotechnology pioneer, where early office staff were cut in on the initial public offering.

If you have the good fortune of spending the first ten years of your career in an emerging industry, you should reap major benefits. There's only one problem: **It is notoriously hard to predict the future.** After IBM's engineers built one of the first computers, a room-sized monstrosity called a Supercalculator, an IBM executive dismissed it with this comment: "There is probably a worldwide market of five for this."[7]

Many of the greatest breakthroughs in history were totally unprecedented. No one anticipated these earth-shattering changes: Before Antoni van Leeuwenhoek invented the microscope in 1674, all of microbiology was not known to exist! Before computers were invented in the 1940s, a linear computing machine was unimagined. Early science fiction described robots and antigravity cars, but no computers. Distributed computing (for example, the Internet) was also unanticipated, imagined by only one science fiction author, William Gibson, in his novel *Neuromancer*, before it was a fait accompli. Before the structure of DNA was discovered by James Watson, Francis Crick, Rosalind Franklin, and Maurice Wilkins on February 28, 1953, the secret instruction set of life itself was exactly that—a secret. Gene-splicing and the rest of biotechnology were unimaginable before their discovery.

What does this have to do with your career? Try as hard as you can to see the future, you cannot tell what innovations will arise, and arise suddenly, over the coming years. Just as one example of how quickly things can change, the software industry that made Bill Gates the richest man in America, and employs millions of people around the world, did not exist before he dropped out of Harvard to start it.

What industries do you identify as likely to be emerging right now? And which can you imagine coming into existence in the future that might be possible only in fiction right now?

Make a list of industries that you imagine are newly emerging right now, or may be likely to have major breakthroughs in the very near future. Although it is fun to speculate on the wildly fanciful, try to list industries that you believe are possible in your lifetime.

List at least five Newly Emerging Industries.

Next, make a list of jobs you might enjoy that are related to those industries. Remember, one quarter of the managers and executives in the last high-tech boom of Silicon Valley did not have technical degrees. All industries need creative, energetic, intelligent workers of all types, and even the most scientifically complex and engineering-driven companies also need financial and marketing executives, graphic artists, human resources staff, caterers and event planners, facilities managers, customer service directors, speech writers, janitors, sales representatives, personnel trainers, management coaches, technical support staff, budget analysts, government liaison officers, distribution experts, foreign language interpreters and translators, newsletter editors, and so on.

Whether you are interested in the jobs or not is not the point. The point is to identify where your skills and abilities might fit.

Waves in Demographic Trends

Other industries that guarantee a rising tide to lift all boats are those that are certain to ascend the waves in demographic trends. The most obvious of these is the baby boomer tide, that wave of Americans born between 1945 and 1964. They are like a rat in a boa's belly, making their way through society and changing it as they go.

The trend to watch is this: 77 million Americans are starting to retire as of right now. *Seventy-seven million.* What will they need? What services focus on them? This will be the healthiest and wealthiest generation ever to retire and grow old. Right now they desperately need retirement planning services, estate planning services, and certain types of insurance (long-term care, disability, and burial). In the medium term, they will need recreational opportunities, more and more golf courses, more and more RV parks, plenty of tours and cruises, different kinds of insurance, and post-retirement educational opportunities. This generation will not go gray crocheting afghans, you can be sure. And in the long run, they will need assisted living residences, extensive specialized medical services, convalescent and hospice facilities, and such new service businesses as adult day care, exotic burials, law firms specializing in elder affairs, and advocacy associations. Along the way, they will need many types of public and private social services organizations that specialize in their concerns. Smart careerists will ride this demographic wave and *anticipate* these needs, rather than waiting until they become obvious to everybody.

But the baby boomer generation is not the only demographic trend to watch. Hispanics have become the majority minority in this country in the last few years. They are underserved in retail commerce, underserved in media, underserved in electoral politics, and underserved in education. Their numbers give them the clout to shift the direction of the entire American economy, and by *anticipating* these shifts you may be able to find niches that will continue to expand for years.

Need more examples of demographic trends to bet on? The tastes of every generation seem to catch the old guard unaware: Every generation has new music moguls, fashion visionaries, and other arbiters of cool who rise up right in the midst of well-established businesses that just don't get it. The existing players are unable to address these new market opportunities, and the upstarts blindside them by identifying and commercializing the trends first. Snowboarders and sailboarders were ignored by established sporting goods manufacturers, allowing newcomers to stake out a niche all to themselves. An acquaintance of mine made $10 million before he was thirty, designing, manufacturing, and selling extreme sporting goods over the Internet before selling to an old-line sporting goods manufacturer playing catch-up. By reason of your youth alone, you may have access to trends that old-timers just can't see.

Again, you don't need a permanent advantage from a demographic trend. If you can just get lucky enough to pick one that will deliver a ten-year growth spurt, you will have opportunities to advance that will far exceed spending a decade in a more mature industry.

Which demographic trends do you think will drive industries over the next five to ten years? Which are particularly likely to result in rapid career growth? Can you identify ways to get in on the ground floor of a trend-riding industry?

Make a list that you have some confidence in. Use your imagination. It doesn't matter if these industries actually exist or not. For example, you don't need to know if there are elder rights law firms; it is enough if you just believe that they will be needed in the near future.

List at least five Demographic Wave Industries.

Now make a list of jobs you might enjoy that are related to these industries. How could you, considering your skills and interests, find opportunity in each of the trends you have identified? Again, whether you are interested in the jobs or not is not the point. The point is to identify where your skills and abilities might fit.

Remember, you don't have to become a gerontologist to work in an assisted living center. These facilities will need marketing and public relations officers, recreation specialists, administrators, accountants, salespeople, regulatory compliance administrators, and so on.

Make a list of possible jobs in these industries now.

One final note: Every year several magazines publish lists of "hot jobs," with promising titles like "Hot Jobs for the Next Decade" or "Where the Jobs Are Now." After you build your own trends lists, you can look at these as well. However, look with a jaundiced eye. I have had several complaints about these articles over the years.

First, it doesn't matter if there will be a great need for actuarial accountants in the coming years if you have no interest in or aptitude for actuarial accounting. So by featuring the job instead of the underlying trend, readers are led to think (a) they must be actuarial accountants, and (b) they are losers if they pursue a career not seen on the list.

Second, most published jobs lists have struck me as remarkably unimaginative. In my workshops, I find undergraduate students with better visioneering skills than professional labor economists and the magazine writers who cannibalize their data. The articles are full of old, obvious career choices. Almost never have I said, "Wow! I never would have thought about that job." In a weird sense, these jobs-of-the-future articles tend to look backward instead of forward.

Third, many of the jobs featured do not require a college degree. One hot-jobs article listed "truck driver" as a major opportunity. I don't want to malign any college graduate who thinks she would like to drive a truck for a few years, but it would be an unusual career counselor who would suggest it.

Fourth, they sometimes suggest jobs that are counterintuitive to current trends, choices that just don't pass the smell test. A few years ago, one article listed "secretaries" as a hot growth area! This is highly unlikely, as most organizations, large or small, old and well established or young and newly emerging, will continue to routinize all clerical functions and even eliminate the very position.

Fifth, and perhaps my most important objection, there is a conceptual problem in such published lists. If the country needs 127,000 more shoe salespeople, that's not what's really important. What is important is the ratio of job openings to the ratio of interested and qualified workers. It's the supply relative to the demand that determines the success of workers. Let me spell this out: Which is more important to a job search—that the country needs 127,000 more shoe salespeople or that it needs 10,000 more aerosol engineers? The numbers alone will make it seem that the real opportunity is in shoes, but it's not. The country may need only 10,000 additional aerosol engineers, but there may be only 3,000 such graduates in the coming decade. This means that the 3,000 aerosol engineers will have storied careers, while the 500,000 people who are qualified to sell shoes are going to be treated like dirt in the job market.

Think about it, and then do your own thinking and visioneering.

Aptitude and Interest Tests and the Role of Testing

Some career counselors don't recommend career tests or use them in their practices. Others believe they are useful and invest a great deal of time becoming certified in specific tests and their administration. Who is correct? Both are.

Aptitude and interest testing are useful tools that can provide students with career ideas, but they may have dangerous side effects. One of the worst occurs when students place too much confidence in test results. They may believe that test results are a formula that *must* be followed, or worse, a fate that cannot be escaped.

Students are often surprised by their test results. I've heard complaints about one test or another that didn't "understand" or "discover" the real them. Students may feel "defined" by their test results, and subsequently feel limited in their career choices. For example, I saw one ambitious student struggle with test findings that suggested she should serve in a support role, when she viewed herself as a natural leader. She was bewildered by the readout that presented a picture of herself that she did not identify with. Taking the test proved to be a disturbing experience for her.

Young people can be impressionable and mercurial. Your test results can be influenced by how you feel on the day of the test. For example, after a great outing with friends, you may show up in testing more extroverted than you really are. Or if you suffered through a cocktail party hosted by your parents the night before, the opposite results may be indicated. If you just wired up your quadraphonic sound system, test results may indicate you have more interest in working with your hands or solving engineering-type problems than you really do. Some tests are more resistant to this type of variance than others, but all are subject to it.

On the other hand, when a testing process is conducted by a certified and skilled test administrator, there is less risk of misunderstanding the results. The administrator will tell you not to overinterpret the test findings, that they simply supply more information to consider when thinking about your goals and options. And a good test administrator will tell you never to let the findings alone determine what career to choose, or to avoid.

If you want to pursue a career direction contraindicated by a test, go ahead and explore it.

If you abhor a career direction indicated by a test, go ahead and avoid it. This is the fundamental rule to grasp before taking a career test of any kind.

There are different types of tests, which primarily fall into the categories of **prescriptive** and **descriptive**. Prescriptive tests will likely tell you to pursue or avoid certain careers, and descriptive tests purport to tell you things about yourself. The output of a prescriptive test might be a list of recommended employment options. They are designed to identify and guide you to possible job choices complementary to your personality, talents, and interests. The results will indicate a few specific career options that you should investigate, which might be a match for you. The output of a descriptive test will tell you something about your personality, and what kinds of work environments and tasks you should seek or avoid.

I love asking mid-career adults about the career interest and aptitude tests they took in college or the military. Many have worked in similar or complementary fields, but none is doing exactly what a career test suggested. This means test results should not be blown out of proportion in the larger context of your employment explorations.

For example, I took an interest test in high school that said I should consider a career as a park ranger or a military test pilot. Looking back, I realize I was very excited by my biology class at the time, and this interest probably led the instrument to indicate I should be a park ranger. Likewise, the test identified my high tolerance for risk taking and somehow concluded I should be a military test pilot.

These were not particularly useful findings because, for one thing, very, very, very few people become test pilots. One does not just walk onto a military base and say, "I'd like to be a test pilot." Also, I have a personality that resists authority. Even though test pilots are risk takers, they take those risks within the military command and control structure for maintaining discipline in the ranks. Many people would thrive in this environment, but not me.

As to being a park ranger, I need more prestige and grandiosity than most park ranger assignments would provide. I need a big audience for my work, and I thrive on attention and ego gratification. This is neither a good thing nor a bad thing; it's simply a fact about my personality. And it's exactly the kind of thing you need to know about yourself for wise life planning.

In other words, the test identified one area of my personality and made certain inferences about me, without successfully identifying how those inferences might conflict with other areas of my personality.

Other career tests are designed to serve the goal of self-discovery. They will indicate things about your personality you should consider when choosing a career direction. For example, if a test suggests you are introverted, you need to know that not many truly successful salespeople are introverted. Some, of course, but not many. Or if a test reveals that you love to brainstorm and think conceptually, but you hate details, you need to recognize that this trait would probably conflict with an entry-level accounting job.

However, let me say it one more time: If you want to pursue a career in accounting and a test reveals that you hate details, go ahead and pursue a career in accounting. Why? Because (a) the test could be wrong in your case, and you really do have a talent for details, and (b) the field of accounting needs conceptual thinkers, too. It's important to remember that Albert Einstein had trouble with basic mathematics, and where would we be if he had decided to avoid physics?

Finally, on the topic of career testing, it is my opinion that such testing should never, *not ever,* replace soul searching and career counseling. No matter what a test says, you need to sit down and do some honest, introspective thinking about *your* skills and strengths and interests. And you need to meet with your college career counselor and other mentors and advisors to talk about yourself: your interests, your employment ideas to date, your aspirations, what's important to you, and so on. No matter how sophisticated the testing services available to you at your college or university, don't skip the soul searching and the one-on-one counseling.

That said, let's discuss the most popular career tests, their strengths and weaknesses, what they can do and what they can't do. Not all tests are created equal. Some are little more than academically sanctioned astrology. But then again, I knew a top executive who had her astrological charts prepared before every major interview, so who knows?

Strong Interest Inventory (SII): The Strong Interest Inventory allows students to see how their interests compare to those of a wide variety of professionals in various fields. It also exposes them to occupational titles and may give them ideas for further research.

Myers-Briggs Type Indicator (MBTI): The Myers-Briggs Type Indicator is extraordinarily popular in business settings. It attempts to describe the strengths of various personality types and suggests environments that match or don't match a student's type.

StrengthsQuest: StrengthsQuest is based on millions of interviews and surveys of top performers, conducted by the Gallup organization. It allows you to identify your five greatest talents and strengths. Accessible through the book, *StrengthsQuest*, or the website, www.strengthsquest.com.

Birkman Method: The Birkman Method is an assessment tool that attempts to reveal workstyle, lifestyle, and other interest preferences, as well as to identify basic personality needs and how they might match or not match a given setting.

The Enneagram: The Enneagram is also a type indicator, revealing how strongly an individual may possess or lean toward one of nine personality types: Reformer, Helper, Achiever, Individualist, Investigator, Loyalist, Enthusiast, Challenger, or Peacemaker.

Kiersey Temperament Sorter: The Kiersey Temperament Sorter helps students understand which of four main personality types they favor—Rationalist, Idealist, Artisan, Guardian—and how they might best succeed in interacting with others.

Campbell Interest and Skill Survey (CISS): Similar to the Strong Interest Inventory, this survey attempts to match interests and aptitudes to actual career choices by indicating how closely an individual's responses match those of successful practitioners in various professions.

Structure of Intellect (SOI or SI): Based on the theories of psychologist J. P. Guilford, Structure of Intellect is intended to be a test of applied intelligences in these categories: Reasoning and Problem Solving, Memory Operations, Decision Making, and Language Skills.

System for Interactive Guidance and Information (SIGI): SIGI is an educational and career planning self-assessment system, designed to assist in career choice based on values, interests, skills, college major, and other aspects of academic preparation.

The Kolbe Assessment: The Kolbe Assessment is a test of natural abilities and instinctive approaches to work and problem solving. It is designed to provide personality understanding that can then be applied to career choices.

Other Tests: There are many proprietary tests currently being developed and validated by testing theorists, and some of them are quite good. If your career center uses one that is not discussed above, it may very well be a good instrument. However, some tests are quite expensive, some are very new, some have narrow applications, and so on. As in all forms of testing discussed here, if your gut feeling is that a test is wrong or mistaken about you, you're probably right; **and no test replaces introspection and counseling.**

5

Advanced Issues in Life Planning: More than Enough Ideas

You should now have more career ideas than you know what to do with. You have compiled and thought about the following information:

- Every Job Ever Held by Everyone in Your Extended Family

- Your Earliest Career Idea

- Your High School Career Fantasies

- Your College Career Ideas

- Industries Worked in by Your Family

- Industries in Your Area

- Careers Associated with Your Major

- Your Top Five Issues

- Jobs Associated with Your Top Five Issues

- People You Admire, and What They Did/Do for a Living

- Accomplishments or Traits You're Proud Of

- What You'd Do If You Won the Lottery
- What You'd Do If Prestige Didn't Matter
- What You'd Pay to Learn or Get to Do
- What You Could Sell
- Your Career Values Survey
- Newly Emerging Industries, and Possible Jobs
- Demographic Wave Industries, and Possible Jobs
- The Results/Findings/Ideas from Career Testing

How are you going to sort through all these possibilities and decide where to begin your exploration? Well, before you start, you need to consider several more subtle issues. Although it is relatively easy to make lists of jobs held by our uncles and aunts, it is not always so easy to identify exactly why we are attracted to a particular job. First, we have to consider a few advanced life planning concepts; in particular, the concepts of happiness, threshold needs, flow, signature strengths, and alignment. And we'll talk about the three main sources of life planning error; namely, confusing what you're good at with what you like to do, thinking you have to get every passion fulfilled at work, and believing that your particular interest or talent needs to be the only thing you do at work.

The assignments that follow are different from many of the previous exercises, which were about volume, not quality. The new ones are more qualitative, requiring more introspection. A few solid truths discovered here will be more valuable than creating a large volume of responses that you don't find really important or profound. My workshop students have reported thinking about these issues sometimes years after taking the workshop. Think about that as you consider each assignment.

What Makes You Happy?

Your objective in career planning is to meditate upon, identify, and explore what makes you happy. How hard is that? It turns out, it's harder than it sounds. For example, when considering what makes someone happy, a person tends to concentrate on that which he doesn't have. If something is missing, it often takes on a disproportionate value.

Take air, for example. If you're like most people, you take breathable air for granted. In normal times, you would agree that air doesn't make you happy, particularly.

But if you aren't getting any air, it's all you can think about. You want it so badly, you imagine that air is what you need most to be happy. But once you get air again, you are not happy about that fact beyond the first few moments. Then in no time at all, you are concerned about something else.

This is an example of a threshold need. You need air, certainly, but beyond enough to breathe, more air does not make you more happy.

When imagining the work life you want, be careful not to assign disproportionate weight to things you simply haven't had up to this moment. Take money, for example. If you are a broke college student and you don't have any money, you may be overly interested in money. You may imagine that money is what you need to be happy. But once you get money, you may not be happy beyond the period of time it takes to get used to it. In no time at all, you are concerned about something else.

This is not to say that money, or air, is not important. But the point should be taken that, beyond a threshold level necessary for adequate survival, it does not in itself lead to happiness. So be cautious about identifying status, money, or power as major requirements for your happiness. It may simply be that you haven't enough status, money, or power to suit you—to get above your threshold needs—and the moment you do, it will cease to be of interest and will no longer satisfy.

There is a mythology in our materialistic American culture that fine houses, fancy cars, and "trophy" possessions are major components of the good life—of happiness. But are they? Many Americans work terribly hard and sacrifice their health and well-being, their leisure pursuits and family relationships in order to pay for all those toys.

> Success is not the key to happiness. Happiness is the key to success. If you love what you are doing, you will be successful.
>
> —*Dr. Albert Schweitzer*

If you want to learn more about the history of the American work ethic, read *Blood, Sweat and Tears: The Evolution of Work* by Richard Donkin. You'll be ready to trade some of that material success for other rewards.

Consider what makes up a long and happy life. What do we know about what leads to happiness? Well, more and more, actually.

There is a relatively new academic discipline called *happiness studies*, which explores what it takes to keep humans happy. Kenneth Sheldon at the University of Missouri discovered in a Templeton Prize–winning study that self-directed, internally relevant personal growth makes a person happy. Pursuit of external rewards such as financial wealth and social status does not. Says Dr. Sheldon, "The more you pursue goals of popularity, riches and beauty, the less happy you are," while "the more you pursue intimacy, community or personal growth, the happier you are."[8]

There are studies of lottery winners and overnight-successful entrepreneurs that indicate this: Sudden wealth tends to make people more unhappy than they were before their windfalls. There's even a name for this condition, "sudden wealth syndrome," coined by Marin County psychologists Joan Difuria and Stephen Goldbart, who had been treating the ills of Silicon Valley's instant millionaires. They founded the Money, Meaning, and Choices Institute to study and treat the syndrome.

Building a business up from nothing makes an entrepreneur happy; selling it off for wads of cash does not. The ramifications of this finding are profound. Pursuing our passions will make us happy. Meaning makes us happy. Making a difference on an issue that is important to you will make you happy. That's why your Top Five Issues are, perhaps, the most important piece of work you have done so far in this book.

Interestingly, lack of stress is not associated with happiness. Many people with highly stressful lives are quite happy, while many people who lead virtually stress-free lives are miserable. Being bored is actually associated with an increased risk of mortality. Some people, it seems, are literally bored to death.

The stress itself is not as important as control over its causes. There is an important relationship between **responsibility** (which can cause stress) and **authority** (the ability to address the causes of stress). A job featuring responsibility with authority could be heaven. A job featuring responsibility without authority is usually hell. Unfortunately, many entry-level jobs are structured exactly this way; they feature responsibility without much authority, at least at first.

> Happiness lies not in having what you want, but in wanting what you have.
> —*Arthur Watkins*

Strong marriages or similar long-term partnerships are important to contentment. Long-term friendships and successful relationships with adult siblings have been associated with longevity. Bonds with community or religious organizations promote happiness, resilience, and longevity. Having pets has been shown to improve health and longevity. Working at a job you love has been associated with longevity and resistance to disease. Avoiding television news promotes a greater sense of personal safety and well-being. Finally, being optimistic in your general outlook contributes to happiness and longevity.

Although there is no brain gym or mental workout routine that will make you a grinning idiot if you live in hell, you can learn to make choices that will make you happier. In fact, you can learn to simply be more happy. As Martin E. P. Seligman established in his landmark book *Learned Optimism*, you can become more optimistic and presumably live longer because of having done so. Dr. Suzanne Segerstrom at the University of Kentucky has documented in a Templeton Prize–winning study the positive effect optimism has on the human immune system and reduced mortality. In the simplest sense, optimistic people have more to live for and more reasons to want to be alive. Think about it.

Seligman is also the author of the idea of "signature strengths." The gist of this concept is happy people are good at identifying their natural strengths and building a life that involves opportunities to use those strengths often—every day. (For more on signature strengths, see his book *Authentic Happiness: Using the New Positive Psychology to Realize Your Potential for Lasting Fulfillment.*)

All of this is important, but it doesn't mean that money and prestige are *not* important. It is just that, beyond your threshold requirements, *more money or prestige will not make you happier.* Later in the book, when we talk about alignment of employment choices with other life goals, you'll need to define those threshold requirements for yourself. The point here is to help you look at the bigger picture of what makes humans happy, rather than at the air or money that you lack right now.

Peak Moments versus Flow

When I ask most college students to think back over their lives and identify the times when they've been the most happy, they tend to provide what are called peak moments. Peak moments are like a good sneeze—very satisfying, perhaps, but not long in duration. They are intense and short, and often involve a physical reaction; that is, you feel a peak moment in your body, in a wave of exhilaration or relief.

A peak moment is going down a ski slope that's far too advanced for you, flying over a mogul, and then there's this weightless instant when you realize *you might actually live through this.* That's a peak moment.

A peak moment is being the finalist in a spelling bee: the very last person to stand and deliver, but you've never seen or heard the word before, so you guess, *and you guess right.* That's a peak moment.

A peak moment is walking across the stage at graduation time.

The problem with identifying peak moments as happiness is that they are so fleeting. They last a matter of minutes, at most. But that's not the only problem: they often are attached to an activity that involves a major investment. Skiing takes time to master, and a bad day skiing is cold, miserable, and wet. Winning a spelling bee involves hours and hours of study. Graduation comes only after sustained and diligent academic performance. Years to study, minutes to graduate.

The ultimate illustration of this point is having sex and then having children. Sex may be a peak moment, but children last quite a bit longer.

So whenever you think about peak moments, think also about the commitment involved, or the ramifications of pursuing the moment. That's the bigger part of the idea, the greater commitment, the larger experience.

Let's consider a career in sales. There are many salespeople who are addicted to making the deal. They love it. They thrive on it. They live for it. Whether they're selling shoes or Chevrolets or shares in blue chip stock, there's nothing better than closing the deal, clinching the sale, getting the Yes!

But they actually hate to sell. They hate to get up in the morning and slog through lead lists and make new contacts and butter up the gatekeepers and beg for time and lug around presentation materials and live on the road and get yelled at by the boss and miss their friends and family. They hate to sell.

Closing a deal is a peak moment. The rest is a salesperson's routine. Some people would love this life, would find it exciting, but that's not the point. The point is to see beyond the peak moment to the rest of the picture.

Life is made up of a series of days. **You'd better enjoy your days, if you plan on enjoying your life.**

The problem with concentrating on peak moments is there are too few peak moments with too many days in between. Pay attention to the days in between.

Another more sophisticated way to think about happiness is this: Try to identify "flow" periods, rather than peak moments. One of the pioneers of happiness studies as a discipline is Dr. Mihaly Csikszentmihalyi of the University of Chicago, who identified and defined a state called "flow." A flow experience always involves an activity or task that requires some skill, that consumes all your attention, and that is so captivating and satisfying that you lose track of time or possibly even of your surroundings. You are totally immersed in the activity. It is so intrinsically satisfying that you are thinking of nothing else.

Artists and high-performance athletes often experience flow when practicing their art or sport. But a cab driver having a stellar day whizzing around a city can experience flow also. A mother playing with her toddler can experience flow. A musician practicing all alone in his loft can have an entire day of flow. A retail store manager who is busy just the right amount and who has all the answers for every customer can have flow. A suburban father who decides to clean out a garage or shed can have a whole afternoon of flow. A college student who is writing a paper when it's coming together just right can have flow. A person in the midst of an argument who seems to have the right rationale at every stage of the discourse can actually be in flow, too.

Flow is not about any external fact. It is not about power or image or prestige or compensation, but about the task and the performer in an insular bubble of successful activity. No one can give you flow, grant you flow, or award you flow. You just experience it.

Days that offer a high incidence of flow turn out to be happy days indeed.

One of the most interesting things about flow is that it is entirely a relative experience. One person can be having a flow experience while sitting next to another person—who appears to be having the exact same experience—who is in fact having a terrible, horrible, no good, very bad day.

If you take flow to the next level and imagine a series of days that are dominated by flow, the experience is this: **The universe seems to be conspiring in your favor.**

Have you ever had times like this? A particularly successful few days, or even longer? Can you identify periods of time, from minutes to hours, when you were captivated by a task that was going well, that was so intrinsically satisfying that you lost track of time or your surroundings?

Make a list of the times you have experienced flow. This is a bit conceptual, but it is an important consideration if you're trying to build a happy work life. With thoughtful introspection, you should be able to recall several periods when you have had flow experiences. Make your list now.

Once you have your list, ask yourself what you were doing. What was the task involved? Then, of course, identify the jobs that might provide opportunities to pursue such tasks, or others like them, under similar circumstances. Identify the tasks you associate with flow, and identify the jobs that might contain those tasks now.

For more on flow, see Csikszentmihalyi's books, *Flow: The Psychology of Optimal Experience* and *The Evolving Self: A Psychology for the Third Millennium*, or the more than one hundred articles he has penned on this concept. And watch out for overemphasizing those peak moments.

By the way, you can actually learn to watch for what makes you happy by designing your own Mood-O-Meter. Build scales representing days, weeks, months, years, and significant periods of your life (such as "senior year") and start tracking your happiness. Over time, you will start to notice what makes you happiest and what brings you down. Then you can adjust your plans and activities accordingly. This takes a considerable commitment over a long period of time, but it's worth it if you want to learn more about what makes you feel good. Here is an example:

Mood-O-Meter

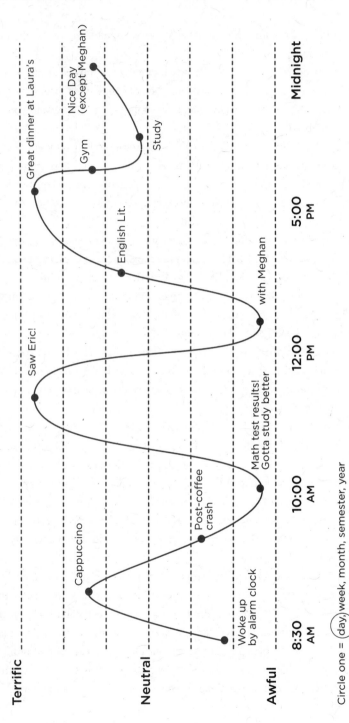

Terrific

Neutral

Awful

8:30
AM

10:00
AM

12:00
PM

5:00
PM

Midnight

Woke up
by alarm clock

Cappuccino

Post-coffee
crash

Math test results!
Gotta study better

with Meghan

Saw Eric!

English Lit.

Great dinner at Laura's

Gym

Nice Day
(except Meghan)

Study

Circle one = day, week, month, semester, year

The Three Main Sources of Life Planning Error

The three main sources of life planning error are (1) confusing what you're good at with what you like to do, (2) confusing avocations with vocations, and (3) confusing one aspect of a job with the whole job. Let's consider them in order.

#1 What You're Good at versus What You Like to Do

What you're good at is not the same as what you like to do. Of course, there will be some overlap, but these two lists will be distinct. The easy list to make is the list of what you're good at. What you're good at is overt. People can see it. Even you can see it. People will tell you that you are good at skill X; they'll praise you for exhibiting the skill, or you may win awards for it, and you can see with your own eyes that you are better than others at it, or that your abilities with skill X are more impressive than your abilities with skill Y or skill Z. You probably know what you're good at, what you do better than others, or at the very least, what you do better than some of the other things that you do.

So it's an easy list to make.

A harder list to make is a list of what you like to do. Out of all the things that you do, what do you enjoy doing? The problem with this list is that it is not overt; it is covert. It is inside you, not visible to others, and hard for even you to discern. Few other people are going to be able to clue you in on what it is you like to do, although a skilled counselor can help. No one is going to give you an award for liking to do something. However, this is the more important of the two lists.

Everyone involved in career planning will tell you that in the long run, it is more important to pursue the things you enjoy doing than the things that you are good at, especially if you don't really like to do them.

When you enjoy doing something, you'll do it for intrinsic rewards. You'll do it on your own. You'll do it more often. You'll do it every chance you get. You'll pay to get to do it. You'll invest in training and lessons and tools. You'll do it when it's difficult, and you'll do it when obstacles are thrown in your way. You'll do it when others tell you to stop.

Here's the punch line: You'll do it until you *are* good at it.

When I was in college, I took a creative writing class with some very talented writers. I wasn't one of them; I was about middle of the pack in skill level. Some of my colleagues were brilliant. One stood out from the others, however, as the worst writer of all. Everyone in the class knew it, except him. He had no talent, no sense of rhythm, very little creativity, no sense of story, and only a modest command of formal structure.

But he liked to write. He wrote constantly. It was all bad, of course, but there was rather a lot of it. He turned in—and this is no exaggeration—ten times as much material as anyone else in the class. He wrote longhand in thick spiral notebooks. When these were full, he would pull posters off the wall and scribble bad poems on them. At a party, he would disappear, and we'd find him in some basement storeroom, tapping out more bad material on a borrowed laptop. We thought he was more of a madman, really, than a writer.

You can anticipate the outcome: out of that class, he is the only full-time professional writer today. He is editor of a magazine, and has published a novel. I've read the novel. It's good.

There are historical precedents for my college friend. Jack London, author of the classic young adult adventure book *Call of the Wild*, collected his rejection letters on a wire in a shed in his backyard. The wire had six feet of rejection letters strung on it before he sold his first story. He went on to become the highest paid writer in the history of American letters. He liked to write, and he also did it until he was good at it.

There are several studies that indicate that wealth in America is often created, not by people who are interested in wealth per se, but by people who are obsessive about something. They worked on a problem so obsessively that they solved it before or better than anyone else and, as a result, were rewarded financially. Bill Gates of Microsoft and Sam Walton of Wal-Mart were exactly this type of person. They didn't set out to get massively, obscenely rich. That was a byproduct of their efforts. They set out to write microcomputer operating system software that worked, and to run a retail store well, respectively.

So, please make two lists: What I Am Good At and What I Like to Do. Watch for overlap, as this can create a powerful advantage. And as you are choosing career directions, pay more attention in general to what you like to do.

#2 Vocation versus Avocation

A major source of life-planning error is the idea that your job has to satisfy the whole you. In other words, every aspect of your personality has to be fully engaged, every skill you possess put into use before the job is truly "satisfying."

But this is rarely the case. You've got a lot of life going on outside of your job, including friends, kids, charities, hobbies, classes, club memberships, and other major endeavors that have nothing to do with what you do for a living. So you can have many avocations in addition to your vocation.

There are certain pursuits that we may be very passionate about and interested in that do not tend to pay enough to earn a living. These make excellent avocations rather than vocations, for example, music. If you are committed to music, it doesn't mean you have to pursue music for money. You can pursue music as an avocation, for the sheer joy of it.

CASE STUDY Tim C.

Tim C. is a software release manager for a software engineering company in Boulder, Colorado. He makes buckets of money at his job, but he also has another passion—music. He plays standup bass for a fusion jazz group every Friday and Saturday night. They get a small gate plus free drinks. As he told me, "I'd do it for free, but they treat us better when they have to pay us something." When his job takes him to a new town, he finds a new group to join. If he can't find a group, he forms his own. He's done this ever since leaving college. Highly paid technology professional by day, funky fusion god by night. Yeah!

CASE STUDY Laura M.

Dr. Laura M. is an emergency room physician in Portland, Oregon. She loves the fast pace of emergency medicine. It's one of the few arenas where a doctor still has full control over treatment modalities, and it's over when it's over. Says Dr. M., "Most doctors carry a patient load. They're really never off duty. But when I finish a shift, I get to go home and know that the patients are either fine or in the capable hands of someone else. It's great." But there's another side to Dr. M. She is an Olympic contender in a fencing sport called *épée*, which is a heavier version of the conventional foil. In other words, Dr. M. is a world-class sword fighter. She trains every day she's not on duty, and she leaves her job several times a year to compete around the world.

CASE STUDY Lance B.

Lance B. is a young attorney practicing in San Francisco. He is the type of corporate attorney John Grisham writes novels about. He structures billion-dollar acquisitions for global companies. He wears $1,000 suits on his dress-down days. And he works really, really hard. Lance also lives in Tiburon and takes the ferry across the bay to his job in the financial district. That gives him almost an hour every morning and every night to relax, and the way Lance B. relaxes is to work on a novel on his laptop. He recently had his first one accepted by a publisher and is already about halfway along on his second. He told a journalist, "I like to write, but I also like the law. And it is a very rare writer who makes half as much as I do in law. Sure, it'd be great if I became the next John Grisham, but meanwhile, I'm not going to quit my day job." Indeed.

Music, art, theater, and dance can be big passions that you develop outside your work life. Other pursuits that can fall smoothly into this category include religious service, community service, involvement with a 12-step community, personal athletics, athletics coaching, outdoor adventuring, nonprofit fundraising, cooking and culinary arts, interior decorating, and so on.

Make a list of activities or pursuits that could become **Avocations** for you. Don't decide right now that they don't belong on your day-job list. Just make sure to include anything you could be passionate about outside your work life.

#3 Aspect versus Whole

Another stumbling block to life planning is the idea that what you like to do must be the primary thing you do on the job. Sometimes this happens just because we aren't thinking creatively enough. Or it may be an identity issue; in other words, we may overidentify with the thing we like to do, and believe we must *become* it instead of *do* it.

A classic example is someone who likes to write. He may think he needs to become a writer instead of looking for opportunities to do writing. So he makes a list of jobs that allow him to be a writer and only a writer, such as poet, novelist, journalist, copywriter, grant writer, or tech writer.

A much bigger world would open up to him if he looked at careers in which writing was a required skill, and a key to success. These options may include such widely divergent jobs as legislative assistant, management consultant, public relations assistant, rabbi or minister, politician, attorney, editor, college professor, or even government lobbyist. All of these jobs offer ample opportunities to write, and continued success requires an ability to write well.

So think creatively as you consider which jobs might challenge and satisfy you. Seek opportunities in which what you like to do is an *aspect* of the job. But try not to overidentify with a job function by thinking it has to be the *whole* job or the only thing that you do.

CASE STUDY John H.

Dr. John H. is a chemistry professor and premed advisor at a small college in Oregon. He is best known on campus for writing and starring in "Magic with Chemistry," a very funny demonstration he performs every fall to get more students to take chemistry. He is also the school choral director and the producer of a barbershop quartet. Dr. H. does not himself sing, at least not in performance, but he loves to work with musicians and singers and enjoys the challenge of bringing out the best in a musical performance. He once told the student newspaper, "Directing a musical group is a little bit like chemistry. There are rules that determine what you can do, what you can mix together, if you want a certain outcome." He has taken his love of music and performance and made it an aspect of his job as a college professor. It is a part of what he does, but not the whole thing.

CASE STUDY Dave C.

Dave C. has a story that is both similar and very different. He discovered scuba diving while still in high school. He was crazy about it and got certified by two certification organizations, NAUI and PADI. In college, he made extra money as a scuba instructor through the phys ed department at his university in Georgia. "I looked into all the careers you could have that involved scuba," he told me. "You can teach at a dive shop in any resort community in the world, which pays peanuts, or you can get into underwater salvage and underwater welding, which pays major bank. The only problem is the work is sporadic, and the people you have to work with are [not what I had in mind]." So Dave is currently in graduate school studying underwater archaeology. "I'll be a college professor most of the time, and a field archaeologist every chance I get." He enjoys the academic life and has found a way to combine his interests.

CASE STUDY Clarissa H.

Clarissa H. is a personal friend of mine, who was always good at math. Her father had been a high school math teacher, and she felt some family pressure to become a teacher or a college professor. "I didn't want to teach," she told me. "I don't really like people that much, and you have to do the same thing over and over again. I wanted something else, even if it meant letting down my father." So she got a job with an economic consulting firm, designing analytical methodologies to assess financial outcomes of hypothetical business scenarios. "We do things like say how much company A was harmed by the activities of company B. Or how much money a top executive would have earned if he had not been killed on the job. It's more creative than you might imagine. They love me because I can come up with a perfectly reasonable methodology to support any number they want." So Clarissa gets to do math every day, without being a mathematician.

Be creative as you imagine jobs that would interest you. Think of some of your favorite things to do, that you can imagine doing professionally, and then think beyond the obvious to which jobs might allow you to practice that skill or talent.

Title one list "Skill, Talent, Activity" on the left side of the page, allowing plenty of room on the right side; then fill in the right side with "Creative Ways to Get Paid" for each skill, talent, or activity.

One More Chance to Create Options

It's time to start sorting through all the industries, job descriptions, and career fantasies and create a list of possible jobs you'd actually like to explore. Relax. This is not a major commitment! You're not deciding what you're going to do for the rest of your life; you're only looking for a few ideas that are so interesting you'd like to look into them a little further. You can drop one later or add one back in that you decide to pass over at this point. But it's time to narrow the field and get this massive career ideation project down into a reasonable number of jobs you'd like to investigate as you proceed to the next part of the book.

Let's build a list of at least five jobs that you believe would be very satisfying for you. The best way to do this is to use a method I call holistic assessment: start by holding everything you know about an option in your mind simultaneously, and then decide how much better or worse one choice is than the others. There is no formula or point system or computer program you can run the data through that will provide some kind of ordinal ranking. Holistic assessment truly is the best sorting device. You're just going to have to weigh all the options and decide.

Consider everything I've asked you to think about so far: all the exercises you completed and all you've learned about yourself through introspection, testing, and counseling. What do you feel would be some promising places to begin your exploration? **Which jobs have a high probability of providing work that you would enjoy and find meaningful and intrinsically rewarding on a daily basis?**

Try to vary your choices a bit, and try to include at least one or two that you had not really considered before doing the life planning exercises.

Write down five Possible Career Choices.

Now, here's one more chance to define and weigh your options. Let's explore what it is you like about each of your choices. One at a time, choose an option from the selection above and list the things you like about it.

Once the left side of the paper is filled with qualities that are appealing to you about that job, use the right column to make a list of *other jobs* that would also supply the aspect that appeals to you. In general, these should be jobs you could and would be willing to do, but as an exercise in creativity, they can be any other job that would include the aspect that appeals to you.

Then, make another list of the three main things you don't like about the job you're considering, and list jobs that would not have those limitations.

What follows is an example from a student at a workshop in Massachusetts.

If any of the jobs in your right-hand column start to look more attractive than the job you're diagramming, it may be time to consider pursuing it first.

Job: Writer for a newspaper

What I like about it:	Where else I could get that:
Opportunity to work with words in an environment where words really matter	College professor H.S. teacher Attorney Advertising copywriter Writer for other media (online content, magazines, TV, film) Editor in publishing Poet
Opportunity to be creative	All the writing positions above Party clown Actress Teacher Pastry and dessert chef
Get to work on a project basis, and work mostly on my own	Baker Organic farmer
Intellectual prestige, identified as one of the "smart crowd"	College professor H.S. teacher Most other writing jobs (not TV)
Ability to make a difference on issues I care about, mainly poverty, disenfranchised and voiceless groups, federal budget priorities, income inequity, public art	Social worker Politician Advocate or activist Soup kitchen manager Maybe some type of government bureaucrat, a policy position Some kind of job with a city or state arts commission Corporate extortionist (just kidding!)

Three things I don't like about the job:	Jobs that would not have that problem:
Print media is dead	Online content writer
Lots of night work	Almost any office-type job, the 9-to-5 world
You usually have to start out for some newspaper in Podunk, writing about church picnics and praying for a plane crash or bank robbery.	Almost every other job I have considered is urban, with the exception of college professor, where you have to go wherever you can get a job, even if it's Podunk.

Considering the exercise you've just completed, now list your top five choices for jobs you'd like to consider exploring. If nothing has changed, write them down again anyway. Get used to them.

Write down five **Possible Career Choices.**

How Do You Envision the Future?

When you imagine yourself five or ten years from now, what do you see? How will you be living? Let's consider some sample questions about what you envision for yourself in the future:

- Are you a fast-charging world beater, always seeking a new challenge? Or are you comfortable making a difference in a smaller sphere of influence?

- What kind of car do you drive? Do you drive at all?

- Do you own a home, lease a condo, rent an apartment? What does your home look like? How is it decorated? How much did it cost?

- How many hours a week do you work? Do you have to work weekends? Holidays?

- What do you wear to work? Suit? Business casual? Anything you want? Before heading out to work, what do you look like?

- Who do you know? For example, who are your colleagues at work, and what types of work do they do? How closely do you interact on the job? Do you interact socially?

- Do you mostly work by yourself, or are you interacting and cooperating with others all day long?

- What do you do on your vacations? Where do you go?

- Who are your friends, and what types of people are they?

- What do they think of your job? What will others say about you?

- What professional issues are you working on?

- What personal issues are you working on?

- Where do you live in the country? Do you live and work in urban, suburban, small town, or rural locations?

- How much do you spend on housing, transportation, clothing, and meals?

- Do you have a family? If so, what is your role in the family? Are you the primary breadwinner? Or do you split home and career exactly fifty-fifty?

- Is there enough money?

- Are there children? Who is in charge of them? Who would take care of them if they were sick?

- Do you travel on the job?

- What do you do when you come home from work?

- How much energy is left for the other aspects of your life after you're done working?

- Do you practice a religion?

- Are you active in local politics?

- Are you in graduate school? Planning to go soon?

What can you see?

Even if you don't have detailed answers to these questions, you do know quite a bit about your expectations of the future. At the very least, you probably have a clear idea of your financial goals and your work-life balance goals.

Your question now is this: Do the job choices I'm considering align with my financial and work-life goals? **This is an extraordinarily important question.**

Most people do not ask themselves this question until they run into a lack of alignment. That is, they find themselves without something that is actually a threshold need for them. Then they're gasping for air or money or time, and that lack of air or money or time becomes an overwhelming crisis in their lives.

Life is about compromise, and adult life involves a lot of compromise. However, for each of us there are certain things over which we are not willing to compromise, and if we were to, we would become unhappy.

The key is to see this in advance.

So as you consider the job options you are going to explore, do you see any that don't align with your threshold needs? Do you see any that, as attractive as they are in some aspects, have other aspects that you would find ultimately unacceptable?

Likewise, are there any "needs" that you've been hanging onto that you now see are expendable? Are there any "requirements" that would keep you from pursuing a job that would be delightful in every other aspect?

Let me give some examples of both cases. First, let's consider the needs. I always ask my students where they would like to live, what they want to wear to work, and how long they imagine their commute to work will take.

If anyone tells me they want to live in Atlanta or Los Angeles and they want to commute to work in ten minutes, or even in thirty minutes, there's a problem. There is no short commute in these two cities. So, you have three options: decide a longer commute is okay, decide you want to live in another area of the country with less traffic, or live in the building you're going to work in.

Suppose you want to be a scriptwriter but you don't want to live in Los Angeles. This is a problem. While it is true that there are plenty of scriptwriters who are successful who don't live in Los Angeles, most of them started out in Los Angeles. They became successful in Los Angeles. And yes, you can try to be a good Muslim without going to Mecca, but that's not what the Koran says. If you want to have realistic career plans, one part of the plan has to align with the other parts of the plan.

Let's consider what you want to wear on the job. The standard options are suit, business casual, casual, uniform, and T-shirt casual. If you want to be a bank officer or a Fortune 500 executive, but you just can't stand the idea of wearing a suit to work every day, well I've got news for you: Something has to give. These two ideas are not compatible; they're not in alignment with one another. It's compromise on one or compromise on the other.

Likewise, if you want to be a social worker and drive a BMW, you're going to have to realize that it's likely to be a very old BMW. Very old. You may decide to tweak your career objective just a little. For example, if you want to help people have better lives, become the executive director of a chain of successful weight loss clinics. Then you could drive whatever car you want. Several of them. In different colors.

Just as there are needs you may choose to abandon, such as not living in Los Angeles or wearing casual clothes, likewise there may be job choices you need to abandon if your needs will not be met. There may be career choices that, once you consider the ramifications, are simply not that attractive after all. Remember, all needs are valid, and threshold needs are crucially so.

Now let's look at some examples of alignment. The first two are success stories in life planning, and the last is an expensive, miserable, irreversible failure.

CASE STUDY Tatiana R.

Tatiana R. was interested in working in a veterinarian's office. It was one of her top five career interests after working through the program presented in this book. So she started visiting veterinary clinics and talking to support staff. She quickly learned that except for the vets, almost everybody earned minimum wage or very little more. She had no interest in becoming a veterinarian. With most of the jobs part-time, most of the staff were not trying to live off that income alone. This was well below her threshold income needs, so she dropped it from her list and pursued other interests.

CASE STUDY Lisa B.

Lisa B. had wanted to be a chef since high school. She loved to cook and had a great deal of talent for it. She frequented the best restaurants and was a real "foodie." Although she knew that entry-level wages were meager, she was satisfied that the chefs in top restaurants were paid well. Then her college career counselor asked if she understood that she would be standing on her feet eight to ten hours a day, that most chefs had no social life outside of the restaurant, and that the profession was famous for hot tempers and big egos. "It's not unusual for the chef to yell at the sous chefs and the line cooks," her counselor told her, and reminded her that it took years to climb through the ranks. Lisa decided that she was not willing to work in this type of environment. The really interesting thing about this story is that Lisa said later she already knew everything her counselor had told her, but had never really faced up to it. Now cooking is a major avocation for her, while she pursues a career in counseling.

CASE STUDY "Nancy"

Years ago, I had a career development office in the Financial District in San Francisco. Nancy had set first appointments with me three times and had missed the first two. The third time, she showed up and was ushered into my office. She was tall, very attractive, and wearing a very expensive suit. She sat down, put her head in her hands, and began to cry. I offered her a tissue and assured her that she could tell me what the matter was. She said—and this is an exact quote—"I went to law school because I thought I wanted to be a lawyer, and now all I do is work. I have to work ten to twelve hours every day, including Saturdays, and if we get behind, I have to work Sundays. I'm twenty-seven years old, and I haven't had a date in six months. I don't even know any guys. I'm making all this money, but I don't have time to spend it. I have to buy my clothes from catalogs because I can never leave the office. And I can't quit because I borrowed all this money, and there is nowhere else I can earn enough to cover my student loans." Unfortunately, she was right.

Nancy's case is a perfect example of not considering alignment in advance. Someone else might have been perfectly happy to attend a top-ten law school and follow that up with a job at a top-ten law firm, but Nancy's threshold needs for time and intimacy were not being met. She didn't find out in advance what her future career would really be like, and no amount of money in the world could make up for what she was not getting. Had she asked some young associates in big-time law firms, they could have told her about the hours and the pressure. Uninformed, Nancy was blindsided.

This is alignment: the alignment of your life plan with the reality of your job choices, and the alignment of at least some of your job choices with the ramifications that necessarily go with those choices. Magical thinking simply doesn't work.

All these things matter, but out of all the aspects of job choices to pay attention to concerning alignment, the two biggies are income and work-life balance:

- Will you earn enough money to live the way you want?
- Will the jobs you have in mind allow you to have the kind of life you want *outside* of work?

Just as a caution: Try not to be overly fearful of some of the less-than-savory aspects of entry-level jobs. You should look at every job five to ten years out, and ask yourself if it will satisfy you. Entry-level jobs often entail hard work, lots of hours, much responsibility but little power, and so on. These are the compromises I was talking about when referring to adult life. There's an old saying that applies to this situation: You have to win the game to change the rules. So expect to pay some dues before you get everything you want. But be sure to consider whether the job will lead to what you want five to ten years from now.

And as a further caution: High-risk professions present special problems on the question of alignment. They carry a high risk of failure. This is a ramification of the career choice, but don't remove those high-risk professions that you otherwise remain very interested in. If you still want to be an artist or musician or professional athlete or dancer or novelist or, for that matter, president of the United States, you can leave them on the list at this stage if everything besides the risk is attractive. We'll consider risk assessment and risk reduction more carefully in the career exploration phase, part 2.

Review the top five choices you're considering for exploration. Are there any jobs that, considering all the ramifications of that choice, are out of alignment with your threshold needs? Review the many sample alignment questions in this chapter. Are there any choices that, when you really consider what is involved, seem decidedly unattractive after all? If so, strike them now and replace them with another job choice from your large selection of options. Remember, your final list should have some variability to it and include at least one or two life goals you had not considered before working through the book.

After considering alignment, list the most current **Top Five Job Ideas** that you think you want to explore further.

You're almost ready to look into these employment options. But first, you must ask yourself if there isn't something else entirely that you'd rather do for a year or two first.

6

A Different Kind of Choice

There are many reasons that college graduates choose not to launch a long-term life plan right away upon leaving college.

Some believe that service is a social obligation, and choose to put in a year or two volunteering for the larger good before going on to launch a search for a professional track job. Ironically, young people who join the military and young people who join the Peace Corps are often motivated by the exact same desire—a desire to serve others before serving themselves.

Some new graduates are headed for graduate school and are looking for an enjoyable and structured experience to give them a break in their studies.

Still others are just not ready to give up the feeling that they have their whole lives ahead of them. They may feel that launching a career is the beginning of becoming their parents, and wish to avoid that inevitability for a year or two longer.

And some just want adventure, and are not at all worried about long-term employment. They believe, rightly so, that they can do that later.

So what are your options? Here are just a few possible choices:

Volunteering

AMERICORPS

This is straight from the AmeriCorps media packet:

"AmeriCorps is a network of national service programs that engage more than 50,000 Americans each year in intensive service to meet critical needs in education, public safety, health, and the environment. AmeriCorps members serve through more than 2,100 nonprofits, public agencies, and faith-based organizations. They tutor and mentor youth, build affordable housing, teach computer skills, clean parks and streams, run after-school programs, and help communities respond to disasters. Created in 1993, AmeriCorps is part of the Corporation for National and Community Service, which also oversees Senior Corps and Learn and Serve America. Together these programs engage more than 2 million Americans of all ages and backgrounds in service each year."

AmeriCorps provides two options for young volunteers:

AmeriCorps' VISTA works to bring individuals and communities out of poverty. Working for one year in a nonprofit, public agency, or faith-based group, you will have the opportunity to fight illiteracy, improve health services, create businesses, increase housing opportunities, or bridge the digital divide.

AmeriCorps' NCCC is a ten-month, full-time residential program for youth ages eighteen to twenty-four. Combining the best practices of civilian service with the best aspects of military service, you will work with a team of ten to fifteen on projects in public safety, public health, and disaster relief. Based at one of five campuses around the country, teams are trained and sent to work on short-term projects in surrounding states.

AmeriCorps provides very modest living expenses and a stipend, and sets aside monies that can be used to relieve student loan debts or to pay for future education. You get access to those monies when you complete your term; commitments range from ten months to one year. You do not have to be a college graduate to serve with AmeriCorps, but not all applicants are accepted. AmeriCorps is facing funding challenges at this time, so check the latest reports before trying to sign up.

AmeriCorps
www.americorps.org
1201 New York Avenue NW
Washington, D.C. 20525
(800) 942–2677

PEACE CORPS

This is straight out of the Peace Corps media packet:

"All assignments are for two years plus three months of training in your country of service. Only U.S. citizens may join the Peace Corps. You have to be at least eighteen to join, and most assignments require four-year college degrees. Applicants without a college degree may qualify by having three to five years of work experience in an area such as managing a business or working in a skilled trade."

About 95 percent of assignments require a bachelor's degree. Prior volunteer experience and proven ability to learn a foreign language are unofficial requirements. Your GPA is not as important as your attitude and philosophy of service. Ability to work with your hands (carpentry, painting, construction work, and that sort of thing) is also an unofficial plus. Many Peace Corps volunteers end up as teachers, so teaching or tutoring experience is also an asset. Of the 10,500 who apply, 5,000 are accepted. The Peace Corps is facing funding challenges at this time, so check the latest reports before trying to sign up.

The Peace Corps also has a model returning reorientation program, with good support for the post–Peace Corps job search and graduate school applications, and the Peace Corps alumni network is a lifetime asset for members.

Peace Corps

www.peacecorps.org

The Paul D. Coverdell Peace Corps Headquarters

1111 - 20th Street NW

Washington, D.C. 20526

(800) 424–8580

TEACH FOR AMERICA

This is straight out of Teach For America's media packet:

"Teach For America is the national corps of outstanding college graduates of all academic majors and backgrounds who commit two years to teach in urban and rural public schools and become lifelong leaders in the effort to ensure that all children in our nation have an equal chance in life. Since our inception in 1990, approximately 9,000 exceptional individuals have joined Teach For America, directly impacting the lives of more than 1.25 million students, and taking on leadership roles as alumni to increase opportunity for children. Teach For America places teachers in eighteen locations across the country."

No previous teaching experience is required, but a cumulative GPA of 2.5 is, and a college degree must be completed before the first day of teacher training in the summer. American citizenship is a prerequisite, and expect a background check. Of the 14,000 who apply, 1,400 are accepted. Teach For America's funding was recently severely cut, so check the latest reports before trying to sign up.

Teach For America

www.teachforamerica.org

National Office

315 West 36th Street
New York, NY 10018
(800) 832–1230
(212) 279–2080
(212) 279–2081 fax

Teach English Overseas

Teaching English Abroad by Susan Griffith, Vacation-Work; 6th edition, 2003.

More Than a Native Speaker: An Introduction for Volunteers Teaching English Abroad by Donald B. Snow, TESOL Publications, 1996.

Teaching English Overseas: A Job Guide for Americans and Canadians by Jeff Mohamad, English International, 2000.

Also, I recommend you check out this book on both international and domestic opportunities:

The Back Door Guide to Short-Term Job Adventures by Michael Landes, Ten Speed Press; 3rd edition, 2002.

International Careers

The Global Citizen: A Guide to Creating an International Life and Career by Elizabeth Kruempelmann, www.the-global-citizen.com.

Alternatives to the Peace Corps: A Directory of Third World and U.S. Volunteer Opportunities by Joan Powell, Food First Books, 2001.

Careers for Travel Buffs and Other Restless Types by Paul Plawin, McGraw-Hill, 2003.

Post-Baccalaureate Internships

Google "post-baccalaureate internships" and you'll get a wide-ranging list of options, paid and unpaid, full- and part-time.

Check out Kalamazoo College's excellent resources at www.kzoo.edu/career/externships.

Apply to any organization that lists any internship opportunities.

In addition to the organizations you can find with the resources listed above, consider a year of service with an advocacy or issue-oriented group, or a national or international nonprofit/NGO.

Also, check out the latest on post-baccalaureate internships on my website: www.donaldasher.com/careers.

What follows is a partial list, but remember, many of these will have few or no paid positions:

Democratic National Committee
www.democrats.org/about/interns.html
Internship Office
430 South Capitol Street SE
Washington, D.C. 20003
(202) 863–8000
(and local campaigns and chapters nationwide)

Republican National Committee
www.rnc.org
Internship Programs
310 First Street SE
Washington, D.C. 20003
(202) 863–8500
(and local campaigns and chapters nationwide)

The Green Party
www.gp.org/interns.html
Green Party Interns
P.O. Box 57065
Washington, D.C. 20037
(202) 319–7191 or (866) 41GREEN
(and local campaigns and chapters nationwide)

Sierra Club San Francisco
www.sierraclub.org/jobs/internships_sf/
85 Second Street, 2nd Floor
San Francisco, CA 94105
(415) 977–5500

Sierra Club Washington, D.C.
www.sierraclub.org/jobs/internships_dc/
408 C Street NE
Washington, D.C. 20002
(202) 547–1141

Boys and Girls Clubs of America (BGCA)
www.bgca.org/clubs
(with regional and local iterations nationwide)

American Red Cross National Headquarters
Internship Coordinator
Corporate Diversity Department
8111 Gatehouse Road, 6th Floor
Falls Church, VA 22042
(703) 206–8572

Habitat for Humanity
(decentralized domestic and international operations)
www.habitat.org/HR/

Save the Children
www.savethechildren.org
54 Wilton Road
Westport, CT 06880
(203) 221–4030

Jesuit Volunteer Corps
(organized by region)
www.jesuitvolunteers.org

Catholic Charities
www.catholiccharitiesusa.org
1731 King Street
Alexandria, VA 22314
(703) 549–1390
(and branches nationwide)

The Military

When considering the military as a post-college choice, it is important to remember that college graduates are routed to the officers' corps, and that two-year stint you might have imagined may not be available. The minimum commitment for an officer in the Army is three years after you've completed training, which can vary. If you add flight school, JAG, (Judge Advocate General) or an MOS (military occupational specialty), you're looking at more than a six-year minimum commitment.

All the armed forces—Army, Navy, Marine Corps, Air Force, Coast Guard—will accept college graduates into basic training, but you will face pressure to enter an officer candidate school and make a longer commitment.

The Army has 212 different occupational specialties, and just because you were a French lit major doesn't mean you're going to end up peeling potatoes; you may get routed to the Defense Language Institute to train in special ops. Then again, you're going to have to pass rigorous physical training all the same.

The national recruiting offices for each branch of the military are listed here. You can locate a local recruiting office by going to the website of your favored branch of the military. Start out by consulting with a recruiter for the branch you're interested in. It's a good idea to shop around, not only between branches, but even between recruiting stations within the same branch. I strongly recommend you get some kind of personal introduction to a recruiter, and listen carefully to any veterans or currently enlisted personnel you can find. Because once you're sworn in, you'll complete the hitch one way or another.

Do not assume you can get into the military. Their physical and character requirements are stringent, and many applicants are, in fact, turned down. Prior minor legal infractions and excessive weight are common reasons for declining recruits, even those with spotless academic records.

The national recruiting offices for each branch of the military are

Army

www.goarmy.com

Navy

www.navyjobs.com

Marine Corps

www.marines.com

Air Force

www.airforce.com

Coast Guard

www.gocoastguard.com

A Tour

As mentioned earlier, from the nineteenth century until the 1950s there was a tradition of the grand tour upon completion of college. A young American gentleman or lady was expected to go to Europe to tour museums and hear foreign languages. This was so they would be interesting at cocktail parties. Later, they would marry well and/or join their uncle's brokerage or trading company. Those days are long gone.

But that doesn't mean you can't be a romantic and follow in their footsteps. Just remember, it's your job to pay your own way in this world, so taking a tour does not mean someone else is obligated to pay for it.

If you already have the resources, you can go adventuring and worry about launching a job search when you return. Or you can take an any-wage job, save your money, and then go. You can also work your way around the world. A close friend of mine worked her way around the world as a cocktail waitress, and came back with more money than she had when she left. Many countries have a more relaxed interest in work papers than the United States, so a strong work ethic and a little flexibility can get you far.

You can also take a domestic tour, also known as a road trip. Reconnect with your roots, explore historic sites, visit grandparents before they're gone, explore a spiritual practice, work on a political campaign, find a mentor and build a wooden boat—that kind of thing.[9]

You may decide to replace one or more of your top five job choices, or you may decide to abandon the whole life launch project for now and go on a road trip. If you do decide to pursue one of these activities, remember that you can also pursue employment exploration even while you're building wooden boats or serving in the military. In fact, it would be a waste if you did not use this time to further refine your job interests.

As a final word of caution: Some of these activities are quite competitive, as you can see from the numbers above (applicants/admitted). It is a good idea to have a backup plan, either involving education or a job or a post-baccalaureate internship or an exploratory entry-level job, in case you don't get the assignment you wanted.

NOTES

1. Illustration provided by Dr. Howard Figler in the video, "Job Search Success for Liberal Arts Majors," copresented by the author, University of Tennessee Television Studios, February 26, 2003.

2. "College Experiences and Managerial Performance," monograph by Ann Howard, *Journal of Applied Psychology,* 71, no. 3, 1986:530–52.

Cf. Northeastern University's Center for Labor Market Studies, with conflicting findings, but they measured all liberal arts majors, including the higher percentage that don't take jobs requiring a college degree.

3. *Ted Turner Speaks: Insights from the World's Greatest Maverick*, by Janet Lowe, p. 39.

4. Ferguson Publishing, *Career Opportunities News*, Jan/Feb 2003.

5. Ferguson Publishing, *Career Opportunities News*, Jan/Feb 2003.

6. For an excellent explication of this theory, read *The Company of the Future* by Frances Cairncross.

7. Yes, I'm aware of Kevin Maney's excellent autobiography of IBM's Thomas Watson, *The Maverick and His Machine*, in which he cannot trace this quote reliably to either Thomas Watson, Sr., or Thomas Watson, Jr., or in a variation to the engineer Howard Aiken; yet in each case he reports meetings and interviews where something like this was said. That's sufficient for my point, which is that predicting the future is a dangerous pastime.

8. As quoted in *USA Today*, May 23, 2002, upon conferral of the Templeton Prize.

9. I am indebted to Patricia E. Craig, career specialist counselor at Pasadena City College, for some of these suggestions.

Finding Out about Your Interests in the Real World

PART 2

Go confidently in the direction of your dreams!

Live the life you've imagined.

—Henry David Thoreau

7

Prepare to Learn More

Now that you have at least five job ideas, it's time to explore them further. It's time to discover more about what career paths are like, which jobs in the field might be good entry points, how one advances in a given field, what kind of education is required or which skills you might need to develop, and to winnow and sift your list. In short, it is time to find out more—to be sure these jobs are right for you and that you are right for these jobs.

As you learn more, your interest in some of the jobs and careers under consideration may wane and even be replaced. So you are not at all finished with the work from part 1. You may wish to resurrect a job or two from discarded lists, if you decide to abandon as unattractive or impracticable a job you currently cherish.

Before proceeding further, however, list your **Top Five Job Ideas** (as they stand right now) that you think you want to explore further.

Job Exploration

Introspection is the primary tool for both job ideation and job exploration. And if you were paying attention and you did all the exercises suggested in parts 1 and 2, by now you're pretty good at it.

Career counseling is also a tool for job exploration, as you delve deeper into possible choices with your advisors. It is important to remember that "career counselors" can be parents, faculty, other mentors, and so on, as well as the trained and talented counselors available to you through your college or university career center.

Now that you have some job ideas, here is a complete toolbox for the next phase, job exploration:

- Introspection
- Career counseling
- Class project
- Independent study
- Capstone project
- Campus activities
- Community activities
- Information networking
- Company receptions
- Shadowing
- Volunteering
- Internship
- Summer job
- Post-baccalaureate internship
- Entry-level exploratory job
- Continuing education
- Credential
- Master's degree
- Terminal or professional degree

We'll define each of these and then discuss how you can further explore the job ideas you've developed so far.

One of your goals in all types of job exploration is to take the intermediate steps necessary to get from where you are today to where you want to go. For example, if your goal is to be partner at a top CPA firm or chief of surgery at a prestigious hospital or CEO of a global media company, you need to find out about all the intermediate steps necessary to get there. You need to map out all the job experiences and the typical sequence for obtaining them, the best pre–graduate school jobs and internships to pursue, the educational requirements and the typical schedule for fulfilling them, as well as the interpersonal and professional skills required and how the most successful professionals develop them.

For example, playing golf is a known prerequisite for executive success in certain fields. That doesn't mean that you must learn to play golf. But it does mean that if you choose not to learn to play golf (or go to graduate school, or take an offshore assignment, or master your emotions), you are deviating from what is for some professions a known formula for success. In short, it is your job to discover known formulas for success.

Mapping the steps in between college and a distant professional goal is a critical life development skill. So, as you go through all these methodologies, do not lose track of the fact that you are trying to build a life road map. A graduate degree or an internship is never an end in itself; it is a tool that either does or does not advance you toward your life goals. We'll cover this in greater detail near the end of part 2, but for now, remember your goal and don't get lost in the details of information networking and post-baccalaureate internships.

As you continue your exploration, ask yourself, "What is the next thing I need to do to get to _____?" And the next thing after that, and so on. No one becomes chief of surgery straight out of medical school, so if that's your goal, you're going to have to get more sophisticated about the intermediary steps.

Now let's consider tried and proven methods for doing job exploration.

> Your vision will become clear only when you can look into your own heart.
> Who looks outside, DREAMS, who looks inside, AWAKES.
>
> —*Carl Jung*

Introspection

Introspection is thinking about the life path, its costs and benefits, and yourself, your skills and needs, paying particular attention to identifying your threshold needs.

Career Counseling

Every time you talk to anyone about your life goals and aptitude for pursuing them, you are conducting career counseling. In fact, even when you are in a job interview trying to win an offer, you are doing a kind of career counseling. Although some career counselors are bound to decry this definition as apostasy, I am going to define career counseling as "talking to people about your career" and, of course, listening to what they have to say.

Class Project, Independent Study, or Capstone Project

Many students miss the chance to use their education to explore job options more fully. If you're interested in a job choice, like underwater archaeology, instead of waiting until school is out to explore this option, approach a professor right now and design an independent study class around your job interest. There is no topic so obscure that you couldn't design an independent study class around it, to gain credit toward graduation while exploring your interest. If you have friends with the same interest, you might form a seminar group or even an actual class around it.

Likewise, many schools have a senior project, a thesis, a senior seminar, or a capstone project that students can use to pursue more information about a potential job option. With a little creativity, you can investigate almost any goal from almost any major. If you are interested in medical options and you are a theology major, study the association of religious faith with recovery times from various medical maladies. If you are interested in working in Latin America upon graduation and you are an economics major, obviously you want to study an aspect of pan-American financial issues while still a student.

This is also an excellent way to gain access to people and places normally closed to outsiders. If you are interested in the use of DNA in crime scene analysis, why not design a senior project around it? If you want to know how a new presidential administration picks thousands of political appointees in a matter of weeks, research and write a white paper on the process.

Even if you don't have a strong enough interest to devote a whole class to a particular topic, ask a professor if you can focus one of your regular classroom assignments on an employment interest. In graduate school, a classmate and I were bored and designed a field study to spice up a class. We met human resources professionals in some of the fastest growing companies in America and learned about some unique business challenges created by rapid growth. My primary interest was the impact of rapid growth on the career paths of people already employed by these firms. What we learned in our field study was ultimately far more important to our own employment paths than anything we learned in the rest of class.

By the time your course is over, you'll know more than enough about it to design a job entry point for yourself.

By the way, if you plan to work abroad—ever—please be smart and take foreign languages now. As in the case study below, even one year of a foreign language is better than none. Assignments abroad are increasingly required for advancement in large corporations. Being comfortable with other cultures and languages can be a real, long-term career booster.

CASE STUDY Derrick L.

Derrick L. was an international business major who had taken four years of foreign languages, but not like most students. He took one year of Chinese, one year of Japanese, one year of French, and one year of Arabic. "I didn't go to a name-brand business school," he told me. "So I needed a way to stand out. My advisor thought I was crazy, but I have straight A's in foreign languages. In fact, each one was easier than the last. You just have to learn how to memorize. I knew I wanted to work abroad, but who knows where the hot spot will be? All over the world, business during the day is conducted in English. But what really matters is what happens at night. You have to speak the local language, wherever you are, if you want to be really good."

For an international marketing class, Derrick skipped the usual route of writing about products and production and instead wrote a comparative analysis of business protocols in Asia and Europe. For a senior-level finance class, Derrick studied currency hedging systems used by companies doing business worldwide. Next fall he'll be going to work for one of the largest management consulting firms in the world doing the same thing.

"Definitely it was my two papers that got me this job. Do you know how hard it is to understand Japanese honorifics? You can't send a team to Japan without that knowledge on the team. And with the Euro challenging the U.S. dollar for the role of global currency, my hedging paper should remain relevant for years."

CASE STUDY Caty B.

Caty B. wanted to work with children in women's shelters, so for a class project she wrote a paper: "Slipping Through the Net: How Philadelphia Treats and Mistreats Children in Crisis." She met all the executive directors of programs serving battered women, women in recovery, women under court supervision, and homeless women. Later in her senior year, she knew just which program she wanted to work for, and getting a job was as simple as calling someone she had already met and asking for it.

"They made me submit a resume and go through the interview process, but they let me know that I was basically hired right from that first phone call," Caty told me. She's getting valuable experience in preparation for applying to graduate school.

"I want to go into clinical psychology, which is really competitive now, or get a master's and then a doctorate in social work, which would give me more options. I don't have to decide now, and this is great experience for me either way."

Campus and Community Activities

You can also take advantage of campus and community activities to explore job ideas. Activities are useful for skills development, self-discovery, and job exploration. Later, in part 3, we'll discuss how you can take campus activities and create portfolio and resume material; but for now, let's consider how campus activities might support job exploration.

If you're interested in a profession, obviously you want to belong to the student association related to that profession, such as a student affiliate of American Society of Interior Designers (ASID) if you're interested in interior architecture or interior design. Or the student marketing association or premed society, if you're interested in pursuing one of these fields. But a smart student takes this much further than just finding something to put on a resume. She'll organize events, and bring in speakers, and gain access to VIPs in the profession.

Being more than casually active in a preprofessional club is obvious. But think about the skills you can develop and the career options you can explore in any student organization. The first budgets I ever prepared and some of the first advertising and promotions I ever did were for student organizations, and these experiences helped me tremendously when I started my own business just a few years later. What can *you* learn?

One of your jobs as an undergraduate is to find out what you like to do and what you don't like to do. For example, if you think you might be interested in producing events, see if you can produce meetings, conventions, seminars, or performance events for a student group, even one you're not a member of. If you're interested in working in philanthropy, development, or fundraising, put on a fundraising event for your favorite charity or student organization. If you think you might like a job in accounting or management consulting, work with the treasurer for any student group on campus. Many groups need volunteers for this type of nuts-and-bolts administration, and the skills you will develop are exactly what employers want to see. Besides, you may discover that you don't like accounting, and then you can eliminate it as a future direction.

Look again at the case study of Julie L., beginning on page 14. Notice how she used her sorority connections to maximum advantage, not just for networking, but also to gain real experience to test herself and to gain direct access to VIPs while still a student. One of the secret hot committees on any campus is the public affairs committee, sometimes known as the speakers' committee. You'll gain direct access to VIPs when they visit your campus, and you'll be able to ask them all kinds of questions about your interests. Always volunteer to pick them up and deliver them back to the airport. Others may see this service as a chore, often requiring early mornings, but it's direct access to people who would normally be quite inaccessible to strangers.

Even intramural sports can give you opportunities to develop skills and test your abilities: learning to get along well with others, coordinating complex logistics, being a member of a team, and managing your time well.

Think about all your college activities. Are there any activities you're not taking advantage of that could become part of your exploration efforts? If so, write about them in your life planning notebook, describing the skills and experiences you've gained or hope to gain from them.

Company Receptions

On-campus recruiting schedules, that is, the lists of students who actually get to meet one-on-one with recruiters, often involve certain restrictions. They may be restricted to certain majors, cite minimum grade point averages, require at least some experience in the field, or insist that candidates be U.S. citizens. But a company reception is almost always open to all; usually, everybody is welcome.

Company receptions are sponsored by corporate recruiters during both the spring and fall semesters. They usually involve a short PowerPoint presentation or slide show, followed by Q&A with several company representatives, including a recruiter, also known as a "college relations manager," or happy, good-looking young people hired in recent years, or both. The reception often features free sodas and logo-laden swag.

The goal of these receptions is to increase a firm's profile on campus, to get the word out about how great the employer is, how wonderful it is to work there, how powerfully intelligent the company's strategy is, and how you'd be a fool not to work there if you were lucky enough to be offered a job.

Most such receptions are hosted by larger companies that can afford a promotional budget that is not tied to a particular recruiting effort. They are usually attended mainly by business and engineering students, but—and here's the sweet part—companies that recruit on college campuses hire all types of students.

This is an excellent opportunity to get all kinds of employment information, as the representatives are sponsoring the reception for just that purpose: to answer your questions about getting jobs at their companies. So even if you're an English lit major, you can learn about opportunities with a technology-based firm.

Company receptions are often scheduled and promoted on relatively short notice, so drop by the career center every week to see what's on offer.

Shadowing

Shadowing is the more adult version of going to work with mom or dad to see what they do for a living. But now it's not your mom and dad you're going to work with, and it's not about what they do for a living but about what you might want to do for a living.

As you are networking, you are going to discover people doing exactly what you think you would like to do someday. Ask them to allow you to shadow them for a day (or a morning or afternoon) to get a feel for what a day in the life of a _____ is actually like.

Organized shadowing programs have long been common in the premed and pre-dental fields, and are on the increase in general business. Some university career centers coordinate shadowing events for all interested students, allowing them to go to work with local executives. These programs allow students to discover more about professional employment.

Several career center directors have privately complained to me that these events sometimes devolve into a polite little PR tour and a free lunch, which is not what they are supposed to be. Properly conducted, the student observer should say nothing and interfere as little as possible with the routine duties of the professional being observed.

In any case, don't wait for an organized program. Try to arrange a shadowing day on your own, especially if you're interested in something a little different, such as nautical engineering or police work or art auctioneering.

Ask your career center for referrals to practicing professionals you can approach for shadowing opportunities, and even ask your career counselor if she'll make the first contact for you, to see if the professional is receptive to such a proposal. Also, use all your own networking contacts to identify midcareer professionals you can approach about a shadowing opportunity.

Even under the best of circumstances, shadowing can be disruptive to the professional's normal work routine, so it is uncommon for a shadowing opportunity to last more than a day or two. For the same reason, it is unusual for people early in their careers to be appropriate sponsors for shadowing.

As in all other job exploration activities, shadowing will help you identify employment that is attractive to you and discover things about it you might like and not like so much. Shadowing also helps you identify jobs that, despite your initial attraction, are *not* that attractive once you learn more about them.

Review the list of information networking contacts you have developed, and identify any that might be good sponsors for a shadowing opportunity. Then make an appointment with your career center to see if they can help you set one up.

8

Are You Ready for Networking?

Information networking means identifying people who will know more about a career interest, and simply making contact with them to talk about what they know. This is how you learn the secret handshake that all industries have. You need to learn the lingo and find out what the unwritten rules are, as well as find out if this path is for you. You need to know typical job titles, which jobs can be considered entry level, and what the requirements really are for both entry level and continued advancement.

The Informational Interview

For example, if you were to go on an informational interview in a publishing house, you would learn that an editorial assistant is a very different position from an associate editor. To a novice, they sound similar, but they are not. An editorial assistant is the lowest possible assignment in publishing, the absolute bottom of the food chain. An associate editor is only three levels from God. An editorial assistant is a gofer, who copies manuscripts and checks facts and proofreads revisions and gets everybody lunch. He also reads at night from the slush pile, trying to find that one gem of a manuscript that will get him promoted. An associate editor reports to an editor who reports to the editor-in-chief who reports to the publisher who answers only to God.

You have to know all this to have a prayer's chance of getting a job in publishing.

But first, you absolutely must have a specific employment idea in mind before you start information networking. You will waste your time, and your contact's time, if you are still undecided on what interests you. So if you are in the "I dunno. Anything," stage of your career development, you need to go back through job ideation in part 1 before you go on.

Remember, ideas may come from any of the exercises you've done so far. Here's a case study of a job idea that is ready to be explored further. Rob had a summer job at a recycling center and got more than a little interested in what happened to the materials that passed through the center.

CASE STUDY Rob B.

Here is Rob B.'s career idea, ready for exploration: "I want to find out more about the global trade in recyclable materials, in particular, circuit boards and computers and other fairly complex commercial and consumer goods full of toxins. Where do they go? Who buys them? What is done with them? I guess I'm interested in all types of recyclable material, but on an industrial scale. I want to find out what kinds of jobs would allow me to trade globally in recyclable materials, by the ton or by the container load, at a minimum. I think I'll start by (a) calling all the computer collection centers I can find, to find out where they sell their stuff, and (b) calling the town recycling center where I used to work. I should be able to just follow the chain to identify some brokers."

You may have some job ideas that are fairly complete, and others that are just being formed, but there is a minimum level of definition required before going out to seek more information. The following ideas are *not* well formed enough to begin information networking:

- Something in advertising
- Something on Wall Street
- Something in higher ed administration

These three career ideas are well formed enough for information networking:

- Something on the visual arts side of advertising
- Some kind of investment analysis position on Wall Street
- A job as an admissions recruiter for a college or university

Information networking is exciting and productive. Your initial idea may be discarded in the first five minutes of doing it, never to be taken up again as you learn about fabulous jobs and career paths that you never imagined. But if you don't come in the door with a specific idea, few people are going to want to help you. You will give your alma mater a bad reputation if you contact alumni and practicing professionals without doing at least some introspection and homework first.

One more time, and this time with gusto! List **Five Career Ideas** you are now ready to investigate further.

Networking Is about Information, Not Power

When we think of networking, many of us will immediately conclude, "I need to find someone who could hire me, someone who is prominent and powerful." Not true! Networking is about information, not power. Assuming you're ready to pick one of these ideas and explore it, anybody in the right industry will have knowledge of value to you. In fact, the ideal contact for information networking is someone doing the job you want to have in three to five years. They are near enough to the entry level to give you useful advice, yet far enough into the organization to give you a sense of the bigger picture. In the case study on page 98, Clary N. met with a prominently successful professional, but it has been so many years since he was a beginner that his advice for her was not that useful.

Where can you find someone who knows about the industry you're interested in? More to the point, where can you find someone who now has the job you want to have in three to five years? By referral through your career center, by referral through your alumni office, and by networking with everyone you know.

Let's consider each scenario. The career center has access to employers, alumni, and currently enrolled students returning from internships and shadowing experiences. They can find contacts for you in any industry, from accounting to corporate law to television to zoology. They will know of employers in the area who might be willing to share information with a polite and well-prepared student. They will have a national alumni volunteer database, that is, alumni who have specifically volunteered to help students like you. A more savvy student will try to gain access to the full alumni database, which includes all the alumni who did not volunteer to be career mentors. This increases your contact base by many thousands of names, but as we will discuss in "Networking Etiquette" beginning on page 101, these alumni must be approached with greater care and consideration.

Most alumni offices will avoid assisting students in job development, as this is not their mission, and they may have had unhappy experiences with student job seekers in the past. However, a personal appeal to an alumni officer can overcome this bias. Just remember that the alumni office at most universities provides referrals only to the most prepared and professional of students. So before you approach them, know what you're after and be ready to explain exactly how you're going to approach an alumna or alumnus.

Career centers and alumni offices will usually not conduct a database search for you of alumni employed in corporate tax law, for example. Usually this will be your responsibility.

Alumni are a great source of employment information for students, because you have a built-in connection with them. They are predisposed to like you and help you. Also, many alumni feel a sense of loyalty to their almae maters, and they relish a chance to contribute to the academic community by helping you. Plainly put, most alumni want to help you!

This is an important principle for you to understand. You are not bothering an alumna or alumnus by seeking career information, as long as you don't ask him or her for a job. If you ask for a job, you've violated an unwritten rule of etiquette. Before we cover more of these unwritten rules, let's consider other sources for networking contacts.

The Networking Game

Everyone has a network. It includes everyone in your family, everyone in your apartment complex or dorm, everyone in your classes, everyone from back home or from high school, everyone you know. A partial list of networking contacts appears on pages 104–106. If you think of everyone you've ever met who might remember you, it's at least several hundred people.

Perhaps you've heard the theory that everyone in the world can be connected through a maximum of six degrees of separation. It turns out that's not quite true, but it's usually true.[1] The Networking Game is based on this principle: For most groups of people, it's not hard to find a connection between person A and person G, and the number of connections rarely exceeds six. If you ask about the *type* of person, instead of the specific person, the number of connections required drops dramatically.

Here's how you play. Gather a group of fifty people together and, one at a time, ask for a career connection. The questions should always start out with "Does anyone know anybody who_____?" For example, a person might ask, "Does anyone know anybody who works in management consulting in Los Angeles?" And someone else might ask, "Does anyone know anybody who is a music agent, or who is a musician who tours with a successful band, or who has a record contract?"

And the next person might ask, "Does anyone know anybody who might be able to tell me how to become a prison chaplain?" And so on.

If you have fifty or more people in a room, two or more will raise their hands no matter how obscure or outlandish the query.

Now here's the secret: *You don't need fifty people in a room. You can just ask the next fifty people you meet and get the exact same results.*

So once you have a job idea, get in the habit of asking everyone you meet, "Hey, do you know anybody who could tell me more about industrial espionage?"

Underutilized Contacts

It is a truism among those who study networking that the most unlikely of connections is in fact quite likely to succeed. So your ex-boyfriend's old tennis buddy's aunt's stockbroker's wedding photographer could be the most useful connection for you.

Students often overlook some important networking channels, or at least fail to develop them systematically:

- Faculty
- Friends of parents
- Parents of friends

Faculty members often know where students from prior classes got jobs, and typically know the whereabouts of hundreds of their former students. Ask, and they can hook you up with grads from three to five years earlier.

Also, faculty belong to invisible networks that students don't usually imagine and cannot see. For example, they are usually involved in professional associations and know other faculty all over the country. They may also be involved in joint ventures and have consulting relationships with a wide range of business, industrial, and governmental entities.

So be sure to poll your faculty for contacts in your desired fields.

Another great networking resource is friends of parents and parents of friends. If your mother has an old friend in the mayor's office and you are interested in city government, it's time to work on that contact. If your best friend's dad is an economist with a think tank that is intriguing to you, it's time to lean on your friend for an introduction. These networks provide virtually guaranteed access to powerful, knowledgeable, and influential people at the height of their careers.

You've already made a list of jobs held by the friends of your parents and the parents of your friends. Are there any people you need to contact this week?

Practicing Professionals, and the Rich and Famous

There is no need to be intimidated by the rich and famous. When I was an undergraduate, I wrote heartfelt letters to a series of famous people asking their advice about a particular matter. About 10 percent wrote back! I have a framed letter from author James Dickey on the wall in my office.

Even celebrities can be approached at public appearances, especially lectures, and you can get a few questions in if you mob them right after the talk.

Accosting the secretary of state or the latest Nobel Prize–winning physicist may be difficult, but I think you should be perfectly comfortable approaching professionals that you do not know and asking if they would have a moment to speak with you about their careers.

As obvious as it may sound, if you want to go to dental school, call or email some dentists. If you want to become a neurosurgeon, call or email some neurosurgeons. If you want to be a CPA, call or email some CPAs. If you want to be an FBI agent, call or email some FBI agents. Whatever your professional interest, don't be afraid to contact strangers who are successful and seek their advice on how to get into and succeed in the field.

CASE STUDY Clary N.

Clary N. wanted to be a photographer, but her father, a banker, was aghast. So he set up a meeting with a friend of the family, a successful commercial photographer with international magazine credits. I sat in on the meeting. The photographer was advised in advance (by the father) to discourage Clary. He didn't, but he did tell her some tough truths. "Your very best work, the most balanced and beautiful photograph you will ever make," he said, kissing his fingertips. "They're going to put a pack of cigarettes right in the middle." He also talked about risk. "Only one photographer in a hundred ever makes a dime from his work, and only one in maybe fifty thousand gets to live as I do." The meeting was in his apartment, thirty-three floors above the lakefront in Chicago. Clary told me later, "I knew all that. What I wanted him to tell me was how to sell my first photograph."

CASE STUDY Maria H.

Maria H. loved accounting but found all the entry-level jobs distasteful. "Then my professor described forensic accounting, and that sounded really interesting," she told me. Maria got a referral from her professor to a forensic accounting specialist. "She told me I didn't even have to get my CPA first, since I have bookkeeping skills.

It's a new field, and there are no real rules as far as who gets to do it. She was really encouraging about the intellectual challenge. It's like working out a puzzle or solving a mystery. And there are opportunities to be an expert witness once you get some experience. Very exciting."

CASE STUDY Kathleen D.

Kathleen D. was a geology major, interested in all aspects of ground water. When she discovered that a classmate's brother was an engineer in a geologic consulting firm, she wangled a meeting with him. He told her that all the big money in geology was in oil exploration and involved extensive travel and field assignments. If she wanted to do work that was more environmentally friendly and didn't involve long-term field assignments, he advised her to consider groundwater remediation consulting. His firm was active in cleaning up groundwater at old industrial sites and testing for groundwater contamination at industrial properties for sale. She had never heard of this job option and was very attracted to it.

Asking the Right Questions

When you connect with a networking source, whether it's in the foyer at a concert hall or by telephone or over a leisurely lunch, what do you ask? You want information about typical job titles and life paths, skills that are required for success, lifestyles of those with this type of employment, and so on. Pay particular attention to jobs that are considered entry points. You want to know what those jobs are called, that is, their most common titles. Also, who does the hiring—what are the titles and positions of the people most likely to hire people like you?

It does you little good to know the career path from SVP to CEO. You need to know how to get in, in the first place.

You also want to know what the jobs are like. What are the daily duties and routines? What are people in this field like? What do they wear? How many hours a week do they work? And so on.

Remember, people love to talk about themselves. In fact, most people consider themselves expert on at least one topic: themselves. So ask how they got started in their field, what their plans are for the future, and what they would have done differently if they had to do it all over again. You will get a tremendous amount of useful information and, unless you are interrogating them like a police detective, the meeting will pass quickly for both of you.

Be sure to ask, Who else does this? Where else should I be looking? When you are an outsider, you don't know things that may be common knowledge to insiders.

For example, you may be interested in advertising, so you would naturally approach advertising agencies. That's great, but be sure to ask people in advertising "Who else does this? Who else should I be talking to?" This will open up a whole new world for you. They'll tell you that advertising agencies are only the tip of the iceberg.

They'll tell you about marketing communications departments (also known as marcom departments) that exist in many large corporations and even some nonprofit and governmental organizations. They'll tell you that there is a whole sub-industry of commercial production companies in Los Angeles that make only television commercials. They'll tell you about marketing consulting companies and public relations firms that look, act, and feel like advertising agencies. And they'll tell you about promotions subcontractors, companies that do things like provide cheery young people to give away cheese squares in supermarkets. They'll tell you about legions of independent contractors, such as food stylists and underwear wranglers (yep, it is what you think it is). And they'll tell you about promotional products manufacturers, direct mail contractors, and fulfillment service bureaus, all of which are part of the advertising industry but not generally known by outsiders. All these companies want the same skill set as advertising agencies but draw much less competition than the highly visible Madison Avenue firms.

Finally, be sure to ask each contact whether you can get in touch with them again if you have further questions, and get their email address to make it easy for them to respond. Always be nice because everyone you meet while doing job exploration could become a critical contact when you get ready to do a job search.

Here are some of the Right Questions to Ask in Information Networking:

"How did you get into this field?"

"Can you describe a typical day? Week? Project? Business trip?"

"What kind of preparation is typical to get into this job? Is it really required, or just the usual approach?"

"What kind of people thrive in this industry? What character or personality traits would you say they have in common?"

"What are the typical entry-level jobs in this industry for new college graduates? What are the usual titles for these entry-level jobs; what departments do they work in; and who hires them?"

"Do you know anyone who is just starting out in this field, say, someone with three to five years' experience? Would it be alright if I called them and mentioned that I was referred by you?"

"What was different about the job than you expected? What was the biggest surprise when you went into this field? Any myths you'd like to shatter for me?"

"Who else does this kind of work? What other companies? Who else should I be talking to?"

"What ensures continued advancement?"

"What is the typical path out of this position or field? What does this prepare someone for next? For example, what's next for you?"

"What would you do differently if you had to do it all over again?"

"What advice do you have for someone like me?"

"How can I get some experience or more exposure before I graduate?"

"Can I contact you again if I have a follow-up question? I promise not to be a pest. Is email the best way to contact you?"

Remember, one of your main goals in information networking is to step back from your eventual goal and fill in all the steps between where you are now and where you want to be eventually. You need to be able to clearly visualize yourself going through the positions, experiences, and skills development required, step by step, to reach your goal.

If you cannot do this, you have not completed a thorough life path exploration, and you'll need to find more knowledgeable people to interview. **Ambition without a clear plan is not sufficient.** And you cannot create a clear plan out of your imagination. This is the most valuable part of information networking: learning the steps required to go from where you are, a college student, to where you want to be, wherever that is. You'll get some bad advice once in a while, but advice from people inside an industry is always superior to advice from people who have never been in that industry.

Networking Etiquette

Information networking is not the same thing as looking for a job. You are conducting job exploration, not a job search. The number one rule of information networking is this: *Never, never, never ask for a job.*

You should be fearless in approaching people for information, as long as you are nice, you are polite, and you will take no for an answer. Although you can make initial inquiries by mail, telephone, and personal introduction, email is a very good way to open a networking relationship. Email is low impact on the recipient. If they want to brush you off, it is easy for them to do so. If they are willing to help you, they can specify how they would like to proceed.

Never ask for a job, and be careful how you talk about salary. It is important for college students to learn as much as they can about salaries and compensation for various career options they are considering, but they have to be careful. Never ask a person how much he makes or how much his company pays. Instead, ask questions like these:

"What could a person expect to make in a position like this?"

"What would be a typical salary industry-wide for a position like this?"

Ask for salary data in ranges, not specific dollar values.

Occasionally during a networking session, you may accidentally stumble across a job opening that appeals to you. You're having a nice, open-ended conversation about their field, their job, and their company; and they may suddenly say, for example, "We hire interns every year for jobs like the one you're inquiring about," or "We have an opening right now at the entry level for someone like you." This creates a dilemma, because in an informational interview you must never act like you're applying for a job. So what do you do?

You have to apply for permission to apply. You must literally ask for permission to apply for the position. That way you are acknowledging that this informational networking meeting is not an interview for a job and you wish to know how to proceed. If you run into a promising opening, do not start acting like you are in a job interview. Instead, ask a question like,

"This sounds like a very interesting opportunity. How would I go about formally applying for a position like that?"

Then, follow their directions. If they encourage you to apply for the position, it is okay to ask,

"May I say I was referred by you? May I mention your name in my application letter?"

If they're really friendly, you can even ask,

"If I write a cover letter and email you a copy of it with my resume, would you be willing to put a note on it and forward it to the appropriate decision maker?"

Be overtly thankful and appreciative of all the help you receive. Learn to write prompt thank-you notes. They don't need to be fancy, and although some career advisors disagree, I think they may be handwritten. They can be this simple:

"Thank you so much for taking the time to meet with me yesterday. You were very helpful. I'll be thinking about everything we discussed as I continue with my job explorations."

Email is okay, but a card by mail is better still.

Special rules of etiquette apply when networking with alumni. Let me be blunt: alumni, especially loyal alumni who are also donors, are far more important to any university or college than a currently enrolled student, and that includes you. If you harass or annoy important and powerful alumni, you could find yourself banned from the career center and from university databases! Don't make a fool of yourself with alumni. If they volunteer to meet you at 7 A.M., be sure to be there on time. Send a thank-you card or email every time, and mind your manners. If you promise to send a resume or say hello to an old professor or call them back when you get a job, then you must follow through.

By the way, knowing how to get information by networking is an important life skill, not just a one-time-only, get-a-job skill. If you learn how to do this effectively, you will be a more effective financial executive or social worker or nurse than if you fail to master the art of networking.

Your task now is to identify people you can approach for information networking purposes. Start by playing The Networking Game with yourself. Ask yourself, "Whom do I know who could help me learn more about _____?"

Make a list of ten or twenty contacts that you'll use to launch your information networking. See the following workshop example from a student at the University of Tennessee, and before you say you don't have a network, refer to the list, People Who Want to Help You, on pages 104–106). Remember, an adult American knows six hundred people. You know hundreds of people. So think systematically about where and with whom you want to start.

Also recall, the best networking contact is someone who holds the job you would like to have in three to five years. As you collect advice from everyone possible, try to get referrals to those who are just beginning their careers in the industry you are exploring. It's great to know the president of the company, but in the long run you'll get more pertinent advice from peers.

Make a list of **Initial Networking Contacts** with whom you can begin this process.

SAMPLE INITIAL NETWORKING CONTACTS

For information on positions in finance and investments management

POTENTIAL CONTACT	RELATIONSHIP	POTENTIAL VALUE
Dr. Laurence Byrd	Pastor	MBA, investment banking before becoming pastor
Randy Follis	Roommate's uncle	Works as a financial consultant at Goldman Sachs
Daniel Campanello	Youth Director at church	Stockbroker somewhere
Philip Mason	Alumnus, friend of a friend	Audit staff, E & Y, less than three years

Martin Sanborn	Cousin	Has many contacts in banking business in Atlanta
Steve Knox	Friend	Financial consultant at American Express financial services
Walter Ehrlich	Professor Ehrlich's son	Trader at ?? Wall Street (will find out)
Mr. Hardawick	Parents' friend	Was financial advisor at Morgan Stanley Smith Barney
Mary Jo Johnson	Cousin's friend	VP at Wachovia
William Dahlton	Church member	Senior partner at Ernst & Young
Caroline ___? (not sure of last name)	Friend of a friend	Intern with Carlton, Harris, and Euben in Dallas
Ms. L. B. "Betty" Wallis	Parents' friend	Worked for many years in banking
Ms. Jocelyn Hobart	Mother's friend, sorority sister from college, I think	Works in banking industry in Canada
Ms. Kelley Weiss	Aunt's friend	Analyst recruiter for Bank of America
Mr. Aaron Ascher	Parents' friend	Financial analyst at JPMorgan Chase
Sara Montague-Sproul	Aunt	Worked in banking, now CPA, knows everybody

PEOPLE WHO WANT TO HELP YOU

1. Every alumna or alumnus from your college

2. Every former employer

3. Every branch, subsidiary, affiliate, and parent company of every former employer

4. Every former coworker

5. Every competitor of every former employer

6. Every supplier or vendor to every former employer

7. Every customer or client of every former employer

8. Every venture or business partner of every former employer

9. Every consultant (person or group) to your former employer

10. Every famous person in your targeted industry

11. Every writer at every newspaper or journal or site that covers your field

12. Every friend you ever had

13. Every friend your friends ever had

14. Every spouse your friends ever had

15. Every parent or close relative your friends ever had

16. Every acquaintance, however fleeting, you ever had

17. Your parents, grandparents, siblings, aunts, uncles, etc.

18. Every friend your parents and other family members ever had

19. Every employer or business associate of your parents and other family members

20. All the alumni of all your other almae maters

21. Every professor or teacher you ever had, or who ever worked at any school you attended

22. Every career center officer or career counselor at every school you ever attended

23. Every teacher or professor of your kids, siblings, friends, parents, etc.

24. Every leader and member of your church, synagogue, or temple

25. Every leader and member of every social, academic, or professional club you know of

26. Every neighbor you ever had

27. Every doctor you ever had

28. Every accountant or financial advisor you ever had

29. Every attorney or insurance agent you ever had

30. Every hairdresser or barber you ever had

31. Every dry cleaner you ever had

32. Every masseuse or masseur you ever had

33. Every personal trainer you ever had

34. Every coach and member of every sports team you were ever on

35. Every gym manager or membership director you've ever met (or known of)

36. Every real estate broker you ever had

37. Every auto mechanic you ever had

38. Every veterinarian you ever had

39. Every yenta you ever had

40. Every wedding planner or photographer you ever had

41. Every funeral director known by anyone you know

42. Every doorman or doorwoman in every building in the financial district

43. Every clerk in every corner store

44. Every cabdriver of every cab you take while looking for work

45. Every bartender at every club you shouldn't be hanging out in anyway

46. Everybody you know by first name from AA

47. Every psychic you ever consulted, or thought you consulted

48. All military personnel you ever served with

49. Everybody you ever helped out in this life

50. Start over and talk to them all again[2]

9

Volunteer and Internship Opportunities

Definition of an internship: A short-term, real-world work experience, full- or part-time, paid or unpaid, designed to give the student/employee the chance to learn about the employer/sponsor and its industry in particular as well as the world of work in general, to form a relationship of potential future career benefit to the student/employee, and to give the employer/sponsor the labor, energy, ideas, and future goodwill of the student/employee.

What do volunteer and internship opportunities have in common? They are really different iterations of the same thing. They are more like separate species of the same genus than truly different beasts. Both may be paid or unpaid, and full- or part-time.

What follows are several common misconceptions about volunteer and internship opportunities:

- Volunteer and internship activities require a major time commitment.

- Volunteer and internship activities are difficult to obtain.

- The only way to find volunteer and internship activities is to search for already established programs.

- Volunteer and internship opportunities are summer activities and would conflict with summer jobs or other summer plans.

- You can't get paid for doing volunteer and internship activities.

In fact, the opposite is true in each case. Volunteer and internship activities may *not* require a major time commitment. They can be done on a part-time basis all year round, including during the school year. They can be done on a sporadic basis, during school holidays and breaks. And they can be done during the summer, even while you pursue another commitment such as a job.

Well-organized and established volunteer and internship programs are but one way to have a volunteer or internship experience. The organized programs, especially the exotic and popular ones, may draw lots of attention; but you can set up your own experience by approaching any manager in any organization and asking, "May I be an intern in your office this summer?" or, "May I be a volunteer with your organization during every school break this fall, winter, and spring?"

CASE STUDY The Manager's Perspective—Maureen D.

Maureen D. is a real estate planner for the regional transit district in a medium-sized California city. "I got a call one day from a college student, who asked if we had an internship program. I said no, and then he asked if he could come over and talk to me about what I did and how the department worked. So I said, 'Sure.' The student was smart, had done his homework, and was very gracious. So Maureen invited him to observe a public meeting, where real estate plans were to be discussed. He came, wearing a suit, and kept his mouth shut for the whole meeting. "Then he basically begged me for an opportunity to be my intern," said Maureen. "Who could say no to that? So I had a little problem with HR about what to call him. We decided the best thing to do was hire him as a clerical worker. I think we paid him minimum wage, but I got a lot of work out of him. He was the first intern we ever had. Now we're considering setting up a program."

CASE STUDY The Student's Perspective—Marcus S.

Marcus S. was interested in going to law school, but he had no exposure to the law. So he called a series of law firms in Houston, trying to get appointments to discuss volunteering or internships or even summer job opportunities. "I started with the big firms: corporate law, insurance defense, that kind of thing," said Marcus. "But I got nowhere. So then I started networking through friends of the family, and an attorney that defended my cousin in a DUI told me two things. He said I could volunteer with some legal programs that assist the poor, or I could work with a plaintiff's or criminal defense attorney, a solo practitioner who wouldn't turn down free help. Of course, I asked him if I could volunteer with him, but he turned me down.

"So I started writing to solo practitioners and small firms, letting them know that I was bilingual, and that I was reliable, and that I had a good academic record as a pre-law major at [a local university]. I wrote to whomever's name was first on the letterhead, and I included a letter of introduction from one of my professors. I used snail mail—real old school stuff. I always followed up with a phone call. I got through about one time in five, but that was enough. I worked with [a local attorney] all the way through my junior year, every Saturday morning, all of fall break, all of Christmas break, because this guy didn't take off for Christmas, and all of spring break. He wrote me an awesome letter of recommendation for law school, and I think that's what made the difference."

You can get paid for internships and, in some cases, paid a lot. You can even get paid for volunteering, something that few people know about. Your college or university may have special grants for students to do volunteer and community service work. Ask your financial aid office, your dean's office, and your community service or internship coordinator for information on programs like these.

Also, many companies end up paying volunteers because they may feel guilty taking advantage of young people or because it is easier for them, administratively, to pay you. Human resources departments that are not used to working with volunteers and interns often would prefer to pay you rather than have your status be unclear to them. Finally—and this may be a shock to you—it is no big deal to hire someone at the entry level. If a department head wants to hire you for the summer or for the holidays, usually he can just decide to hire you. Minimum wage is so low now, comparatively, that it is simply not a budget item requiring a lot of discussion.

On some university campuses, the co-op and internship programs are academic programs. These have been proven to benefit students' development, and if you can participate in them, do so. Sometimes, however, on campuses with such academically based programs, students may confuse the university's programs with the total universe of internship opportunities. Remember, an internship can be in the summer, fall, winter, or spring, and can be paid, unpaid, part time, full time, or even just a couple of hours a week.

Don't make the mistake of holding too rigid an idea of what a volunteer or internship activity is. Internships and career-related volunteer activities provide the ingredient critical for job-search success: experience. Every internship and volunteer experience you have should be listed on your resume under the heading Experience.

Only 1 percent of students have no work experience upon graduating from college, and you definitely do not want to be that one in a hundred who is setting himself up for a major job-search hurdle. Looking for work with no experience is like running a race with a one-hundred-pound stone around your neck. Avoid it by seeking an internship or volunteer experience now, or a summer job as outlined beginning on page 119.

Another reason to pursue this while you're a college student: All types of people are willing to help you who will *not* help you the minute you graduate. The minute you graduate without a job, you become just another unemployed person, competing with all the other graduates without jobs *and* all prior graduates without jobs *and* the millions of talented and experienced Americans who are unemployed on any given day. By then, it's awfully hard to get the help you could easily have accessed while still a student.

What follows is a case study of a student who failed to use an internship or volunteer experience to test her career ideas, so it was quite late before she discovered what she didn't like.

CASE STUDY Heather A.

Heather A. was an English lit major in college, and when she graduated she was unsure where her career interests lay. She was interested in language and in children, so someone suggested that she teach. "I really liked children's literature," she said; "It's much more complex than most people realize and besides, I love kids, so I thought, Teach, sure, that makes sense." So Heather signed up for a combined master's in education and teaching credential program. She completed the first year of studies with a 4.0 GPA, and then in the second half of the third semester, she was sent out to observe in an elementary classroom. "I immediately discovered that I don't like kids at all. I discovered that I like *my* kids but not other people's kids." Heather finished the master's degree and the credential, including a miserable stint as a student teacher, but she never sought a job in a school. Instead, she took a job as a department manager in the biggest bookstore in America: Powell's Books, in Portland, Oregon.

Discovering what you *don't* like is one of the least talked about, but perhaps one of the most most valuable, aspects of field experiences. It is important to note that Heather would have been much better off discovering she didn't like the school setting *before* investing in a master's degree unrelated to her future career.

In addition to learning what you like and don't like, and gaining experience to add to your resume, research shows that students who complete an internship are twice as likely to find a job after college that requires a college degree.[3] This is critical for early career success. A shocking one third of college graduates accept jobs that don't require a college degree. Refer to the list on page 114, Documented Benefits of Internships, and you'll see that, overall, the benefits of internships are far too important to pass up.

Write a plan right now for finding a volunteer experience or internship related to your job interests. You may choose not to put the plan into action, but make the plan anyway. Identify internships that would support your job interests, and develop a scenario for volunteering related to your job interests before going further.

Internships: Putting Off the Job Search and Acquiring Experience While You're at It

Interning is a great way to spend time putting off the job search and acquiring valuable experience and references. Having both experience and someone who can attest to your skills will increase your chances of landing a great first job. There are internships for every field you could be interested in, located around the country and, in some cases, around the globe. If you're lucky, you'll be able to forgo that part-time dishwashing job by landing a paid internship.

There are numerous resources to help you:

BOOKS

Internships 2003
Peterson's Guides (July 2002)

The Internship Bible 2003
Mark Oldman and Samer Hamadeh
Princeton Review (January, 2003)

The Best 109 Internships
Princeton Review Staff
Random House Information Group; 9th ed. (January 2003)

The WetFeet Insider Guide to Getting Your Ideal Internship
Saleem Assaf & Rosanne Lurie
WetFeet Press (March 2003)

National Directory of Arts Internships
   National Network for Artist Placement
   National Network for Artist Placement; 11th ed. (February, 2008)

The Back Door Guide to Short-Term Job Adventures
   Michael Landes
   Ten Speed Press; 4th ed. (2005)

In addition to these great directories, look at the career section of your local bookstore. These are some of the recognized standards, but there are great new guides coming out all the time.

WEBSITES

www.eco.org

   The Environmental Careers Organization has a section of its website dedicated to internships in the environmental field. Internships range from lab and field positions to government work. Intern with companies or nonprofits.

www.dcinternships.org
www.twc.org
www.washingtoninternship.com

   If you have always wanted to work in Washington, D.C., check out these sites for internships.

www.tvjobs.com/intern

   The intern section of tvjobs.com lists opportunities with major broadcasters such as NBC, CNN, and ABC. These aren't backroom positions on cable-access shows you've never heard of. You can be interning for *Rivera Live, Moneyline,* or *Nightline.*

www.nassembly.org/nassembly/html/search.html

   The National Assembly provides a directory of internships in youth development agencies around the country.

www.inroads.org

   INROADS prepares talented minority students to become professionals in business and industry. The organization places African American, Hispanic, and Native American high school and college students in internship positions and prepares them for corporate and community leadership.

www.idealist.org

If finding an internship with a nonprofit somewhere around the world is your cup of tea, Idealist is your dream resource. After your internship you can return to this website to look for a job.

www.donaldasher.com/careers

My website has great information on internships.

INTERNET SEARCH

Running an Internet search can lead to internships you would never find elsewhere. Sometimes print and web internship directories do not include little-known organizations or internships that may be just right for you. It may take time and dedication in the search process, but there's a good chance you'll find what you're looking for and more.

Begin with Google (www.google.com). Use "internships" as your primary keyword plus the field you're interested in (chemistry, sustainable agriculture, public health). You can be as general or as specific as you want. Remember to put multiple-word phrases into quotes.

If you want to limit your results, use the Advanced Search option. One of the most valuable limiters is specifying the domain to be searched. If you want to look for internships at colleges or on their websites, choose to limit your search to .edu. If you're looking for nonprofit organizations, type in .org. If your search is producing too many sites outside the U.S., specify .com as the domain to limit your results to a greater number of U.S. sites. If you're going global, try including search terms that identify the part of the world you'd like to be in, or limit your search to domains in the country of interest (.au, .jp).

If you're looking for semester-long or summer internships, modify your search by including the term "semester" or "summer." Although it is not necessary, you'll have more accurate results if you put the terms in quotes with internships (i.e., "summer internships").

Use the keyword "internships" and include one or more words that provide more detail, and you'll discover thousands and thousands of possibilities. No matter what variations you use, you're sure to find interesting possibilities.

COMPANIES

If you already know a company or companies you'd like to intern for, give them a call and ask. Large corporations often have an office that places interns. Check out the website of your corporation of interest or call their human resources department.

Smaller firms are even more accessible. Once you've made a choice, email anyone in the company, tell them what you're looking for, and ask them to whom you should send a copy of your resume. Then, be persistent. It's up to you to prove to them you're seriously interested. A small company always loves an unpaid intern. While that may mean getting a part-time job on the side, it also means you get your foot in the door and gain solid experience to show other employers.

Finally, if there is one company that particularly appeals to you, research and identify every other similar company and apply for internships with them, too. Don't wait for them to come looking for you. That's never going to happen. It's your job to go looking for them.

DOCUMENTED BENEFITS OF INTERNSHIPS[4]

- More likely to land job in industry of choice
- More job offers at graduation
- Higher starting salary
- Greater satisfaction with first job
- Extended exposure to potential employer
- Twice as likely to land job requiring college
- Improve knowledge of industry, function, job titles, career paths
- More rapid advancement than non-interns
- Gain something substantive to put on resume
- Gain job reference and hopefully letter of recommendation
- Solid lead with at least one potential future employer
- College credit (maybe)
- Salary (maybe)
- Learn what you don't like

"Good" versus "Bad" Internships

Not all internships are created equal. Some allow you to rotate through different departments and learn broadly about an industry and the career options within it. Some are simply boring minimum-wage jobs with a fancy name. So, what are the defining features of a good internship?

A good internship should allow you to learn something as well as to work at something. So if you're considering an internship offer, try to find out what you will get to learn.

CASE STUDY An Internship from Hell—Paul H.

Paul H. answered an ad posted at his career center for a "marketing intern." He reported to a printing shop down a narrow alley in the financial district. The print shop had an oversized reputation, so despite his misgivings, Paul accepted the position of marketing intern, a minimum-wage summer job. The first week, Paul realized he'd made a terrible mistake. The owner had implied that he needed Paul to develop a marketing plan for the business, but everything Paul suggested was shot down with, "We tried that. It didn't work." Instead, the owner wanted Paul to walk into offices all over the financial district and hand out brochures. That was the entire job.

Paul begged the owner for more responsibility but was told that if he didn't like the internship he could quit. Paul did quit and got a job selling tires. It wasn't marketing, his area of interest, but he made far more money, and by the time school started he had substantial savings. So his summer wasn't wasted after all.

Even a bad summer job can be converted into a good internship with a little creativity on your part. The print shop owner above was immune to good advice, apparently, but the student below made the best of a bad situation.

CASE STUDY A So-So Summer Job
Becomes an "Internship" Success—Ruth Ann W.

Ruth Ann W. returned to her small hometown on Florida's Gulf Coast at her mother's insistence. "She wasn't keen on me going away to college in the first place, but she just flat wasn't going to allow me to work in a big city." Ruth Ann got a job at the local general store, a small grocery, hardware, and dry goods emporium popular with residents and tourists. "I saw right away I was going to have to do something to keep from going crazy," she told me in a workshop. "So I told the owner I'd analyze the sales-per-square-foot of his entire operation—something I'd just learned about in class—and he said, 'Sure, go for it.'"

So in between stocking shelves and ringing up customers, Ruth Ann analyzed sales records. Her analysis showed two problems: some items weren't selling at all, and customers seldom saw most of the store's offerings. "By the time I left, he had agreed with my plan to move the soft drinks and beer to the back of the store and to remove a big shoe polish display that he'd had for fifty years. I'm going to do an after analysis this spring break and see what the impact has been." So Ruth Ann turned a summer job as a cashier into a genuine business accomplishment.

Ruth Ann plans to summarize her work in the style of a business plan with a supplemental project-in-progress report. A good volunteer experience or internship often involves a work product: some project or report or work sample that you can show to other employers that represents your accomplishment and your abilities.

Also, look for internships with structured social integration components. Will you be expected to grind away alone at your project, hidden away in your work group? Or will there be opportunities to meet people in a social setting, perhaps a training group or a softball game or a conference? This is certainly not a requirement of a useful internship, but it is a defining feature of the very best.

And of course, internships are a standard trial for future employment with the sponsoring organization. Some industries primarily hire from the prior year's internship pool. For example, publishing, the film industry, television and radio, international relations, engineering and technology firms, and many nonprofits and arts organizations prefer to hire first from the internship pool. In fact, in a tight labor market, everybody tends to hire from the internship pool. After all, don't we all prefer to try on the shoes before we buy them?

Freshman year is a great time to start looking for internships. So is the sophomore year, the junior year, the senior year, and as we'll see later, the year after you graduate. In fact, right now is a good time to look for a job-related volunteer or internship experience.

Remember that volunteer and internship experience is really the same thing; you can get it in the summer, fall, winter, or spring, and it can be paid or unpaid, part time, full time, or even just a couple of hours a week.

DEFINING FEATURES OF A GREAT INTERNSHIP

- Opportunity to work at or slightly above your skill level
- Formalized acculturation program
- Established program with committed resources and a clearly assigned supervisor or mentor
- Exposure to various departments and/or functions
- A defining project and, if possible, a resulting product, such as a report or plan
- Established channel of consideration for permanent hire

CASE STUDY Paige G.

"Thanks to a suggestion from my flute professor, I started looking for internships early in my college career—anything in performing arts management—or anything related to music. I looked on the Internet at symphonies and arts companies, things like that. It was harder than I thought to find internship information, so I just started sending resumes to different places and hoping that I got something.

"I had done some things in music before but not much. I basically had all high school stuff on that first resume. I had gone to fine arts camp. I played in county band, sang in county choir. I was on the student council, a member of the Key Club, and a member of the National Honor Society. I just wanted to show I was involved, disciplined, and motivated.

"I wasn't really getting anywhere, but then I found out the programs had education departments. Major symphonies, opera companies, ballet theater, regular theater-they all have education departments within the management side of their arts programs. I found this out by haunting their websites. So I wrote to the education directors, and if they weren't listed by name, I just wrote to the education department. I never heard back from most of them, so I don't know how many got through. This was in January and February, so I wasn't freaked out yet. I could always get a summer job back home. It wouldn't be what I wanted, but it would be something to do.

"There was an actual education intern position listed on the Pittsburgh Opera website, and I applied for it. I was surprised to find out later, most college students don't apply for internships like this. Only about ten people applied, when I had imagined hundreds of applicants. So I wasn't hoping for much, because I really thought all these other people had to be applying for this same internship. A couple of weeks went by, and I got a phone call from the education director. She wanted me to come for an interview. I don't have a car, so my dad actually took time off from work and drove me to Pittsburgh for the meeting. The education director asked me a lot of questions about what I liked to do, mostly trying to learn about my personality and attitude, I think. She didn't ask many questions about my skills.

"They were looking for someone to be more of an office worker, who would occasionally handle an arts project but mostly do paperwork for the department. It wasn't supposed to be project oriented, at first. I was fine with that. I was just happy for the chance to get experience in my field, in music. I was happy. I felt lucky. Before I left the interview, the director told me I had the position, so I didn't have to wait to find out.

"So I moved out to Pittsburgh for the summer, and for about three weeks I just did office work. I tried hard to learn as much as I could, to do as good a job as

I could. Remember, I had no real experience, and I was learning about what the education department did, about its programs, and how they ran them. Then, three weeks into the job, I was asked if I wanted some project work. I would be reviewing books about opera that would be used in their teacher workshops in the fall. I was nervous. I was so afraid I wasn't going to be able to do it right. I had just finished my freshman year in college! But I reviewed five books. I recommended one of the five, and I explained my reasons for picking the book and why it might be useful for teachers to use in teaching about opera to high school students. When they saw my reviews, they agreed with me, and that was the book used in the fall teacher-education workshops. In fact, they still use that book.

"Once I had proven that I could do something besides data entry, they tried me out on all kinds of projects. I put in a lot of extra hours to get stuff done on time. They were so impressed that I usually got stuff done ahead of time, and that's why they kept giving me bigger and better projects. The most important project I worked on that summer was unbelievable. I wrote lesson plans for a consortium of opera companies sponsored by Opera America. They're on the New York City Opera website right now. So teachers all over the country are using lesson plans I developed as a summer intern! I wrote ten lesson plans, and eventually three of them were adopted.

"It's amazing how many internships are out there, and what's even more amazing is that probably only half of them are even listed on the Internet. I'm now the student coordinator of the internship program for the honors college, helping other students find internships. If I had a single piece of advice for students, it's this: The best time to apply is early. Don't even look at the deadline. Apply one or two months ahead. When you call to check on your application, it's a lot better to hear them say, 'We haven't actually started looking at the interns this year, but we'll hold on to your application,' than 'Sorry. You missed the deadline,' or 'Sorry. We already picked someone else.'"

10

Summer Jobs, and "The Most Important Summer of Your Life"

Most of us have three summers in college—four, if you count the one before it starts. By going backward from graduation, you can develop a clear plan for how to spend your summers.

Here are five things you can do with any given summer:

- Find a paid or unpaid internship directly related to your post-college graduate school, or life launch plans.

- Take the highest paying job you can find to earn money for college.

- Volunteer for a good cause.

- Go to summer school.

- Relax, travel, or have adventures.

Perhaps you think it doesn't much matter which of these options you choose in any given summer, but it very much does. It particularly matters what you do in the summer between your junior and senior years. Why? Because this is the most important summer of your life.

The number one indicator of the first full-time job you will hold after college is the last full-time job you hold before you graduate from college.

So this is *not* a summer to build houses for charity or work at a summer camp or goof off in Europe, unless you want to do those same things after you graduate.

You may have paid your way through school painting houses in New England every summer, but the summer before you graduate, you should concentrate on building your future.

If you are headed for graduate school, this time is a precious indicator of your seriousness. Need two good choices?

- Find a paid or unpaid internship directly related to your area of interest for graduate study.

- Go to summer school and take courses in the subject you would like to study in graduate school, preferably at one of the universities you will be applying to.

If you are going to launch a career after college, there is one summer option that is superior to all others:

- Find a paid or unpaid internship directly related to your post-college life-launch plans.

Why? Let me repeat this: The number one indicator of the first full-time job you will hold after college is the last full-time job you hold before you graduate.

But what does "full-time job" actually mean? What's the difference between a summer job and an internship or a volunteer experience? Nothing. The point is that whatever job or internship or volunteer assignment you hold in the summer before you graduate, it should be directly related to your post-college employment goals.

Don't worry if you are a senior reading this, and last summer you washed cars in Las Vegas for reasons unknown to anyone. You can still change your fate, but you're going to have to work extra hard on job exploration to be sure you don't end up washing cars after college. See your career center and work on a plan for landing a shadowing or internship experience before school ends, and get ready to do more job exploration *after* you graduate if you don't have time during the school year. Remember, first do employment ideation, then job exploration, and only after you've done these should you launch a job search.

Assuming you still have the choice, if you're grad-school bound you can get a *job-related* summer experience or go to summer school to take *goal-related* subjects. If you're headed for a job after college, you can pursue a career-related summer experience, no matter whether that experience is structured as a volunteer assignment, internship, or job.

But what if, in your internship or your graduate school prep classes, you discover you don't like the employment direction after all? What if you discover, for example, that you don't like financial sales or you don't want to study nano-engineering? Well, it's too late, unless you back up and do these things the summer between your sophomore and junior years. Then, if you discover your original plan is not so attractive, you have time to test another one.

Thus, by planning backward from graduation, you can plan for your summers.

Note: That first summer is a freebie, the summer after your freshman year. Do whatever you want, as long as you will respect yourself afterward. The second summer is a good time to test a job idea, because if you don't like it you can easily move on and forget all about it. The third summer is the most important summer of your life. So plan for it, if you can.

After Graduating, Is It Too Late?

In this country, it's never too late to fix your life path. Graduation is not the last chance you have to do job exploration. You can continue through post-baccalaureate internships, through exploratory entry-level jobs, through information networking and even shadowing, throughout the process of conducting a job search, and through continuing education. So if you're already a graduate, or a really busy senior, don't spend too much time reviewing the college planning calendar below and move on to the following sections just for you.

Calendar
You don't have to do it this way, but college sure works better if you do!
(For permission to reproduce this calendar on your campus, call (415) 543–7130 or go to www.donaldasher.com.)

FRESHMAN YEAR

- Take a wide variety of courses to try to find your major.

- Take a foreign language (whether it's required or not).

- Find a sport you will enjoy every week for the rest of your life.

- Learn to see your faculty outside of the classroom by dropping by during their open office hours to discuss the class, curriculum, paper ideas, what's going to be on the test, how best to study, who's who in the department, and so on.

- Realize that you can't graduate in four years by taking a minimum load; familiarize yourself *now* with graduation requirements (distribution requirements, minimum credits, major and minor selection, departmental rules). Don't become a senior who has to take required freshman-level courses!

- Get by without a car; your grades will be higher.

- Live on campus; your grades will be higher.

- *Avoid the credit card trap!* Use a debit card.

- Join at least one academic club.

- Join at least one activity to make the world a better place.

- Maybe join at least one activity solely to pursue an interest.

- Learn that college is not just classes but also guest speakers, clubs, movies, outdoor recreation, political exploration, and social opportunities, etc.

- Go the career center in the first semester and learn how to (a) register for announcements and notices, (b) write a resume, and (c) get an internship. Competitive internships are selected over the winter and in early spring!

- Try to find friends who are going to be successful in life, and conversely, try to avoid distracting, loud, irresponsible, and sometimes fun people who are ultimately going to fail at college.

- Find the help desk in the library, the writing center or academic support center, the counseling office, the medical clinic, and other sources of help and support.

- Try not to work long hours at a wage job, so you can adjust to college.

- Watch your grades!

- If, and only if, you are an engineering, nursing, or music major, declare your major and meet with an academic advisor to plan the sequence of courses that will allow you to graduate on time.

- If, and only if, you are potentially interested in a career in medicine, find the premedical advisor and learn how best to prepare yourself.

FIRST SUMMER

This is a "free" summer.

- Pursue a service opportunity or some kind of big adventure.

- Travel abroad.

- Take any kind of wage job.
- Work at an internship or summer job in an industry or field that you would potentially like to pursue after graduation.

SOPHOMORE YEAR

- Prepare in the first semester to get a summer internship (see Second Summer below). .
- Test your interest in one or more majors by deepening your class load in those subjects.
- Continue to see faculty outside of the classroom.
- Become involved in departmental activities, such as guest speakers, receptions, symposia, committee work open to students, and especially the informal events such as barbecues, softball Saturdays—whatever they're doing together.
- Continue with an academic activity.
- Begin to think seriously about what you're going to do after college.
- Start going to all career fairs and asking lots of questions.
- If you're comfortable with your major and settled into college, consider taking the second semester abroad.
- Get by without a car; your grades will be higher.
- Live on campus; your grades will be higher.

SECOND SUMMER

This summer "counts" and is not free; try to do one of these:

- Work at an internship or summer job in an industry or field that you would potentially like to pursue after graduation; if you discover you don't like it, you can still change direction successfully.
- Work at an academically related internship that supports your graduate school plans.
- If, and only if, you can't find one of the above, go to summer school to beef up your chances of graduating on time and/or to prepare for graduate school.

JUNIOR YEAR

This is the year that sets up success after graduation!

- Prepare in the first semester to get a summer internship (see Final Summer opposite).

- If you have not done so by now, settle on a major and meet with an academic advisor to plan the sequence of courses that will allow you to graduate on time.

- Consider a semester abroad (first semester is preferred over second, but this is not critical).

- Continue to see faculty outside of the classroom.

- Continue to be involved in departmental activities.

- Continue with an academic activity.

- Consider adding to your list of activities (academic, service, sports, interest); consider seeking a leadership role in one or more, especially if you're grad school bound.

- Begin to talk about your future life launch plans with fellow students, faculty, alumni, visiting speakers and VIPs, friends of the family, and parents of your friends.

- Visit alumni and professionals in your chosen field for a "shadowing" day, or at least an informational interview.

- If you are applying for a graduate fellowship (Rhodes, Watson, Marshall, etc.), most successful applicants start in the first semester of junior year to prepare their applications; find the scholarship advisor and plan your application strategy.

- Research graduate schools: look up prominent graduate faculty in your field of interest, read articles in the academic journals for your field, look at www.petersons.com and other grad school guides.

- Begin to correspond with faculty in graduate schools of interest.

- If grad schools on your list require the GRE, plan to take it late in the second semester or in the following summer.

- If grad schools on your list require a GRE subject test, register in February for an April sitting.

- If headed for medical school, register in March to take the April MCAT; you can take it again in August if you don't like your score.

- If you're headed for law school, register in November to take the December LSAT or in January for the February sitting; you can take it again in June or October of the following year if you don't like your score, or know you can do better the second time around.

- Visit all the graduate schools you can during the school year.

- Try to go to an academic conference in your field.

- Watch your grades! These are the last grades that will show if you plan to apply to graduate school next year.

- Get by without a car; your grades will be higher.

- Live on campus; your grades will be higher.

FINAL SUMMER

This is the most important summer of your life; don't fool around!

- Now it's critical to find an internship or summer job in an industry or field that you would potentially like to pursue after graduation. Ask for a letter of recommendation before leaving at the end of the summer.

- Work at an academically related internship that supports your graduate school plans.

- Continue to talk about your after-college goals with everyone you meet; continue to visit professionals in their workplaces whenever you can.

- Try to go to an academic conference in your field. Visit some grad schools if you can. Meet professors who might be mentors in grad school. Correspond with graduate faculty in your area of interest.

- Prepare for and take the GRE or LSAT in June if you still need to (you don't want to do this in the fall, with classes and applications to graduate school).

- Prepare for and take the MCAT if you didn't like your first score, or know you can do better the second time around.

- If, and only if, you're headed for graduate school, consider going to summer school at one of your targeted institutions. Take classes related to your grad-school plans, and watch your grades!

- If you're applying to medical school, be sure to get all your applications in at the earliest opportunity, on the first round (the first week of June is recommended).

SENIOR YEAR

- First week of class, visit your career center and explore all support available to you that will make this transitional year a success; get that final resume polished and pursue interview training from the career center.

- Prepare in the first semester to get a life-launching job or post-graduation summer internship; plot out a year's search activities with your career counselor.

- First week of class, meet with professors about your graduate school plans, seek their advice, and identify potential authors of letters of recommendation.

- In September and October, get all your non-med graduate school applications in (deadlines will vary, but apply at least thirty to sixty days early).

- Schedule any GRE subject tests if you still need to. If grad schools on your list require a subject GRE test, register in September or October for the November sitting.

- Continue to talk about your career goals with everyone you meet; continue to visit professionals in their workplaces.

- Begin to systematically identify alumni who can give you career advice; learn how to conduct an effective informational interview.

- Build a networking list of professionals in your targeted field who can help you find a job.

- No matter what your major, participate in the on-campus interview cycle if you're interested in the industries that send recruiters to your campus.

- Get by without a car; your grades will be higher.

- Live on campus; your grades will be higher.

SUMMER AFTER COLLEGE

If you land a job before graduation,

- If headed for business school, consider taking the GMAT during this summer and applying this fall to enter business school with one year of experience, the following fall to enter with two years' experience, and so on.

- Remember, every August for the rest of your life, ask yourself: "In one year, do I want to be in grad school?" Watch out for the extensive lead time to get into a graduate program.

If you're admitted to graduate school, this is a "free" summer;

- Pursue a service opportunity or some kind of big adventure.
- Travel abroad.
- Take any kind of wage job and rest your mind.
- Work at an internship related to your academic interest.

If you're launching a career but don't have a job yet:

- Use the career center to run a systematic search.
- Find a post-baccalaureate internship or summer job in an industry or field that you would potentially like to pursue as a career.
- Stay in touch with professors who may refer you to positions.
- Try hard to find work you're interested in, even passionate about, that requires your college degree and your accumulated skills; try hard not to freak out and settle for any income you can find.

Post-Baccalaureate Internships

Post-baccalaureate internships have been around for many years, but they are newly popular as all types of organizations have come to realize how valuable interns can be, and that there are in fact twelve months in the year. For example, Monica Lewinsky was working in the White House as a post-baccalaureate intern.

Post-baccalaureate internships run anywhere from four months to a year, and some run even longer. They are available with start dates from June to May.

For more on post-baccalaureate internships, see Michael Landes's *The Back Door Guide to Short-Term Job Adventures.* Also see chapter 6, A Different Kind of Choice, beginning on page 73, and check out the internship resources.

CASE STUDY How Post-Grad Internships Saved My Career—Jesse K.

"It took me forever to get a job. I blame it on the economy, and the fact that I have a natural tendency to want to avoid being rejected. That stopped me from pursuing some avenues of my job search as doggedly as I probably should have.

"When I was a senior, I was too busy to run a job search. I was doing an honors thesis in sociology plus carrying a full load of classes, so I decided the career thing would just have to wait.

"After I graduated, I started perusing the Web, trying to get a feel for which companies were located in the area. I'm from Honolulu, and my college was a real ivory tower kind of place, so I didn't have any idea what was out there. I like this area. It's great for young people. There're a lot of kids my age doing art and making music, and compared to Honolulu, everything is easy and cheap.

"I became a regular in the career center. Since it was summer, everything was laid back, and I could put in several hours a day in their media center. They had computers, books, videotapes, file cabinets full of leads, and they didn't care if we brought in sodas and snacks. Some of us had a regular club going in there.

"The career center people decided they liked me, and they began to help me make some connections. I was interested in advertising, publishing, and journalism anything in those areas. I connected with someone on the development staff who said she knew people in advertising. She took me to a cocktail party in the [Waterfront District], and I tried schmoozing with people. It actually worked! I got an informational interview out of it, but the guy's firm wasn't doing so well, and he kept telling me I had to go to grad school right away, which was the last thing I wanted to do. Later, sure, but not right away.

"He did steer me to an alumna at an art house, sort of an upscale graphic design studio that also published books and a magazine. They liked my thesis, and just like that, I got an internship. I was assigned to work on a book on the commercialization of sexuality in graphic design, and I was doing a lot of other projects simultaneously. The boss was really incommunicative, and I never really knew if I was doing what she wanted. I spent all my time on the phone trying to get permission to reproduce images for a book that was actually very critical of the images, so it was a little tricky. 'What's the book about?' I was asked, and I had to find a way to get permission without revealing too much.

"I hadn't really been told that I would spend so much time contacting people, and I wasn't sure I was gaining any skills I'd be able to present to my next employer. And there was another problem: I didn't think the book was all that good. Not to brag or whine or anything, but I'd just finished a research project of my own that had more academic rigor and originality. At the time, I didn't think I was gaining all that much from the internship, but it gave me something to put on my resume. I asked for a letter of recommendation upon leaving, and it was pretty strongly favorable, so it wasn't a bad stepping-stone after all.

"Then I did the solitary job search thing for a while, sitting around in my apartment making lists of everyone I knew. I was determined to use networking contacts and friends, make connections; but like I said, the economy around here is tight. Everyone

I talked to would say, 'Well, all my friends are unemployed, too,' or even worse, 'I'm unemployed, too,' so it was slow going. I ran into one of my friends from the career center club, who told me he'd given up on applying for jobs and was only applying for post-college internships. Summer was over and internships were easier to get, or so he thought. So I tried that, too, but got nothing. No jobs either. It seemed that three years' prior experience was a minimum requirement for every job I discovered.

"Pretty soon it was mid-fall, and a friend asked me if I wanted to work at [a retail store] for the Christmas season. I was running out of money again, so I went for it. It really felt like a step down to be told in detail how to fold a shirt, but I made some good friends, and I liked that it was keeping me busy. But I was starting to get depressed. In a way it was motivational, because I realized, Hey, I have a $200,000 education, and I'm not going to fold clothes for long. This is temporary. I'm not going to allow this to become my future. Besides, I knew I'd be laid off come December 26.

"In the middle of this, I got an email from [a weekly newspaper] asking if I was still interested in an internship. I didn't even remember that I had applied for one there. They asked for a new resume, and I emailed one with a PDF of the recommendation letter from the last internship, the one with the art house. I almost didn't believe it, but they asked me if I wanted to start on Monday. This time there was no pay, but I figured with the money from the [retail] job, I could afford to do it. So I was working from 8 A.M. until the store closed at 9 P.M.

"I was happier than I had been since college. I'd go down to the paper, develop my own story ideas, get some editor to give me a green light, report on it all day, then go to the store to cover my rent. They threw you right into it with no training at all. I would have liked for someone to tell me what to do, but that's just not how it worked. If they took your stories, you got to stay; if they didn't, they kicked you out. They accepted three or four of my stories, so I got to stay.

"One of the stories I wrote was on Christian psychedelic rock. They took the story, but it never came out. My three months were up, and that was the maximum for the internship. The retail job had already ended, so I had nothing again.

"From there I got another internship, this time at a literary magazine. Although it paid, it was really a form of intern exploitation. The guy ran the whole 'zine with interns. He didn't know what he was doing, and he talked to himself constantly. He was obsessed with my digital camera. He kept having me take pictures of this ether bottle he'd had since the sixties. I think it meant a lot to him. But somehow we got the 'zine out, and I got another cool credit on my resume.

"All this time, I was asking all my contacts for leads to magazines, advertising agencies, and newspapers. I'd also just joined this band. I'd played drums and had been in a band of one kind or another since high school. I asked the bass player, who worked for [a major newspaper], if he'd drop off my resume down at the paper. He was very reluctant to do so. He said he didn't have any pull and was just an editorial assistant himself. Besides, he said, he was in the business section, and I didn't have a business background. Finally he agreed to do it.

"The paper called me a week later about a copy aide position. That's like a gofer who can spell, but I didn't have any other leads so I pursued it. I had three interviews, which I thought went reasonably well; but they called me and said, 'No, you're not right for this position, but in a few weeks we'll have something that will be a better match.' I thought, Yeah, right. But in two weeks I started to call them.

"Right then my Christian rock article hit the stands. I sent the paper a copy, and they called me right back. They wanted me to interview for an editorial assistant position in A&E. That's arts and entertainment. I'm compiling music listings now, and I'm submitting reviews. It took a long time, but this really is my dream job. I get free tickets to everything, and my life has completely turned around. Overnight it changed. It's like I'm suddenly popular.

"I think the internships were the key. I had the time to do them, and they helped me build a resume. Without those internships, I'd be doing some go-nowhere job that doesn't require a college education. My friend that got me that retail job has his bachelor's degree, and guess what he's doing right now? Folding shirts.

"It didn't hurt that my band mate took my resume to the newspaper's HR office, and gave it that little extra push. The job I ended up getting was publicly posted, but because my resume was on top of the pile and I'd already interviewed, I was sort of the default candidate. I was qualified but so were a lot of other people.

"My advice for other students? Get as much experience as you can, even if you have to work for free. And keep trying, even when it's tough and looks hopeless, because you deserve a job that's mentally challenging."

An Entry-Level Exploratory Job

What do you do after you graduate, and you don't have a job, and you're not sure what you want to do, and you have bills coming due, and so on. End of the world? Hardly. You can explore any field by getting any job in that field.

Job searching is really the topic of the next part of the book, but there is one principle you have to get right here: **It is just as easy to get a job that will advance your career interests as it is to get a job that will make you miserable.**

So before you give up on your employment aspirations, pick a field you're interested in and seek *any* job in that field. If you're interested in publishing or sports or the wine industry or the Methodist church or nonprofit hospitals or museum curating or dairy farm management, get any job in the field of choice. Then, from the vantage point of a job within that industry, it is much easier to do job exploration. In fact, once you're inside, moving around within an industry is much easier than trying to get in as a college student or even a recent graduate.

Many people give up and settle for less than they want, when they find themselves faced with the need for a job fast. But *fast* is a relative term. Would you put in three months to find a job in the field of your dreams? Here's the punch line for the third or fourth time: It could take you three months to find a job you'll hate, so why not go for it? Why not go for a job in an industry you'll love? Why not pick an industry you're interested in, and—even though you're not sure, and you haven't done all your homework, and you didn't get a great internship, and maybe you goofed off in Europe or at some summer camp for extreme sports—**it's not too late to do job exploration.**

Why not do it from inside, while drawing a paycheck and supporting yourself as an adult?

Those of us in the career planning business occasionally tend to place too much emphasis on the planning and too little emphasis on the career, as in the real jobs that real people have. So much involves chance, and circumstances and events beyond planning. Too much is made of the right way to do it and too little of the way it's actually done.

CASE STUDY Rob S.

Rob S. was an accounting and finance major in college, who moved to New York City immediately upon graduation. He guessed that Wall Street and corporate jobs were not going to match his personality. He didn't mind working hard, but he didn't like wearing suits or getting up before noon. So he took a job as a doorman for a nightclub. "Just don't say 'bouncer,' because I weigh maybe 155 pounds with all my clothes on. Other people were in charge of security. My job was checking IDs. No ID, no entry. Very simple." The general manager liked Rob's attitude, and before long he was second signature on the nightly cash count. When the bar manager didn't show up one night, Rob became the bar manager. Rob dropped the pour cost 15 percent the first month, and that really got the manager's attention. Rob was made assistant manager for the club. Then he was promoted two times more. In a little over four years, Rob went from doorman to chief financial officer of a corporation with three clubs, and his income went from $15 an hour to over $150,000. Rob is twenty-seven years old. His company is seeking to buy more clubs.

CASE STUDY Todd W.

Todd W. majored in intellectual history at a liberal arts college. He returned to his hometown without doing a thing about his post-college plans. "My folks didn't have a basement," he told me. "They had a trailer parked by a pond in the middle of a field. So I graduated college to live in a trailer." Todd liked the idea of working in the newspaper business, but had no writing portfolio besides a series of college term papers on the concept of individual liberty. Nevertheless, he walked into the local newspaper and asked for a job as a writer. "I don't need a writer," the publisher told him, "but can you sell advertising?" Todd sold advertising like no one before him. "I have a simple technique," he said. "I never take 'maybe' for an answer. 'No' is okay; 'yes' is better, but nobody ever says 'maybe' to me." Todd works for a company that owns newspapers in edge cities and suburban areas all over the country. He's been in the newspaper business for one year, and he's already been transferred to a bigger market. "I may continue in sales, or I may get to train to take over as publisher for one of the papers. Either way," he says, "I don't think I'm ever going to have to live in a travel trailer again."

CASE STUDY Marta S.

Marta S. went to Europe after graduation and spent a small inheritance goofing off in Italy and France. She perfected her French and picked up enough Italian to get by. "The biggest thing I discovered," she related, "is that Americans do not have the best lifestyle in the world. We think we do, but we don't. The French and especially the Italians have it better. In large cities and small towns, Italians still take a stroll after dinner. Typically they discuss art and culture and the meaning of beauty. This is so not like America. So I started to look around for where I might find the most European lifestyle, and I decided it was in Napa Valley, the wine region north of San Francisco." Marta started as a hostess in a wine tasting room, was promoted to assistant manager, then manager of retail operations. She is at the same time pursuing an apprenticeship with her employer's winemaker. "I'm even considering going to [the University of California at] Davis for a master's degree in the enology program," said Marta. All of this enthusiasm started with a $10-an-hour job for the tourist season.

Millions of ambitious college graduates have succeeded after beginning with an entry-level job, and so can you. If you have great enthusiasm for the industry, you'll rise rapidly. In fact, there used to be a tradition on Wall Street that college graduates would start in the mail room and take one to three years to get promoted out of it. If you need to get a job fast, try to be picky about the industry, but don't be picky about the job.

It is much easier to move around within an industry than it is to break into it later. In fact, some industries can only be entered from the entry level. If you have a keen interest in the film industry or the restaurant business or the music industry or fashion design, it is better to start now, as a recent college grad, than to become successful in another field and then try to migrate in later.

Ask yourself these questions:

- Have you already graduated from college?
- Do you need to support yourself right away?

If the answer to both is yes, you should consider an entry-level exploratory job. If the answer to either question is no, then you should look again at internship, shadowing, and post-baccalaureate internship opportunities.

Write an analysis of the appropriateness for you of an entry-level exploratory job in your career journal.

If you were going to approach one or two or three industries for any entry-level job, which industries would they be?

Just remember that an entry-level exploratory job is still job exploration. Don't settle for a job unless you find you like the industry *and* it has potential for advancement.

And don't be afraid to make mistakes! If you get into a field and it's not a keeper, move on! A little failure is part of any successful life. Walt Disney's first cartoon production company went bankrupt. Elvis Presley got a C in high school music, and his teacher told him he couldn't sing. Edgar Allan Poe was expelled from college. Einstein dropped out of school without completing his degree. Bill Clinton has had more comebacks than the Staten Island Ferry. John Grisham wrote three novels that didn't sell; his fourth, *A Time to Kill*, was rejected by sixteen agents and a dozen publishing houses before launching his best-selling career. To cheer yourself on during your career exploration and job-search process, read Joey Green's delightful book *The Road to Success Is Paved with Failure: Hundreds of Famous People Who Triumphed over Inauspicious Beginnings, Crushing Rejections, Humiliating Defeats, and Other Speed Bumps Along Life's Highway.*

11

More Education

Lifelong learning used to be a requirement for only the most elite professions such as medicine. Today it's a requirement for everyone. Lifelong learning is the hallmark of a modern life path.

You simply cannot continue to advance without continuing to learn, either on your own or through formal educational programs, for the rest of your working life. It doesn't matter if you're a blue-collar worker-droid or a customer service representative or the chief science officer for a biotech company, we all have to keep learning to keep our jobs at all.

> Education is the great engine of personal development. It is through education that the daughter of a peasant can become a doctor, that the son of a mineworker can become the head of the mine, that a child of farmworkers can become the president of a great nation. It is what we make out of what we have, not what we are given, that separates one person from another.
>
> —*Nelson Mandela* [5]

But what about using education as part of employment exploration, that is, to see if you want to go into a field in the first place?

Education is a great way to explore job ideas, but you need to investigate before you overinvest. Remember the case study of Heather A. on page 110, who did two years of graduate study for a career she didn't like after all? You want to use education to explore job ideas, not commit to them before you've explored them.

I have a warning, however, and I do mean to be blunt: It may be tempting to use education not to advance your life planning but in fact to avoid it. Avoid using a return to education as an escape from the job market, from the hard work of doing introspection and idea exploration and finding a life-launching job.

Ask yourself, "What is the minimum amount of education I could obtain that would let me know if this is a good career direction for me?"

Only when you're sure it is a good initial direction—that it's a match for your aptitudes and interests and in alignment with your future vision for yourself—can you make a commitment to the maximum amount of education available.

Here are your options, roughly in order of investment:

- A one-day or weekend class from an open university–type organization or a training and seminar company
- Annual conference for a professional association
- Continuing education courses
- Sit in on a university class in an area of interest
- Credential
- Master's degree
- Doctorate

If you want to learn more about the import/export business, raising pigmy goats, interior design, becoming a corporate concierge, becoming a talent agent, or what have you, one-day seminars are available in every major city from open university–type seminar companies. These are a great way to get an insider's peek at an industry and to make connections of real value if you do decide to pursue the issue.

Look around for a one-day or weekend seminar in your area of interest before you invest in more expensive and time-consuming options.

Attending the annual conference of a profession that interests you is a great way to discover more about it. You can get a student pass or sometimes a one-day pass. Plan your day so you can see the optimum mix of keynote lectures, professional development workshops and seminars, and other presentations from leaders in the field. And be sure to go to the vendor booths, as each represents a potential employer should you decide to pursue the field. Professional conferences can be expensive, but if you can afford it, the benefits in terms of idea exploration are huge. It's like trying to get a drink of water from a fire hose. There are very few places offering so much expertise and so much good advice in such a concentrated time and space.

Practicing professionals, professors, and your career center can tell you about professional and trade associations in your area of interest, or you can look them up in the *Encyclopedia of Associations*.

The trade associations and licensing authorities affiliated with certain professions require practitioners to take continuing education courses on a regular basis. These courses vary in length from a few hours to a semester-length class. They are not that accessible to students from outside the profession, and many classes will be highly specialized. However, once you're in a profession, seek as much of this type of training as you can, as it is key to continued advancement.

One university class can make a huge difference if you're trying to break into an industry you know little about. Remember, all industries have a secret handshake and a secret lingo that you have to learn before you can get a job in the field.

CASE STUDY Debbie R.

Debbie R. is just completing an undergraduate degree in biology and has had several internships in fisheries management. She spent the summer before her senior year on a boat in the northern Pacific as an observer. But she decided that ichthyology was not the field for her. "I like scientists a lot, but you have to get a Ph.D. to get anywhere. Until you do, the pay is very modest, to put it politely. I wanted something more commercially viable." She thinks it might be biotechnology, so she's taking a class this year: Introduction to the Biotechnology Industry. Debbie says, "I'm learning which positions exist and where I might fit, and besides, the professor is well connected. If he likes you, one phone call and you've got a job."

One class while you're still a student makes sense, but if you've already graduated, putting off your job search to take a class may not. It may be better for you to get an entry-level exploratory job, as described in the previous section. Obtaining a credential, a master's degree, or a doctorate should be considered only if you are quite confident of your life path and wish to bolster your skills and employability. Let's cover those options here, even if they are not usually used for employment explorations.

A **credential** is a post-baccalaureate sequence of courses, usually about four or five, that provides some demonstrable expertise in a specified field or discipline. Credentials are particularly useful for nonbusiness majors who want to pick up expertise in business topics such as human resources or marketing, and for all graduates interested in areas such as substance abuse counseling. Most major universities now offer the credential as an option between a bachelor's and a master's degree program.

A **master's degree** typically takes two years of full-time study, but there are many other options available now. You can get a master's degree by going to class at night or on weekends, or by participating in cycles of full-time, on-campus study followed by periods of independent study. You can also pick up a master's degree quickly, in as little as one year, by taking one of the many degree programs that feature continuous study (no holidays and no breaks).

Doctoral study is a major investment in time, money, and effort, and is certainly not something you should enter into lightly. Discuss plans for this degree with your academic advisors and your career center or center for graduate and pre-professional school advising. Also, for all your graduate school planning needs, check out my book *Graduate Admissions Essays*, the best-selling guide to the graduate admissions process.

Online education is a great way to finish a degree program or pick up a class that is difficult for you to obtain otherwise, but it is not a great way to get all of your post-baccalaureate education. I have interviewed a number of students who are not happy with online education and dropped out before completing their programs. A key question to ask of any graduate program, online or brick-and-mortar, is "What is your attrition rate? Of those who don't finish, what are their reasons?" Any program with a dropout rate in excess of 50 percent is one to avoid, or at least to investigate carefully.

Although I am a big fan of graduate education overall, employment exploration is usually done with low-investment options such as one-day seminars or a class or two. The following section contains more on this, and later in the book we'll discuss the benefits of graduate education and the best time to go to graduate school. For now, concentrate on the job exploration applications of acquiring more education.

Jobs That Require More Education or Interim Experience

Now let's consider a different aspect of education: Do some of the jobs you're targeting require an advanced degree as a minimum credential for entry? Further, are there jobs you're targeting that require interim experience as a prerequisite for entry? It's not a problem if you answered "yes" to each of these questions, but you need to fill in the blanks.

If some of the jobs you are targeting require more education or more experience than you currently have, you need to identify interim jobs that will move you toward your goal—jobs you can hold now that will advance your career and educational goals.

For example, to become a CPA in most states you need three years of supervised auditing hours. Many practicing CPAs will also pick up a master's degree sooner or later.

To get into medical school, hands-on clinical exposure is a real plus (some premed advisors call it "the hidden requirement"). You get extra points if you deal with actual bodily fluids and actual medical procedures, instead of the usual read-to-recovering-patients types of experience.

If you want to go to law school, but not this week, it is beneficial to identify jobs that will give you exposure to practicing attorneys. (What lawyers do for a living is nothing like what you see them doing on television; for example, even litigators are in court less than 5 percent of the time.) By the way, there are a lot of unhappy attorneys in this country. Be sure to ask ten or twenty of them whether they would advise you to go to law school today, and listen to their advice.

If you want to be a research scientist, you're probably aware that you're going to have to get some kind of lab job first, cleaning test tubes or entering data or mopping up spills of exotic effluvia.

If you want to get a Ph.D. in clinical psychology or a master's degree in family therapy, you would be well served by all of these experiences: (a) volunteer with a suicide prevention, teenage runaway, or AIDS counseling hotline, (b) get a job as a residential counselor at a halfway house for troubled teenagers, (c) serve as a research assistant, paid or not, to a Ph.D. doing original research in virtually any area of human behavior, (d) work with emotionally disturbed or developmentally delayed kids, and (e) get any assignment you can on the inside of a locked psych ward, whether volunteer or paid.

If you want to be a film producer, you have to get an assignment as a gofer, then a script reader, then get an assignment on a production. (See Trevor K.'s case study beginning on page 147.)

These are the kinds of directly related and increasingly responsible preparatory jobs that lead to successful admission to graduate school and successful attainment of jobs with high entrance barriers.

Don't forget any educational hurdles that may stand between you and your life goals. If you want to be a grade school teacher, you may have to complete a teaching credential program, complete a supervised student teaching assignment, and pass a certification test. Meanwhile, you can work as a teacher's aide, or volunteer at a school, or do independent tutoring, or teach SAT prep, or get a job with a private school that doesn't require a state credential, or go to work for one of the private educational diagnostics and study skills coaching companies that seem to be in every city now.

In addition to its job exploration value, taking a university class can help you get an assignment once you decide it's in a field you want to pursue further. Perhaps you need to take just a few courses to prepare you for your chosen career direction or for graduate school. If you are an anthropology major who knows she wants to work in marketing, take a marketing class to show the interest is genuine. If you are an English major who knows he wants to work in biotechnology, it might be smart to take a class related to biotechnology to prepare for success.

This is what led to John's success in the next case study. He didn't need the class to explore his interest so much as to prove his interest to others.

CASE STUDY John A.

John A. majored in biology at an elite college. He had a good academic background but had done no post-college planning. After graduation he had a series of survival jobs in Oakland, California. His lack of direction was making him miserable, his parents were on his back, and his girlfriend left him for a guy with a greener wallet. When he had what he calls his "career epiphany," he had three part-time jobs, one making lattes at a coffee house, another as a playground aide at a private school, and one checking IDs at the door for a club that specialized in world music and poetry readings. On some days he worked from 6 A.M. to 1 A.M. "I was working at all these lifestyle businesses, the kind of places that make a city a great place to live, and suddenly I realized it wasn't an accident. I really relate to the special aspects of a city that make it livable, that provide its residents with a high quality of life," said John.

So he decided to go into city planning. He applied for every single job in city planning that was within a two-hour commute in all directions. John found nothing, zip, nada for over a year. Then he learned that he could take classes as an "external student" at UC Berkeley. He signed up for a city planning class and then updated his resume. At the top, he added that he was an "enrollee" in this class. He pulled information from the class announcement and listed it under Education with a line, Topics will include. . . . Now the top part of his resume was about a class he hadn't taken yet. Guess what? He got a job before the class started with an affordable housing redevelopment agency. To his credit, John continued with his urban planning curriculum by going to night school, and he will soon have his master's degree.

Your educational options include taking a seminar or workshop lasting as little as an afternoon, taking a class at a college or university, or getting a credential.

If you want a job that requires advanced education or interim experience that you don't currently have, write a plan for gaining that experience or education. What is your plan to succeed? How will you prepare yourself to be competitive? Write it out now.

Advanced Degrees and Long-Term Career Success

As I said earlier, I am a big fan of education. Once you find the field that is right for you, you should immediately develop an education plan that will maximize your value in the marketplace.

To put it simply, going to school pays off, and going to graduate school pays off in a big way. Whatever your field, you should pursue as much training as you can afford, in terms of both time and money, and from as many sources as you can find. Once you're in a field, continuing education is available as professional development through your professional association, through vendor training, university courses, advanced degrees, and even special seminars and summits for policy-level decision makers. There are programs sponsored through Stanford Business School and Harvard Business School, among others, that are limited to corporate presidents and CEOs.

A college degree is really just an entry-level ticket to the professional world. One in four employed people have a college degree. How rare do you think it is for someone to get a doctorate? Not rare at all, as over forty-thousand earned that distinction last year alone, joining the several million who already have one.

Advanced education is actually necessary in many fields. Increasing specialization makes continued training necessary for continued success. And there's simply a lot more information in our world today than ever before. According to John Avery's book *Information Theory and Evolution*, the total amount of new information produced in 2001 and 2002 equals all the information accessible from all prior human history! Thus the need for more education just to handle the burgeoning amount of information in all fields.

Also, higher education is used by employers to sort through job applicants. In the same way that you hope your bachelor's degree separates you from those who don't have one, workers holding master's degrees hope to distinguish themselves from those who stop at the undergraduate diploma. An acquaintance recently forwarded to me a job posting from someone seeking a "secretary, master's degree preferred." So this creeping credentialism has become a real career issue. Don't be blindsided by it.

According to the U.S. Census Bureau, those who complete a master's degree earn, over their lifetimes, $400,000 *more* than those who stop at the baccalaureate. Those who complete a doctorate earn $1.3 *million* more than those who stop with

INCOME AND EMPLOYMENT BY DEGREE ATTAINMENT

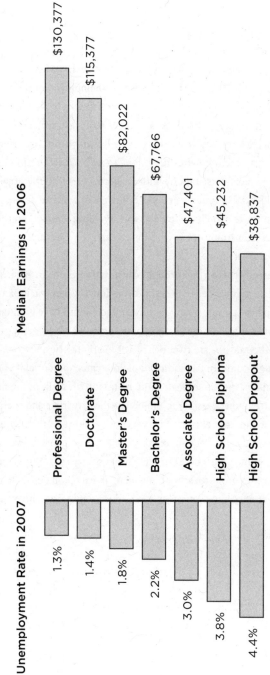

Unemployment Rate in 2007

Professional Degree	1.3%
Doctorate	1.4%
Master's Degree	1.8%
Bachelor's Degree	2.2%
Associate Degree	3.0%
High School Diploma	3.8%
High School Dropout	4.4%

Median Earnings in 2006

Degree	Earnings
Professional Degree	$130,377
Doctorate	$115,377
Master's Degree	$82,022
Bachelor's Degree	$67,766
Associate Degree	$47,401
High School Diploma	$45,232
High School Dropout	$38,837

Source: U.S. Bureau of Labor Statistics

a bachelor's degree. And those who complete the M.D., D.D.S., D.V.M., and J.D. (doctors, dentists, veterinarians, and attorneys) earn $2.3 *million* more than those who stop at the baccalaureate level.

So, education pays off.[6]

Also, look at the table on the previous page. Notice that with each degree attained, income goes up and, perhaps just as important, unemployment goes down. Some of you liberal arts majors may want to know what happens to liberal arts Ph.D.'s who cannot find teaching jobs, and there are many who face this fate: they are forced to accept an increase in pay from the private sector, from government, and from nonprofits that snap them up after they "fail" to find a teaching job.[7]

It is true that you can rise rapidly with an employer without worrying about your educational credentials if your employer doesn't worry about them. But a problem arises when you try to switch employers, when you put yourself on the open market and face competition from others who have taken the time and trouble to keep up their educational credentials.

When does education become a competitive issue in hiring? When your competition all have advanced degrees and you don't. When you look to your left and to your right, and the people sitting in those cubicles both have graduate degrees, it'll be past time for you to consider it. The best age at which to get a graduate degree seems to be in the mid-to-late twenties or very early thirties.

This is a rough guide, not an indicator of your career potential if you do it another way. For one thing, your career may really be taking off right in the middle of those years, so that you couldn't possibly accommodate the extra time and energy for graduate school. And graduate school is not for everybody. I don't want to panic anyone who is just glad to get out of college in one piece and has no plans to ever go to graduate school. Let me remind you: There are many other sources of training and professional development besides graduate school. In whatever ways you decide to enhance value, remember, to get maximum return on your education budget, invest it early.

> The man who doesn't read good books has no advantage over the man who can't read them.
>
> —*Mark Twain*

12

How about High-Risk Choices?

Some jobs present special challenges for prudent planning, in light
of the low probability of success and the correspondingly high risk of failure.

We all plan on being wildly successful in our employment, but the statistical fact
is that exactly half of us will have below average success. The most highly paid film
actors and corporate executives are so extraordinarily well rewarded, each earning
millions of dollars per year, that it is hard to imagine either needing more.

But what about the moderately successful film actors and business executives?
Well, here their experiences diverge. The moderately successful business executive still
earns something like $50,000–$100,000 per year, while the moderately successful
actor may earn—and this is no joke— nothing at all.

The median income in the Screen Actors Guild (SAG) is so low that half the
dues-paying members in the largest union representing the acting profession don't
earn enough to pay their rent.

Let's consider other examples. A "failed" salesperson still earns $30,000–$50,000
per year, while the "failed" athlete earns, again, nothing at all. The starting salary
for an NFL lineman is well over $100,000, but the really important datum is that

the average tenure for an NFL lineman is less than two years. And that's if you get to play pro ball at all. Of course, there are quarterbacks and other star performers earning millions of dollars per year, but there are a lot more athletes earning the contractual minimum.

Similar analyses can be conducted for baseball and basketball players. And fashion models and couturiers. And novelists and scriptwriters. And painters and sculptors. And photographers and songwriters.

Many are willing, yet few are called.

So what do you do if you are a bright and prudent young person who wants to pursue employment in acting or photography or poetry or opera or Christian psychedelic rock?

This is an intensely personal quest; each of you will have to make your own decision, and it may evolve over time. There are, however, a few approaches others have used with success:

- Give it your all for a few years, and if you haven't become a household name, pursue your backup plan.

- Make your high-risk interest an avocation, and pursue another career that allows you to satisfy all your threshold needs.

- Pursue your passion without a plan to stop doing so, but find out how most poets, etc., support themselves.

> First, you must eat.
>
> —*Advice from Wallace Stegner to each*
> *incoming creative writing class*

Of course, you can use the approaches in combination.

First, if you decide to go for it, you will need to eat and pay rent while you give it a shot. As you progress with your job explorations, you will need to find out how other people typically support themselves during the lean times that are common early in these types of careers. For example, when networking with writers, you'll soon discover that they often teach at private schools without a credential, or get MFAs and teach at writing workshops or colleges and universities, or work as editors in publishing, or write for newspapers and magazines and online content providers, or work in public relations or advertising. The myth of the cab driver–poet is exactly that. Studies have clearly established that you are much more likely to write a magnum opus if you work around people who love and care about words than if you don't.

If you can count on family support, you may decide to use it as a cushion while you try out film making, wildlife photography, or such. For those with the resources, this is certainly an option.

In any case, your exploration of high-risk jobs and careers is intended to establish a plan for putting food on your table while you wait to make it. This is not the same thing as a backup plan. It is a front-end plan so that you can survive while you pursue your passion.

Finally, you need to anticipate what you will do if you don't make it. What will you do if you're an athlete and get injured, or you write a novel that's never published, or you make glass sculptures for ten years but decide you'd really like to own a car that starts? And how long will you try before you think, "I gave it a good try; time to go on to something else"?

Consider some of the case studies we've already seen. Lance B. was an attorney who wrote novels during his commute (page 62). Clary N. was a photographer looking for a way to get started (page 98). James W. was a novelist who crashed and burned (page 21). Here are a few more from among my own friends:

CASE STUDY Bobby G.

Bobby G. is a successful novelist, who writes six hours every day in the Library of Congress in Washington, D.C. He writes longhand with pencils and transcribes his work onto a computer every night. "I wrote six novels before the first one sold," he told me. "Then I got a three-book deal. Before that, I was one of America's working poor. I did every kind of temporary office job just to survive. I even lived in my car a couple of times. I was arrested once for failing to pay parking and traffic tickets. We've criminalized poverty in this country, and it is literally illegal to be as poor as I was. But I made it." He has no regrets and writes every day.

CASE STUDY Mike M.

Mike M. played guitar in a band in the San Francisco Bay Area. A couple of times they almost had a recording contract. "We never got that deal, but we toured and got gigs, we had followers, we had buzz. We were not gods, by any stretch, but we were minor divinities. It was a constant hustle. That's how I learned to market things. You have to constantly try something different; you have to be smarter and more clever than your competition." When Mike got married, his wife wanted to have a baby, and he decided to leave the band. He went into sales management and vaulted himself into six figures within two years. He attributes his success in business to the promotional work he did for his band. He still jams occasionally with his buddies but says he doesn't miss the scene.

CASE STUDY Bill S.

Bill S. was a successful fine art photographer living in Manhattan. He had solo shows and was sometimes mentioned in art magazines. He shot pictures every day, and his loft was his dedicated photography studio. Bill was audited by the IRS for deducting 100 percent of his living quarters as a business space. The IRS sent agents to the loft, and Bill showed them the hammock he hung between hooks to sleep on. He passed the audit. But after six years, Bill realized he wasn't really getting anywhere. He had done everything he possibly could in photography except repeat himself. And he was tired of sleeping on a hammock in a studio. So he signed up for a post-baccalaureate premed sequence at Columbia University. He was the first person in the history of the program to make a perfect score on the program's biochemistry exam. He's in medical school now, at the top of his class.

CASE STUDY Daria R.

Daria R. is an artist living in Seattle. She has solo shows and for years has made commissioned pieces for Bumbershoot, a regional music and arts festival, and for the Nordstrom retail chain. Each of her friends owns at least one piece of her art. "For me, this has nothing to do with money," Daria once told me. She supported herself after college by working in clubs, but now she is married to a film cameraman, who supports the family. Daria has income from her art, but she'd keep doing it anyway, even if it didn't bring in a dime.

CASE STUDY Andrea M.

Andrea M. is an actress. It is her identity, not her goal. After graduating from college in Philadelphia, she went to Manhattan and tried to break into Broadway. It didn't happen. So she went to acting school and met people involved in off-Broadway and non-Equity theater. She performs regularly in these fringe but legit venues, while supporting herself in any way she can. "This is what I am going to do. This is who I am. I don't really care what anybody else thinks about it. All my friends are actors, too, so I don't have to explain myself to them."

I think it is important to remember that Harrison Ford gave up on his acting career and decided to be a carpenter in Hollywood before the first *Star Wars* film made him a household name.

Who knows what will happen to you as you pursue your dream. But remember, first you must eat.

As you explore high-risk options, be sure that you are realistic about what it will take to succeed. Many of these professions take decades to master. The apprenticeship for a freelance writer is often ten years. A ballet dancer will often have a dozen years of training before becoming a professional performer. An opera singer will also have years of extensive coaching before earning a chance to step out of the chorus.

And some goals may be all but out of the question. It is virtually impossible to become a ballet star if you start at age twenty. You could become a dancer, yes, but a starring career with such a late start is not likely.

In life launch exploration, your goal is to road test a few carefully selected job ideas. You will need to leave the safety and security of the student life and enter the real world as a seeker of advice and counsel. You'll need to find working professionals and ask them, "How did you get started? What's the key to success? What's the secret handshake? What advice do you have for someone like me?" Then listen to their advice.

Don't limit yourself, but pursue high-risk options with your eyes wide open.

If you're interested in a high-risk career option, write your answers to the following questions in your life launch journal:

- What is your plan to learn more about what it takes to succeed?
- How will you eat and pay rent while you pursue this goal?
- How long will you pursue it if it doesn't produce any income?
- What is your backup plan, and what would trigger you to put it in play?

CASE STUDY Trevor K.

"I wrote an English honors thesis during my senior year of college, and I just had no time to worry about a career. After graduation, my mom gave me this big fat career guide. It was dense reading, and it seemed to address older people. Or people who really knew what they wanted to do, which I did not. I had no idea what I wanted to do. I had a hard enough time picking a major, and now I had to pick a career? It seemed impossible.

"So I went to New York and got a job waiting tables. It wasn't about a career; it was about making some scratch and seeing the world. I waited tables about five months, saved up some money, and went to Europe—all over Europe. I found out traveling was great, and you learn all that cultural stuff, but unless you have a trust fund, it's not a real life.

"Then I moved back in with my dad in San Francisco because it was free! I went to all the Giants ball games, and I got a job copying journal articles. It was a weird job and probably illegal: going to libraries all over the Bay Area and finding obscure articles, copying them, scanning them, and forwarding them to this service in New Jersey. I got really good at it. I knew everything about every library—UC Berkeley, Stanford, all the publics—I was an expert. Pretty soon it only took a couple of hours a day. I was making my own money so my dad put rent on me, but it wasn't much; it was no problem.

"But then my dad kicked me out. 'I'm paying my own way,' I said, and he said, 'Yeah, but you don't have a life. You can't hang around here like this.' So that's when I went to look at career books again. One of them had these check-offs. You could pick your preferences off a list, and I checked advertising because it was near the top.

"So I started to look for a job in advertising but got no traction. Nobody would even talk to me. English lit prepares you for everything, but in another way, it prepares you for nothing. In terms of employability, I thought I had no sellable skills. But I knew how to write. In the end, that was a tool, a critical tool. There's no business that doesn't involve writing, whether it's speeches or memos or grant applications or position papers or orders for lunch. Most people, I've come to realize, do not know how to write. But I've learned now that you can't put that on your resume and expect anyone to hire you.

"While I was looking for a job in advertising, I met somebody who was working on a presidential campaign [in Washington, D.C.]. My dad wanted me out of the house, so I thought, Why not? So I went to D.C. with her and got involved in a campaign. They loved me because I could do everything. I could do research, write letters, call people, feed lines to the press, negotiate between big egos. I was good under pressure. The campaign started taking off, and our guy was getting a lot of attention. Washington is the networking capital of the world. In politics, your currency is who you know. I made it my business to know everybody. But then there was a crisis in the campaign, and my boss was squeezed out. I was told to go to the Denver campaign office or lose my paid position. I was living out of a suitcase anyway, so it meant nothing to me to move to Denver.

"Within a couple of weeks our guy folded, and there I was in Denver, renting a room with no furniture. One of the other campaign workers had talked her way into a job as a personal assistant to a studio head from Hollywood, who was a major donor to [the candidate]. She wanted someone to help her drive to L.A. I said, 'Sure.' So I left my stuff in my room and drove to L.A. with her. I tried to get her to hook me up with the studio guy, but she said she couldn't do that; she hadn't even started yet.

"I only knew one other person in L.A., an old family friend, so I looked him up. He offered me a couch for a couple of days. I was talking up my writing and research skills and telling stories about the campaign, when the guy's girlfriend said she knew of a job that might be coming up, a powerful director who might need an assistant. I wasn't even sure I wanted to stay in L.A., but then I got the itch. I decided to go get my stuff in Denver. The cheapest way to get there was by bus, so I bought a bus ticket and had a hellish ride back.

"When I got off the bus two days later, my cell phone rang. It was eight o'clock in the morning, and it was my friend's girlfriend. '[The director] wants to meet you tomorrow. Can you get back here by 8 A.M.?' I said, 'Sure.' I had no idea how I'd do it; then I looked down the street and saw a car lot. I had a debit card. So I bought a used car with the last dime I had in my account and drove twenty hours to get back to L.A. I shaved in a gas station restroom and put on a fresh shirt. At 8 A.M. I was at this guy's office. He kept me waiting for four hours. He had the biggest coffee table I'd ever seen, with every newspaper and magazine. It looked like a newsstand. Most of them looked like they'd never been opened. I remember thinking, In the campaign we had to sharpen each pencil down to the nub. Here they'd probably say, 'That pencil's not fresh. Here's a new box.' This is a better place than politics. It was a weird thought, but I hadn't slept in two days.

"I read magazines and waited. At noon I got the interview, and got the job right on the spot. I started the next day at 6 A.M. That was four years ago. I started at the bottom, but now I'm a script fixer. I guess English lit pays off after all, but there's more to it than that. Hundreds of people move to Hollywood every day, and it's survival of the fittest. The people who meet the most people, who make the most friends, who can make themselves the most valuable, the ones who are always available, who can work without sleep, who never say no, who never whine or complain—they get to go on to the next job. You have to put yourself in the position where you're the one chosen. I use the skills I learned in D.C., every day. Politics and Hollywood are really part and parcel of the same devil. Everybody is always looking for the next big thing. Hollywood is really just one big job audition, all the time. But you'll never be bored."

The Entrepreneurial Option

Almost anyone will tell you that you should work for someone else for two to ten years before starting your own business, that you should learn as much as you can about an industry before going out on your own. This is excellent advice, some of the time.

There are several reasons you may want to start up a business:

- Entrepreneurial fire, that is, you can't keep yourself from starting a business. You are someone with a high threshold need to control your environment and a high degree of self-reliance. You may have already started one or more small enterprises in high school or college.

- To create revenue. The motivation is a short-term need to generate cash flow. You may not be particularly concerned with the long-term outcome.

- To learn more about an industry by using the business as a sort of calling card. If you own a business serving a particular industry or locale, you will have a built-in reason to get to know everyone in that industry or locale.

- To create an enduring, successful, profitable business, either to keep it and run it or to build it and sell it.

Only in the last case is it important for you to have two to ten years of experience before launching a business. For long-term success, it is true that you should master a field before launching a business in that space. However, for the other reasons, you really can just go out there and try something out.

For example, if you can't get a job of any kind, you may need to start a business in order to generate some cash to cover your expenses while you strategize your next move. Whether you keep looking for a career-launching job or relocate for more promising economic conditions or decide you need to pursue some training, starting up a business can create a safety net for you. Low-tech entrepreneurship has been the salvation of many students and recent graduates with mounting bills and no jobs in sight, needing to do something about their cash flow situation. Students have launched moving companies, house painting and cleaning companies, newsletter designing services, lawn and gardening services, babysitting registries, T-shirt screening businesses, advertising promotions companies, and so on, to create revenue.

Have you mastered a skill that you can teach others? Perhaps it makes sense to start a poetry writing workshop or teach oboe or tutor chemistry or lead a French conversational group. These types of endeavors can generate modest cash flow, allowing you to continue with your search for a professional-level position.

Before taking a job that you know you will hate, consider creating a job that you know you will enjoy, even if it is just a temporary source of cash for you. Buy a copy of *Kick Start Your Dream Business* by Romanus Wolter and get started.

One of the oft-overlooked benefits of starting your own business is to gain access to people who would not talk to you or hire you otherwise. Starting your own business can also be a great way to learn more about jobs you're interested in, *and it can give you some valuable experience to put on your resume.* Here are some examples:

If you're interested in events management, consider starting a car parking service that you can promote to caterers in your city. Buy or make some white vests and put a logo on them. Voila, you have a reason to approach every caterer and events management company in town, providing valet parking for their next event.

If you are interested in the commercial real estate leasing business and just can't get the time of day from any commercial property management company, design a window dressing business for empty stores. Empty stores are bad for business, so the idea is to make them attractive. You can provide through-the-window art gallery space for local artists, sell window displays to other businesses, or just make attractive and creative displays that draw the attention of passersby. Your entire investment could amount to a few sheets of painted plywood to use for screens. Then approach every chamber of commerce or neighborhood business association in your area, as well as every building owner and leasing agency. .

If you're interested in working in advertising but can't get a job, stop looking for a job and start selling your services as your own independent business. Develop a brochure and sell web design services or graphic art and design or e-commerce programming infrastructure or specialized translating services, and so on.

The business needn't be directly related to have success with this model. I interviewed a student who developed fliers for his computer troubleshooting business, which he used to get a job unrelated to computers.

CASE STUDY Ian F.'s Amazing Story

"Everybody hates their own computer, and everybody's computer has at least one thing on it that doesn't work or doesn't work right. So I made up fliers that said 'Laptop Wizard. I will fix one problem on your computer absolutely for free to show you the value of my consulting services.' I focused on laptops because I wanted to meet with the actual bosses, not office managers and secretaries. Everybody handles their own laptop. Then I got this list of the fifty largest businesses in my area from the local newspaper. They publish it once a year, and it listed every owner or CEO by name. I sent my flier, which was really a coupon, to each one. This is kind of a big small town, so I don't know if this would work everywhere, but it sure worked for me. I'd go into an office, and I'd schmooze up the boss while I'm fixing his [or her] computer. I got a lot of follow-up business. In a sense, I was making $50 an hour to run a job search. I didn't really have a career plan. I know you're supposed to, but I was just looking for what was available, what was growing, who had strong business. I found a job selling architectural specialty items, custom windows and doors, architectural stone, columns and cornices, garden statuary, cabanas, that kind of thing, to designers and builders throughout the state. The pay is great, and they even gave me a company car. I never would have been able to get in the door without the Laptop Wizard concept. The weird thing is I was an ag[riculture] major in college, and computers were just a hobby of mine."

So starting a business can be a bridge to professional-track employment, or it can become a career in itself. It is important to know that many of the largest companies today were started with a few thousand dollars, including Microsoft, Hewlett-Packard, Apple, Sony, Intel, and Mrs. Fields Cookies. I started my own business with $2,000 and a used computer, and it's still going strong after nineteen years. I have four brothers, and every one of them either owns his own company or owns a major piece of the company he works for, so I can't see anything wrong with the entrepreneurial option.

What makes the American economy the envy of the world is the entrepreneurial spirit. With an idea, some gumption, and a handful of money, you can start a company. And if you fail, no harm, no foul. You can fail in America, and it is not a permanent stain against you, your alma mater, or your family name. If you fail, you pick yourself up, dust yourself off, get a job, and go on with your life. You can try again later, or you can take the experience and let it make you a better manager in whatever position you pursue.

Finally, you may have heard a version of this widely held belief: The overwhelming majority of small businesses fail within five years. It turns out, this just isn't so. The Small Business Administration conducted a study of 12,185 companies and found that 67 percent are successful after four years.[8] Many business owners sell or close perfectly successful businesses to retire or pursue other opportunities. In other words, not all closed or merged companies are in fact failures. Many of them provided the founder-manager with years of good income and volumes of valuable experience. Chances of success go up if the founder is college educated, if the start-up phase is managed from a home office, and if the founder starts with sufficient capital to carry the business into profitability. By the way, for several years now the majority of new businesses in this country have been launched by women. Altogether, the entrepreneurial option may be right for you, either now or in the future. Just remember, when you own a business, you are never not at work; and if the floor needs sweeping, you are Chief Floor Sweeper. Whatever you think, don't think it's not going to be a lot of work. If you were going to start a business now or in the future, what would it be? Write a business concept and launch plan in your life launch journal now.

Resources

Although the most important resources are grit and determination, there are organizations specifically oriented toward helping young people who have the entrepreneurial itch. A little advice and counsel on how to develop a business plan and how to do a break-even analysis can be useful. Check out the following resources:[9]

Collegiate Entrepreneurs' Organization (support and community)
www.c-e-o.org

Young Entrepreneurs' Organization (support and community)
www.yeo.org

Young Entrepreneur (support and community)
www.youngentrepreneur.com

The Student Success Manifesto (a guide)
www.successmanifesto.com

Young Entrepreneur's Guide to Starting and Running a Business
www.nfte.com

> When you die you won't regret the things you did, so much as the things you didn't do.
>
> —*Mark Twain*

CASE STUDY Art Major and Entrepreneur—Max K.

"I was an art major at [a liberal arts college in St. Louis], with a concentration in sculpture. My media were slate, stone, wood, and metal. Most people specialize, but I was rather eclectic in my interests. I tried not to, but I accidentally graduated, so I had to get a job. I became a finish carpenter, building houses in upstate New York. My dad was an architect, so my toys as a kid were real tools. Most kids get a plastic hammer and saw, but I had real ones. Actually, quite a few of the carpenters

I worked with had college degrees, now that I think about it. I did trim, cabinets, wood floors. I liked it.

"I was living with five guys in a big house with a huge garage. I tried to start my own business designing handmade furniture out of that garage. But I didn't know [anything] about marketing, and I didn't know how to relate the hours I spent working on a piece with its real market value. So I was going broke making beautiful furniture. I taught myself how to steam and bend wood, how to make furniture on a structural level. Skills that turned out to be really useful later.

"Then I moved to Austin and got a job as a waiter. That's the best fall-back job in the world. You get instant cash, and you meet cool people. Restaurants always have cool people. Plus, you have plenty of time during the day to work on other projects. My employer discovered I could make and fix things, and I became the maintenance guy for a chain of concept restaurants. I started doing design work on the side, like logos, ads, identity packages, and I got a job doing engineering drafting. Which I knew nothing about. I drew stuff that was impossible to build.

"I decided to build a portfolio, thanks to a dream I had about animation. Not a dream as in a goal, but a literal dream after watching the original *Batman* movie, and when I woke up I wrote it down. I wanted to do art animation, not character animation. I thought it would be perfect, to draw, do the music myself, and put in a soundtrack. And I liked the idea of having a captive audience. People have to sit down to see your work, not like at a gallery where they can walk by. So I needed a portfolio to get into art school. Around this time, I had a gallery opening in Austin, of drawings. I was doing about eight things at once and applying to art school.

"I was accepted to [art school in Chicago]. I worked as a waiter again, doing some drawing on the side. I started a business drawing 'portraits' of people's houses. I made up sample cards and drove around the fanciest neighborhoods handing them out. Lots of people commissioned me to do drawings of their homes. So, between that and waiting tables, I got through art school. After I graduated, my student loans started coming due. I found out that [a major movie studio] was hiring animators, but they wanted people to draw character movements at twenty-four frames a second—very old school, very boring. There was a job in Kentucky working for public television, which I applied for and didn't get. And I saw a job working for a lighting design company that needed product management and some design work as well. I needed an income, so I applied and I got it.

"So I drew production documents for lighting fixtures. I also caught on that the designers had a great lifestyle. They made their money on royalties, and this appealed to me, because it's kind of like gambling; you never know what you might get. You might get a little, or you might get a whole lot, and the weird thing is I'm not a gambler, but this appealed to me. I had another dream, and it was that I should go into business for myself as a lighting designer. I started saving every nickel and dime I could. I socked away $15,000 and I sold an invention to Nordic-Trac for $11,000, and that made the difference. I bought all the computer equipment I needed, and I started designing lights. I worked seven days a week, every day for a year, to get some royalties flowing. I worked every day until about 1 a.m. Then the next day I'd do it again. Following day, same thing. For a year.

"Now I'm getting my own label. I have a factory in China that produces my designs. I still work seven days a week, because I'm into it. It's great to be independent."

NOTES

1. Just for the record, "six degrees of separation" was coined as a concept in 1967 by Yale psychologist Stanley Milgram. It has since been discredited, as Professor Milgram did his original research within a bounded community, namely, college professors at elite universities, and their immediate friends. So within a bounded community, six degrees of separation may apply, but once you leave that community, it doesn't hold true. No one knows how many degrees of separation lie between you and a sheep herder in Botswana, but it's probably far more than six. For more, see Dan Vergano, "Three big flaws in 'six degrees of separation' theory," *USA Today*, January 14, 2002.

2. An earlier version of this networking list appeared in Donald Asher, *The Overnight Resume*, Berkeley, CA: Ten Speed Press, 1991. Used with permission.

3. Saul Reyes, director of career services, Jacksonville University, personal conversation.

4. Principia College findings: Students with internships were twice as likely to have a job offer at graduation. Jacksonville University findings: Students with internships were twice as likely to get a job requiring a college degree. San Francisco State findings: Students' number one indicator of the first job they will hold after college is the last full-time job they held before graduating. NACE press release, November 26, 2002: 54 percent of hired grads have internship experience on their resumes, and 32 percent of new hires come from employers' own internship pools.

5. Nelson Mandela, *Long Walk to Freedom* (Boston: Back Bay Books, 1994, 1995), 166.

6. Although these data seem to indicate that doctors, dentists, vets, and lawyers earn more than those completing doctorates, the educations of many doctorates are fully funded, while those completing professional degrees may have to borrow—and pay back—significant student loans. Further, when broken down by gender, the data show that female doctorates earn more than women with professional degrees. This may be more information than you would ever want to know about income and educational attainment, but there it is.

7. "The Job Market for Ph.D.'s: Two Views," in *Occupational Outlook Quarterly*, Winter, 1996–97. In short, the outcomes are great as long as you consider that success might include more than one definition (for example, if you can stand not being a college professor). These data clearly show that the penalty for not accepting a tenure-track position is an increase in pay. See also "Perspectives on the Job Market for Ph.D.s," in *NACE Spotlight* (23, no. 16). A little bit like "the glass is half full," but nevertheless, useful. See also Chris M. Golde and Timothy M. Dore, "At Cross Purposes: What the Experiences of Today's Doctoral Students Reveal about Doctoral Education" (a white paper based on a survey funded by the Pew Charitable Trusts, January, 2001). This is also the data source for the above NACE article. Additional information and findings available at www.phd-survey.org clearly show that most doctoral candidates do, in fact, want to become professors.

8. As reported in *USA Today*, February 18, 2003.

9. I am indebted to nationally syndicated columnist Daniel Kehrer and "BizBest" for these resources, as published in the *Reno Gazette-Journal,* May 27, 2003.

Now It's Time to Actually Get a Job

PART 3

Dance as though no one is watching you,

Love as though you have never been hurt before,

Sing as though no one can hear you,

Live as though heaven is on Earth.

—Souza

"I was a business admin major with a concentration in marketing. I was graduating in December, so I was off the regular recruiting cycle entirely. I'd been working for a [retail] outlet during school, but I didn't consider it a career job. They made me assistant manager, which gave me something to put on my resume, but basically I was just a college student with no experience.

"In the fall, I ran my job search by playing around on the Internet. I found some career sites and took some tests that spit out lists of career choices based on your answers. I was trying to find out what I could see myself doing—what I was interested in. I didn't take them too seriously, but actually they were pretty helpful. Through those, I read some job descriptions, and they would either appeal to me or not.

"I knew there was a decision that had to be made. I had a time constraint because I was graduating, and I knew I would not be moving back home. I knew I had to support myself.

"My search was still mostly on the Internet. I'd type in [to a search engine] all the companies I could think of, and visit their websites to see what jobs were posted and how to apply. I emailed my resume all over the place, and a whole lot of nothing happened after that. I think I was aiming too high, or applying for jobs that I wasn't completely qualified for. I thought it was a shot in the dark that might work. But later I realized I was going for things that probably a thousand other people were also applying to.

"A couple of times I got to the second level, where they ask you to fill out an interest form with more information, but that was as far as I ever got. I was never contacted once by a human. For some reason, I just kept doing it even though I thought it was pointless, right up until . . . I got my first real job.

"Since I was still living in [a college town], I started spending a lot of time at the career center. I started reading a lot of their books on interviewing, resumes, cover letters, etiquette. And I got to a point where I could read them pretty quickly. I'd flip through them and see what was new, what I hadn't seen before. I read about twenty of them and got a lot more sophisticated about everything.

"I put together a more impressive resume, and I wrote much better business correspondence, cover letters, and thank-you notes—all kinds of things you can send to companies. A lot of the interview books I looked at were helpful, because they helped me see this from the employer's side: what they're looking for, how they look at a candidate. And I learned to tailor myself to each job better.

"A lot of the books emphasized networking. I tried it, but I just don't know that many people. I'm from Michigan, and I went to school in Missouri. [My school] has a great reputation in St. Louis and Kansas City, but I just had college friends, and we were a long way from St. Louis or Kansas City. I did ask the parents of friends about opportunities at the companies where they worked. But it didn't seem like that was going to go anywhere for me. I got a couple of leads out of newspapers and employment magazines, but in the end I didn't want to waste my time on that.

"At the career center, they have this huge database, and every company in the country is in it. You can search by SIC code, size, revenue per year, location of headquarters, and branch locations. It helped me a lot and put me in touch with companies I would never have heard of otherwise. Some were small, and some you'd have no clue what they did without the description and SIC code. I had about three lists going, all different types of work. Next, I made geographic choices. I pretty much just stuck to St. Louis and Kansas City.

"Now I had a plan. A process. I'd look at a company's website, then I'd start emailing and calling them. I'd ask if they had any openings for marketing majors and recent graduates. If they were interested, I mailed them a resume with a cover letter in the U.S. mail. Emailing resumes was discouraging. I don't think they look at them, and everybody does it. So I mailed mine out in nine-by-twelve envelopes, so they weren't folded. It cost me about two bucks apiece, counting materials, but I thought it was worth it. Sometimes I sent several a day, but I made a phone call each time, and each letter was addressed to a specific person about a specific opportunity. I didn't waste my time anymore just blasting resumes out. I was getting picky. I knew what kind of jobs I wanted.

"Then I started getting interest, and getting interviews. On some interviews, I bombed, including one where I really wasn't prepared. I didn't have any answers to their questions. I didn't know what they were looking for. I was really nervous. But with every interview, I got better. I know how they want you to answer certain questions. By the end, I wasn't nervous anymore. I was always prepared.

"I was a seasoned job seeker now. I knew what I was doing.

"Then I discovered job fairs. I went to a couple, but the competition was stiff. I found out about an entry-level job fair in Kansas City. That was better all around. I'd be competing with other college students and recent grads. I could handle that.

"I bought a very nice suit. I printed my resumes on really nice paper. When I got there, only about 20 percent of the candidates were wearing suits, and of them, a lot looked borrowed or pulled out of some clothes pile. Some people were wearing T-shirts, and I was embarrassed for them. I really thought I was the most professional-looking student there.

"I got in line for an advertising company, and the rep immediately said she was putting my material in a special pile. She called me the next day and invited me to come for an interview. So I drove two hundred miles to the interview. I had my first meeting with the human resources manager; then I took a math test and an Excel spreadsheet test. Then they asked me if I wanted to wait around all day to have an interview with the media director. I said, 'Sure.' So I waited around all day, then had a group interview with five people. Questions came at me from five different directions. It was definitely a little intense. I know I wouldn't have passed this interview without all the practice I'd had earlier.

"They put me through some out of the box–type questions, where there's no correct answer, to see how creative I could be. I felt a lot of pressure to come up with something impressive, something unique. They asked me, 'You're driving down the street in a two-seater car, and you pull up to a bus stop. There's an elderly lady headed to the hospital, and your best friend, and the person of your dreams. Who do you pick up and why?'

"I told them all three of those people would fit in the car, because they are the same person. The elderly lady is the person of my dreams, and the person of my dreams should be my best friend, so they're all the same person. They told me they'd never heard that answer before.

"Then they switched it around and tried to intimidate me. Told me the job was really stressful, a lot of pressure, a lot of hours, if I made a mistake it could be a *huge* mistake, and all this with low starting pay. I just held my ground. The interview came to an end, and I left there completely wrung out. I collected business cards from everyone, and before I even left town to drive the two hundred miles back home, I stopped and wrote six thank-you notes and dropped them in the mail. I wrote them right on the hood of my car.

"Then I had the longest week of my life, waiting for an answer. I emailed a couple of specific questions, things I already knew or didn't really need answered, just to show them I was still sincerely interested. A week later, they called and offered me the job. I tried to negotiate the salary, but they wouldn't budge. They said that's how advertising works. Start low and advance quickly. So I accepted. I've been working there two weeks as of today. My search took four months."

13

Start with a Job Target

So far you've been working on job ideation, generating scores of creative ideas about positions in industries that might interest you. You've also explored some of those ideas by seeking insider knowledge from careerists in those industries. Now you're ready to go out there and get a job in the field.

First, let's confirm your direction. What three jobs are you most interested in pursuing? Remember, a job is in a specified industry, plus it involves having a pretty clear idea of what you want to do in that industry. To seek it, you have to know what a typical title would be for someone in that job function. Once again, if you cannot reach this level of specificity, you're probably not ready to get a job: you probably need to do more idea exploration.

The job you seek now needs to be a job you can obtain now. If you've done career exploration properly, you've filled in all the steps between being a college student and obtaining a major career goal. So the jobs you're after now are appropriate first steps toward that bigger goal. Career goals such as astronaut, judge, and president of the United States need to be supported by appropriate first-step jobs or internships.

With this consideration in mind, what are two objectives for you right now that you'd like to pursue, and what is one dream opportunity you'd like to try to land, even if you think it's a long shot? List them here:

Job target #1:

_____

Job target #2:

_____

Dream opportunity:

_____

You're going to have to select one of these as the first target you will pursue. Job search requires focus, and while you can look for two or three different types of jobs at the same time, you need to start with just one. Learn how job search works before trying to run two or three simultaneous search projects! So, circle the job target you want to use as the first target to pursue.

Before you start working on one of your other targets, get a few dozen applications out on the first one.

Job Search Strategy

Most career books devote many pages to putting together a proper resume and being prepared to interview well. These seem to be cornerstones of the career development process as it is practiced in career centers today. However, I'll let you in on a little secret: The resume is not that important.

Your strategy is much more important than your resume.

I've made over $1 million writing resumes for executives in transition, so you'd think if I had a bias, it would be in their favor. In fact, I've written three books on how to write resumes, and two of them dominate their niches, so I think I know what I'm talking about when it comes to resumes. Yes, a perfect resume will get a complete idiot a job. But a mediocre resume with a good job search strategy will get _anyone_ a job much faster. Strategy is much more important than the resume itself. **How you use your resume is much more important than what's written on the page.**

And I'll take a stance that is even more iconoclastic: **You don't need to interview well if you interview often enough**. If you interview often enough, you'll learn to interview well. Spend your time learning how to get interviews rather than learning how to prepare for interviews, and your time will be better spent.

I'm not inviting you to do a sloppy job with your resume and with your interview preparation. That's not my point. But I am saying that strategy is more important, so spend more time and energy on strategy. In short, spend more time on strategy, and less on resumes and interview preparation. You only have so much energy, so use it wisely. Use the resume tutorial on my website, and get it done. Go to www. donaldasher.com/careers/resumes.

A bad resume with a good strategy beats a good resume with a bad strategy *every time.*

The Three Secrets of Job Search

The three secrets of your job search are

1. You get jobs by talking to people.

2. You need one hundred leads at all times.

3. A smart seeker looks for work in channels.

This is the biggest single truth in job change: You get jobs by talking to people. Anything you do that causes you to talk to people will speed up your job search, and anything you do that keeps you from talking to people slows down your job search.

You've already been doing everything you need to do to get a job. If you've been doing job exploration, you've been learning about employers, how they hire, what motivates them, and which people to talk to. You've been talking to people a lot. To get a job, you'll just continue to use those skills, to go beyond exploring a career direction to seeking jobs in a specific field. You get jobs by talking to people, and you are now comfortable talking to people.

What does this say about the Internet? Well, if you use the Internet like a telephone, if you use the Internet to talk to lots of people, then it will speed up your job search. If you use the Internet to keep from talking to people, it will slow your job search. If you use your computer to talk to other computers, your job search could take, literally, forever. Recall what several students in the case studies said about the Internet. Virtually everyone I talked to while researching this book said job listings on the Internet were not particularly fruitful. Use the Internet to research companies and to email actual individuals. Those are the fruitful applications of the Internet in a job search.

You get jobs by talking to people. Talk to everybody during your job search. Talk to people on the bus. Talk to people in airplanes. Talk to people in line at the movies. Practice your Networking Game skills: "Do you know anybody who would know anything about corporate training and development?" "Do you know anybody who would know anything about artificial intelligence?" And so on. Explore the underutilized networking contacts of faculty, alumni, friends of family, and family of friends. In this way, job search is very much an extension of job exploration.

Now that you know where you're headed, you need to be systematic. One way to be much more systematic is to follow the discipline of developing one hundred leads for every job target you're interested in. A lead may be a company, it may be any one of many job openings posted on a company's career site, it may be a person who works in the right industry but in the wrong company, or it could be someone who you think might be able to tell you more about opportunities in a field you're interested in. So a lead can be everyone and everything from a friend-of-a-friend to a newspaper advertisement to a big building you've driven by, with a corporate logo on it. In fact, you may have dozens of leads, and different types of leads, all related to the same company.

However you define your leads, you need one hundred of them. Why? So that you always have something to do. If you have only a handful of leads, you're going to run out of job search activities to pursue on the afternoon of your first day of job seeking. One hundred will keep you busy.

Also, you need one hundred leads so you can make mistakes. You need to have so many job leads that you don't have to worry about totally blowing an interview. So you don't freak out when you realize you've sent them a letter with a typo in it. So you don't cry if they treat you poorly, which some of them certainly will.

And you need one hundred leads because, out of any hundred organizations, one of them needs your services right now. We know from extensive direct marketing research that 1 to 3 percent of marketing targets will fit any category whatsoever. So if you have one hundred leads, between one and three of them need you right now. The same cannot be said about any dozen of the one hundred.

Sometimes there may not be so many leads in a category. If you're interested in battered women's shelters, and there are only a few around, you are going to have to expand your job target (women's social services) or your geographical area (longer commute or possible relocation) to run a proper job search.

There are databases now that have millions of companies listed in them, searchable by SIC code (type of industry the company is in), number of employees, size of revenue, geographic location, number of years in business, and type of business formation (publicly traded corporation, privately held, partnership, etc.). If you don't have one hundred leads, there are quick and easy ways to build out a lead list. (See More Job Sources on page 190.)

Keep your focus. Build your lead list in a certain channel. Don't build lead lists of just any hundred companies. Build lead lists related to a certain type of company.

The smartest job seekers look for work in channels, that is, they look for a certain type of job.

Look for a certain type of job; don't look for job openings.

When you look for a certain type of job over and over again, you become more sophisticated with every effort you expend. Each company you research helps you understand the other companies in this market space. Each interview you go on helps you learn lingo for your next interview. Each article you read helps you learn more about all the companies in this market segment.

By looking for a certain type of job, you will avoid the pitfall of looking for openings (which can cause your job search to take much longer than it has to). Does that sound odd? That you can get a job faster by not looking for openings than you can if you look for openings?

Openings are intoxicating, but they are the fool's gold of job seeking. You read a job description on a bulletin board or company's career site, and you say to yourself, "I'm perfect for this opening." You write a nice letter and you customize your resume and you send it in and you are absolutely certain that they will be calling you soon. And so are hundreds, if not thousands, of other people just like you. And the hard truth is that some of them are very likely to have more experience and higher GPAs than yours.

Have you ever seen little kids hunt for Easter eggs? You know you've seen this, then: One child finds an egg and calls out, "I found one!" Then, even though she is holding the egg up in triumph, all the other kids will run over and look at her feet! That's what happens in job placement. By the time you see the advertisement, someone else already has it in hand, and you're just another little kid looking where the job used to be.

The Hidden Job Market

First of all, you should know that a job is only advertised if an internal, informal placement effort has already failed. It will not be posted on the career site or placed in a newspaper or listed with a recruiter or agency if the manager can find someone to fill it first. In other words, all jobs that are filled by the informal network within a company *are never advertised.* This is the hidden job market.

The term "hidden job market" makes it sound like a conspiracy, but it isn't. It's just good business practice. Why go through the time delay, the expense, and the hassle of advertising a position if you can find someone to fill it first?

This is extraordinarily important for you to know: About half of all open jobs are never advertised. Job market research consistently confirms this. So if you look only for advertised jobs, you're missing half the job market. The advertised jobs are like the tip of the iceberg, while the rest of the iceberg is invisible. You have to find the hidden job market to run a successful job search.

But that's not all: Announced positions draw the most competition.

Where the Competition Is—You Don't Want to Be

Let's analyze the competition at each stage of job creation, starting with the worst-case scenario: an announced opening. An announced opening is any position that is posted on a job board or a company's website, advertised in a newspaper, or placed with an executive recruiter or employment agency. Announced positions comprise 100 percent of the positions that are not in the hidden job market, as well as some that are occasionally considered part of the hidden job market but aren't—and the competition for them is fierce.

If you're going to apply for positions that are posted on job boards or company websites or in newspapers or with executive recruiters, you have to be a very strong candidate. Why? Because you are competing with hundreds of other candidates to win the job.

How many people apply for announced positions? An advertisement for a good job in a medium-sized city will draw between one hundred and three hundred applications. In a depressed economy, it will draw even more. In San Francisco, a posting for a bartending position at a popular nightclub drew six hundred applications. The club held "open auditions" for the bartender spot, and four hundred people showed up. That's for minimum wage plus tips, in a city with one of the highest costs of living on the continent.

I once made a bet with a friend that I could advertise a bad job and still get loads of applicants. She said that no one would apply for a job they new in advance to be "bad." So I ran the following in the Sunday *San Francisco Examiner*: "Hard work, low pay. Fax your resume to (415) 441–0389." That was the entire ad. A total of seventy-two people faxed in a resume for this position. (Running the ad cost me considerably more than my $15 prize, not to mention a whole lot of fax paper!)

It takes a leap of faith to hire a college student, and once a position is announced, an employer can always find someone who requires no such leap of faith. I could hire a red-headed, left-handed person from Australia, with five years of experience and exactly three promotions during those five years, with an Ivy League education, a major in business and a minor in Hungarian, with a 4.0 GPA, who is well above average height, by looking on the Internet. What are the chances that an employer is out there designing a search just for you right this moment? Slim to none.

In short, you could apply for announced openings forever and never get one. People who get jobs by applying for announced openings are overwhelmingly obvious candidates, with impressive and directly related recent experience. College students and recent grads are among the *least* likely candidates to get advertised jobs that draw hundreds of applicants.

Some people consider executive recruiters part of the hidden job market, but not me. It is true that search professionals do not rely on placing newspaper advertisements, but these days, neither do internal recruiters. Search professionals collect resumes 365 days a year. They have their own databanks of thousands of careerists, all pre-vetted, and they subscribe to every resume bank on the Web. Before a position is placed with a search professional, a job description is created and an internal placement has failed. The search professional is simply an outsourced version of the internal human resources function.

Once a position is "announced" to a headhunter, that job is, for all intents and purposes, the same as an advertised position. Hundreds of applicants will be reviewed before two or three are advanced to the decision makers. So the competition here is also quite stiff.

Richard Bolles, author of the best-selling career guide of all time, *What Color Is Your Parachute?*, is fond of quoting research that finds it takes 1,470 resumes to win a job by simply submitting resumes to announced openings.

That's where the tightest competition is. Hundreds of people apply for positions advertised on the Web or in newspapers, and hundreds of candidates are reviewed by headhunters and agencies for each position that needs to be filled.

What about the internal, informal placement stage? This is a pretty good spot to look for work. Once a manager starts to ask around his department for help, he'll learn about just a handful of candidates. Questions like "Do you know anybody who could help us out with this marketing campaign?" will generate a few suggestions. Or he may decide to look at some of the unsolicited applications that come across his desk every day of the year. Or he may call human resources and ask to look at resumes of a certain type. The internal, informal process may generate four to six candidates, sometimes a few more. So your competition at this stage is four to six, much better than hundreds or thousands.

But that's not all: this is where the overwhelming bulk of hiring occurs. So by getting involved *before* an opening is formulated, *you're gaining access to these jobs.* And you don't have to be perfect. You just have to be better than the handful of other candidates who will also be considered.

Obviously, the sweet spot in terms of competition is the point after the hiring manager has decided to hire someone but before she acts on that decision. Your competition here is *nobody*. Most hiring managers will delay at least two weeks between the decision to hire someone and the act of initiating an internal, informal recruiting process. I recently interviewed someone who waited four months between deciding to hire someone and actually acting on that decision, and I've interviewed people in the past who have waited up to a year and a half! If you approach a hiring manager in this window of opportunity, you simply have to be alive, and capable of doing the job. You may even succeed in getting the hiring person to design the job to fit you, rather than seeking a perfect person for an already designed job.

Your competition in the window between the decision to hire and the beginning of the recruiting process is *nobody*. When you're in the sweet spot, you have zero competition.

But what about before that? What is your competition during the period when a manager is unhappy, but before she has decided to make a staffing adjustment to relieve her unhappiness? Your competition at this stage is inertia. You have to present yourself as the solution to the problem the manager has not yet decided to resolve.

What Is the Manager Thinking?

But there is one very big problem with this line of reasoning: how do you know what the manager is thinking? How do you know when she is unhappy, or when she decides to hire somebody, or when she is running an internal, informal recruiting effort? The answer is simple: you don't. That's why you have to go out there and apply for jobs before they're announced.

Here is a universal truth you have to grasp to move forward with your job search:

All companies are always hiring.

When you read in the paper that a company is laying off thousands of employees, remember, *they are also simultaneously hiring.* As less profitable divisions and branches are downsized or closed down altogether, more profitable divisions and branches are actively hiring. In fact, even in contracting areas of an organization, expensive professionals and managers are being laid off, making way for younger, less costly employees to do the grunt work. Nobody takes a $95,000-a-year scientist or engineer and assigns her to an entry-level position, yet organizations have voracious appetites for interns and new hires even in tough times. Even in the worst of job markets, people retire, or quit, or get fired for cause, or go on medical leave, or take inconvenient vacations. There is always opportunity if you can get your material in front of actual managers.

If you approach a reasonable number of employers, one or more is going to fit your criteria. One or more is going to need a technical writer or an analytical chemist or a statistician. But to increase your odds of getting a job you want, you have to look for a specific type of job. Otherwise, you have no access point. You have no particular person in the company who might be able to help you. You don't know *whom* to ask for, and you don't know *what* to ask for.

You cannot walk up to a company's street entrance and yell into the lobby, "Hey, you got any jobs in there?" You have to ask a more specific question.

The Value of Personal Introduction—How Stacey Can Help You

The best way to get into a company is through a personal introduction. If you can find anyone to get you or your resume in the front door, then you increase your odds that some human will actually consider your proposal.

You've made exhaustive lists of all those who can help you. It's time to call in some favors. Fearlessly ask everyone—your aunt, your aunt's friend, your aunt's friend's sister-in-law Stacey—if they can introduce you to someone in a company who might hire you, or hand deliver your resume to someone in a company who might hire you. This is a very powerful technique, because Stacey may be able to circumvent the resume processing machine that is designed to keep people like you out, and deliver you and your resume directly into the hands of her boss.

In other words, you can work the internal, informal selection process even when the company is "not hiring," which is never true, and even when the company is hiring for announced openings.

Most managers would much rather consider a person who is recommended even in the slightest by any existing employee or personal acquaintance. This is just human nature. The boss trusts Stacey. Stacey has presumably seen the candidate, and can attest that the candidate is interested in a job and is not a drooling idiot. The "intelligent" software and, to put it bluntly, human resources itself cannot make that claim.

There's another phenomenon involved as well. After investing millions in intelligent software to sort applicants, managers are now complaining that it just doesn't work very well. There are simply too many candidates and too little to differentiate them. Many careerists have their resumes posted on resume banks continuously, even though they aren't interested in switching jobs, or they live in distant cities, or they aren't a good match despite what the software and the telephone screener say. In fact, some companies have so many candidates that they are just ignoring the job boards and doing most of their hiring through word of mouth.

Stacey is your hero. Find as many Staceys as you can. A personal introduction is worth far more than four monkeys in a room for infinity (i.e., the Internet).

But Stacey has to know what kind of job you want, or she can't help you.

The Peculiar Case of Government and Educational Hiring

Some organizations have hiring processes that would appear to thwart the Staceys of this world. Hiring systems employed by governments and educational institutions are often formulaic. All candidates will meet stringent requirements, no exceptions. And all candidates will be reviewed by the same committee, no Staceys. And three finalists will be interviewed, and the best of them will be offered the position.

But if you analyze the actual hiring done by educational and government entities, you will find that there is often an inside candidate. Teachers and college professors and government employees of all kinds are routinely hired this way.

So even if you are seeking jobs posted by educational and government entities, seek a Stacey to recommend you, and try your best to be the inside candidate. Fail to understand this at your peril: there has never been an employment system designed yet that doesn't offer some advantage to those with friends on the inside.

You Have More Friends Than You Realize

Remember the hard work you did on career exploration? All of those contacts are now your friends. In case you forgot, the most important contacts are:

- Alumni

- Friends of family

- Family of friends

- Faculty

Think about everyone you've ever met. That's a lot of Staceys.

14

Visualize the Job You Want

To visualize the job you want, start by imagining yourself at work. What type of organization is this? I mean *specifically.* What industry is this? What are you doing for this company? What is your title? What do you wear to work? What's a typical day like for you in this job? Whom do you report to? Does anyone report to you? How many hours a week do you work? Where is this job? How long is your commute to work? How do you get there? Do you travel on the job? How much do you earn? Do you work alone or with others? What are your biggest priorities on the job? You've discovered all this in job exploration, and it's time to specify your most immediate goal. Write out your answers to these questions:

What industry do you see yourself in?

What kind of company is this?

What function will you perform?

What would be your likely title?

Where is this job located (city/state/region)?

What is the commute distance?

What will you wear to work?

Hours per week you expect to work?

Report to whom?

Supervise whom?

How much work-related travel is required?

How old is the organization?

How big is the organization?

How much do you earn?

What is your career path out of this entry position?

The Fastest Way in the World to Get a Job—Call and Ask

If you don't have a personal introduction, don't despair. You don't need friends. You don't need anything but gumption.

So, here on page 172 of this book, I am about to reveal to you the fastest way in the world to get a job. This is something that works in good times and in bad, in rural areas and in urban, in Fortune 500 companies and in art collectives.

Decide which job at the targeted organization you would like to perform. It has to be a job (a) for which they have a need, at least conceivably, and (b) that you can perform, at least conceivably. Then go on the Internet and look up everything you can about the company. Finally, pick up the phone and call anyone who works there, anyone at all, and say, "I'm interested in working for your organization as a _____. Who would I talk to about that?" Or you can email anyone in the company and ask the same thing: "I'm interested in working for your organization as a _____. Who would I talk to about that?"

Then, whatever they advise you to do, do it. They'll either tell you to buzz off, in which case you go on to the other ninety-nine leads you have already researched, or they'll tell you exactly how to get that job at that company.

Sound aggressive? Not really. You're just approaching them about a specific type of job. Either they need someone or they don't. If they do, you follow their instructions. If they don't, you go on to the next one.

The telephone is the fastest route to your next job. Email is okay, but nothing beats your phone for reaching a large number of employers quickly.

By rapidly surveying employers, you don't waste time sending letters and resumes that will just be ignored. By getting a name to contact within the company, you will email and mail and call a specific person, who will be able to tell you whether you have a chance at all of gaining employment with the organization.

Yet, again, you have to know what kind of job you want in order to use this technique. You can't just call and ask, "Do ya have any jobs in there?" Well, you could, but it's not a promising entrée.

The Power of Research → Email → Call

Once you have a name, you need a plan for contacting him or her. Research » Email » Call is a powerful contact management system, the same one used by top salespeople around the world.

Research. First, you need to confirm your contact's name, title, gender, and whether they're in town. You can get most of this on the Internet.

You have to work like a journalist and verify the obvious. If your contact's name is Chris Smith, there are twelve different ways to spell it, so make sure you spell it right. Chris can be one of at least two genders. If you address a woman executive as Dear Mr. Smith, it's already game over.

Always be honest! Say, "I'm sending a letter to Chris Smith, and I certainly don't want to make a dumb mistake. Is Chris a Mr. or a Ms.? Great. And how do you spell that? Wonderful. And is she in town this week? Fine. Thank you for your time."

Email. Then send Chris a short email explaining (a) who you are, (b) what kind of opportunity you are seeking, and (c) when you are going to follow up by phone. This email can be quite brief. A bad email used often will get you a job much faster than a great email used seldom. Here is a perfectly adequate example:

> Dear Ms. Smith,
>
> The alumni office at Campus University was kind enough to share your name and email with me. I'm very interested in opportunities in health care administration, and as I understand it you've done quite well in this field. I wonder if you'd have a moment to share any advice, ideas, leads, or referrals with a young person trying to break into health care administration.
>
> I'll follow up with a telephone call to your office tomorrow before noon. You can count on me to follow through precisely. I hope you'll have a moment to speak with me.
>
> Thank you for your consideration.
>
> Sincerely,
>
> Iama Jobseeker

Please note that this is not the same thing as informational networking. You're not seeking to learn about a job anymore, or to see if you're interested in it, or if you have the skills necessary for it. You did that in part 2. You're looking for employment. You're seeking leads on jobs and ideas about organizations that might be hiring someone with your interests and skills.

Unless you know Ms. Smith is recruiting for a known opening, however, don't directly ask for a job with her organization. Ask for her advice, ideas, leads, and referrals.

Ironically, you'll get a job much faster by seeking advice and referrals than by seeking a job with the people you are contacting.

And, unless you're applying for a known opening, do *not* enclose a copy of your resume. For both networking and exploratory purposes, do not use your resume as part of the first contact. Companies have methods for dealing with unsolicited resumes, and most of those methods involve sending them sight unseen to human resources, who will also unsee them. You'll get a much higher response rate by leaving your resume out of the first query.

Set a precise time to call them on the telephone, saying, "I'll call you Tuesday before noon," or, if you're really well organized, try language like this: "I'll call you at 9:05 A.M. tomorrow. I hope we can connect then."

The Thirty-six-Hour Rule. Whether you use email or snail mail, the timing of the follow-up call is critical. It needs to occur within thirty-six hours of your missive landing in their email queue. The timing matters. The world is moving faster and faster. If you say, "I'll be calling you tomorrow morning," they might remember you that long. If you say, "I'll call you in a week if I haven't heard from you first," you'll lose all momentum; they won't know who in the world you are or why you're calling, and you'll have to start over.

Call. The next time you call, you are trying to reach your decision maker. That's why you need to know if she is in town, so you know if she got your note and if she would at least theoretically be available to take your call. You'll need to state again who you are, why you're calling, what kind of job you are interested in, and what you want from this contact. You need to be ready to provide the thirty-second introduction, also known as the elevator speech.

The elevator speech is what you would say if you got onto an elevator at a convention, looked at the name badge of the person standing next to you, and discovered that he was in fact the president of the company you admire most in the world. What would you say between floors one and five that would cause that executive to agree to meet with you?

The elevator speech is a common business metaphor, but I actually had a client walk onto an elevator at Intel, where she was meeting a friend for lunch, and walk out of that elevator with an appointment to meet a vice president in his office after lunch. Here's a script for your own elevator speech: "Hello, Big Boss. My name is Joy Choi. I was referred to you by the Major University Career Services Center. I'm interested in learning more about your field. I wonder if you would have a moment to share with me any advice, ideas, leads, or referrals?"

The elevator speech, or the thirty-second introduction, can also be delivered via email:

I am a college student majoring in psychology. I am interested in sports administration. I am on several campus committees devoted to promoting and producing sporting events, both intercollegiate and intramural. My ultimate goal would be to land in sports marketing and sponsorship sales, but I am also interested in other areas. I got your name from the alumni office, and I wonder if you would have a moment to speak with me about the sports business.

State (a) who you are, (b) why you're calling, and (c) what you want. Be straightforward, be direct, and remember to push hard for referrals. Broken down, here is the skeleton of a typical script for a thirty-second introduction:

Hello, _____. My name is _____. I was referred to you by _____. I'm interested in learning more about _____. I wonder if you would have a moment to share with me any advice, ideas, leads, or referrals.

Construct your own thirty-second introduction right now. Remember to convey who you are, why you are calling, and what you want.

Gatekeepers and Voice Mail

Once you start calling executives, you are going to run into two potential obstacles: gatekeepers and voice mail.

An executive's most important resource is time. As an entry-level job seeker, you represent a very low priority for any organization, including the one that eventually hires you! Gatekeepers are the receptionists, secretaries, and executive assistants who stand between you and your decision maker. They want to protect her time, and you want to reach your intended party. *You do not have the same goals.* However, if you antagonize the gatekeeper, your chances with her employer will be nil.

So how do you get past a gatekeeper? The best way is to make a connection or cite a referral. Going to the same church or synagogue as Mr. Big is going to get you past most screeners. Being a student at Mr. Big's beloved alma mater is another excellent connection. Even if you have no stature yourself, being referred to Mr. Big by someone who does have stature will usually do the trick.

Getting Past the Gatekeepers

1. Cite a referral: "Dr. Johnson from MIT suggested I give her a call." Of course, this has to be true.

2. Email a note informing your targeted decision maker that you will be calling. Then you can tell the gatekeeper, "Yes, she's expecting my call." The best line for the letter is: "I will call you on Tuesday at 10:30 A.M.

You can count on me to be prompt. I look forward to our conversation." It doesn't matter whether or not you say what the call is about.

3. Call once a day until one of you dies.

4. Call at 7:45 A.M., 10:05 A.M., 12:20 P.M., 2:05 P.M., 5:25 P.M.—that is, whenever you think the gatekeeper is off duty.

5. Level with the gatekeeper: "You know, Bill, I've been trying to reach your boss for seventeen weeks now, and he just won't call me back. What should I do?" And don't forget gratitude: "Gosh, I really appreciate how helpful you've been." A little thoughtfulness can go a long way.

Don't play games with gatekeepers. Be honest about who you are and why you're calling. They're professionals. They'll eat you for breakfast if you lie or misrepresent yourself in any way.

Simple persistence is required to reach people with whom you do not share a high percentage of DNA. You need to be ready to try several times to reach someone by phone. The rules of business protocol are very different from the rules of social protocol. In a social setting, if you call someone three times and they don't return the calls, you're supposed to take the hint. But business is different. You are perfectly within the bounds of propriety to call someone once a day until he asks you to stop.

If you are friendly and courteous, and you call once a day, what does an employer learn about you? Three things: You are persistent. You are friendly. You are courteous. These are not bad images to leave with a potential employer who has never met you.

If you are being screened by a particular gatekeeper, try to call when she is on break. The meaner the gatekeeper, the more likely she takes her break precisely on time. So call at 10:05 A.M., and she's not going to be guarding that gate. Or call during lunch, or before 8 A.M., or after 5 P.M. Whoever relieves her probably doesn't enjoy being a gatekeeper at all. It's not his bag. And you may get through.

Another vexing problem for business callers is voice mail. Never leave more than one voice mail message per day, and don't ask for a call back unless you have a strong connection. They won't call you back anyway, but they'll feel guilty about it. Here's a sample script: "Hello. This is Donald Asher. I'm sorry to have missed you. My number is (415) 543–7130, but there's no need to ring me back. I'll try to reach you again tomorrow morning."

If you are dealing with a fully automated system, where you don't have to interact with a single human being, you can just hit redial until your intended contact happens to be at her desk. As long as you don't leave more than one message a day, this is fine.

Building Confidence for Calling Strangers

Although it's never easy to call a stranger, it is a standard business skill. Working adults know how to call strangers, and how to ask for and obtain information from them. You need to learn how to do this to be effective on the job, regardless of what that job is.

You can substitute emailing for almost any use of the phone, but if you're not getting the information you need, you'll have to pick up that cell phone and start punching numbers.

To build confidence for calling, start with your roommate or a friend or your mom and have them pretend to be a secretary. Have them ask you, "What is this call regarding?" And have them say, "She's not available right now; would you like her voice mail?"

Once you're more comfortable, start by contacting someone at a company you consider a long shot, where you don't care if you make a mistake. If they hang up on you, you can say, "So what? I didn't want to work there anyway."

Once you get the hang of it, continue with the companies or organizations where you hope to get some good ideas or useful referrals, or where you'd ideally want to work.

It is a bad idea to start with your first choices, either for networking purposes or for interviewing. You want to practice on some second-string targets first.

And the next time a telemarketer calls you, say this: "Hey, I'm practicing making networking calls for my job search. If I agree to listen to your pitch, will you listen to my elevator speech first and let me know what you think of it?" If they say yes, try out your pitch on them. If they say no, hang up on them. They have way more than ninety-nine more people to call.

Anticipating Objections

Once you reach your designated decision maker, if you have any connection whatsoever with her, make it clear that you are not necessarily applying for a position. You want advice, ideas, leads, and referrals. If some of her referrals are to people at her company, great, but that's certainly not your only goal.

Alternately, you can just bluntly ask the question from a few pages back: "I'm interested in working for your firm as a _____. Who would I talk to about that?" Or, "I'm interested in working for your organization as a _____.

I was told you were the person I needed to contact. What do I need to do to get an appointment with you to explore this further in person?"

Decision makers are going to have one or more of the following objections to helping you:

- We're not hiring.

- I'm too busy.

- Just send me your resume.

- I'm not the person you should be talking to.

Do not be overly concerned about any of these objections. They *are* hiring. They probably *do* have a moment to talk if you are friendly and courteous. They don't really want you to send them a resume anyway, so you may as well do your best to stay on the phone while you've got them. And they *are* the right person for you to be talking to. However, you should anticipate these objections and be ready to respond to them.

It's a good idea to have a little fun with this. Practice responding to the prompts you know you're going to hear:

- What's this call regarding?

- She's in a meeting. Do you want her voice mail?

- She's out of town. What can I do for you?

- We're not hiring.

- I'm too busy. Just go to our career website.

- Why don't you send me a resume?

- I'm not the person you should be speaking with.

Overcoming the Objections

OBJECTION: We're not hiring.
ANSWERS:

- That's okay. I'm not applying for a job. I am interested in your advice.

- That's okay. I'm not in any hurry. I just wanted you to know what I have to offer in case something opens up later.

- That's okay. I just wanted to know if you would take a look at my resume and give me any advice, ideas, leads, or referrals that come to mind.

- That's okay. Perhaps you can think of someone else who might be interested right now in what I have to offer. Your referral would be appreciated by both of us.

OBJECTION: I'm too busy.
ANSWERS:

- This'll only take a moment.

- Yeah, I heard you guys are pretty successful right now. (Then STOP, no matter how long the silence.)

- I'd be happy to meet you early, late, during lunch, even after work. What's best for you?

- What's a better time for me to reach you?

OBJECTION: Send me your resume.
ANSWERS:

- Well, let me tell you what's on it. I'm the one who . . . (then go into your elevator speech).

- What's your email? I'll send it to you while we're chatting.

- I'll bring it to the meeting. What's a good time for you?

OBJECTION: I'm not the person you should be talking to.
ANSWERS:

- But I'm not applying for a job. I got your name from _____.
  She said you were quite knowledgeable about this field. I just want to know if you would have a moment to share with me any advice, ideas, leads, or referrals.

- Actually, I'm going to be applying through your official channels as well, but I wondered if you could give me a little inside information.

- Who should I be talking to? I appreciate the referral.

What Is "Too Aggressive"?

Over many years of working with candidates, I have only run across two who actually were too aggressive. One was an ex-cop, who went to the homes of CEOs in the middle of the night. He'd throw his resume into the backyard with a note scribbled on it: "This is the one I was telling you about." He did get a job this way, but he could have gotten arrested instead. Besides, it's way too creepy for me.

The other case was a misguided recent college graduate, who went to one of my lectures but didn't keep very accurate notes. I found out about her misdeeds while working in my office one day. The phone rang, and I picked it up.

"Are you Don Asher?" the voice on the other end of the line asked, somewhat tentatively.

"Yes, this is Don Asher," I replied.

"And you're the guy who does career development seminars all around the country?" At this, I puffed up, imagining that I was about to get a speaking contract, imagining that she had heard wonderful things about my workshops and lectures.

"Yes, I'm the guy," I said proudly.

"Did you actually tell a college student to call us one hundred times?" The voice was no longer tentative. It sounded downright annoyed.

"Well, I might have," I answered.

"In the same day?" The voice was truly exasperated now.

Apparently, this young job seeker had sat down with a cup of coffee and just hit redial. She kept getting the same gatekeeper and asking for the same executive over and over and over again, until finally the executive took the call and yelled into the phone, "Who told you to do this? Who told you to harass us like this?" The young lady immediately replied, "Don Asher."

So the executive tracked me down to complain.

Just for the record, you may call a company one hundred times over one hundred days, but not in the same day! For most contacts, once a day ought to do it.

These two job seekers were annoyingly aggressive. But what about the hundreds of thousands of other job seekers I've worked with over the years? Well, they were not too aggressive. Out of any 1,000 job seekers, 999 are not aggressive enough, and one is like Goldilocks—just aggressive enough; she does it just right.

Don't worry about being too aggressive, as long as you'll take no for an answer. Worry about not being aggressive enough. Here's a clue: if an employer says to you, "If you call here one more time, we're calling the police," let that be a sign to leave that company alone and go on to the other ninety-nine you have on your active list.

Again: Worry about not being aggressive enough. That's by far the more common error.

I'm not asking you to make house calls, but I am asking you to try at least several times to make contact with anyone who could be a major factor in your success. Get outside your comfort zone, take some risks, and realize the huge gains you can make by properly launching your career out of college. You owe it to yourself, to your personal investment in your education, and to your parents' investment in your education, to succeed at this critical juncture.

Taking No for an Answer

The approach I'm advocating here is designed to elicit a clear response from the employer, and if that response is no, move on! If an employer says, "Hey, we're just not hiring people like you at this time, and I can't help you," that's the good news. You can forget about this employer and go on to another. Contact them again in a couple of weeks, perhaps, but you can certainly stop calling them now.

Don't forget to treat alumni contacts with special care. If an alumna or alumnus doesn't call you back after three to five attempts, it's probably best to pursue another contact.

What If You're Shy?

If you are shy, contacting strangers or asking for favors from people you know only tangentially can be a challenge. One solution is to use email instead of the telephone. That way you can take your time and craft confident-sounding text messages that might be very hard for you to say out loud. So if you are shy, let email be your friend.

Shy people also need to work extra hard to get introductions from family members and close friends. Having a personal introduction is often all it takes to make a shy person much more comfortable with the job search process.

If you're unwilling or unable to call people and unwilling or unable to work your extended network, plan on making twice or three times the number of applications as someone who is able to use these usually more fruitful channels. However, you should not count on getting a job by way of Internet career sites or by posting resumes on resume banks. Being shy does not make these channels magically more viable!

Extraordinary Lengths

If there is an employer that you very much want to join, you might consider making greater and more creative efforts to get their attention. It is not wrong to go to extraordinary lengths if you believe there is an extraordinary rationale for you to be hired by that employer.

CASE STUDY Greg H.

Greg H. wanted to work for a discount broker but was having trouble getting noticed. Throughout his senior year he posted a new resume and cover letter every two weeks on the company's website, but all he got in return were pro forma replies. He couldn't find any alumni who worked at the firm, and he had no friends or family who could help him. He managed to call the person who normally recruited college students, but when he told her he was an English major, she said she didn't have time to talk to him. So he put on his best suit and went to the company's headquarters at 6 A.M. one day. He stood at the front entrance and handed out resumes to anyone who looked like an executive. On top of his resume was a letter, which started like this: "In my pocket is a cell phone. I'm waiting for your call to invite me into the building to discuss my future with your firm. I have always admired your company, and I'd like to tell you why. Just call me at 415–555–4289, and I'll be right up." No one called the first day, so he went back the next morning, same time, same routine. That morning his cell phone rang, and Greg was invited in. He was hired three years ago, and he's on the fast track, having already been promoted twice.

CASE STUDY Patty C.

Patty C. wanted to work for the clothier Levi Strauss & Co., but couldn't get an appointment with anyone at the company. So she wrote a letter explaining that when she'd gotten her very first paycheck, the first thing she bought was a pair of Levis. She sat on the washing machine all that Saturday, washing them over and over to get that just-right, washed-out look. "I love your product," she wrote, and "I think it makes sense to work for a company that makes a product I love." She got an interview. No job offer came out of it, but she was happy to have had the chance to try to sell herself to her favorite company.

CASE STUDY Paul R.

Paul R. wanted to work for a special effects studio that was famously reclusive. "They don't publish their address or phone number, and there's no sign on their building," said Paul. "I couldn't find a personal introduction, but I was able to learn the name of the director of human resources. So I made up a shipping label: A Special Gift from Paul R_____ Creative Services. Then I made a plaster cast of my actual foot, and put a tag on the big toe with my resume printed on it. My cover letter said, 'My mother bet me I couldn't get my foot in the door. Well, if you're reading this, I've already won that bet. Now I'm betting you'll give me a chance to tell you what I can do. I'm looking for just ten minutes of your time. If I can't capture your interest quickly, then I don't belong at your company.'" Paul got his interview.

Fourteen years ago, a publisher I had targeted as my first choice ignored several query letters from me. So I took my two-page book proposal and rolled it up into a scroll, tied it in the middle with a silver ribbon, and dropped it into a shipping tube. It rattled mysteriously if it was picked up or moved. Then I covered the mailing tube with stickers that screamed URGENT in big orange letters. I shipped the package by same-day delivery from a nearby city. I still had to phone five or six days in a row before the publisher finally took my call and invited me in for a meeting. This is the tenth book I've published with Ten Speed Press, and it just proves that making an extra, creative effort to get the attention of busy and successful people is sometimes a great benefit for both parties.

Here's an example of refusing to take no for an answer:[1]

Dear Mr. Steel:

Thank you for your kind letter of April 17. After careful consideration, I regret to inform you that I am unable to accept your refusal to offer me employment with your firm.

This year I have been particularly fortunate in receiving an unusually large number of rejection letters. With such a varied and promising field of candidates, it is impossible for me to accept all refusals.

Despite your outstanding qualifications and previous experience in rejecting applicants, I find that your rejection does not meet with my needs at this time. Therefore, I will initiate employment with your firm immediately following graduation. I look forward to seeing you then.

Best of luck in rejecting future candidates.

Sincerely,

Anthony T. Tyger

15

Troubleshooting Your Job Search

Managing a job search is easy. You start by selecting a target, in other words, a fairly specific idea of the job you want. Then you develop iterations of the target, that is, you identify organizations that could employ you doing that job. Once you have lists of possible employers, you approach each one along multiple fronts, trying their employment websites, writing to known executives, networking with friends of friends who might have an "in" at the organization, and generally trying to get your proposal for a job considered by actual humans. You can approach an employer from many different angles simultaneously. Once you get their attention, if they don't tell you to get lost, then you will be considered for either (a) an opening or (b) a position where there is no opening yet. In either case, you will no longer be seeking general information about the company; you will be presenting your skill set relative to a job that needs to be done. There may be many interviews or just a few, but there will likely be long, frustrating down times between interviews, when you think you've been forgotten. It is your job during these doldrums to make your future employer think about you, remember you, and consider you for employment even when they are distracted by other duties and possibly other candidates. Then, you help them make a decision, you get them to give you an offer, and finally you negotiate the terms.

That's all there is to it.

Seven Stages of a Job Search:

1. Identify job targets (industry, function, title).

2. Identify raw leads (companies, people, ideas).

3. Identify names of specific employees.

4. Turn a name into an appointment.

5. Sell yourself in the interview.

6. Stay alive through the selection process.

7. Close the deal.

You can troubleshoot your job search by asking yourself where the problem lies. If you're running around looking for openings, then you don't have a job target, and you have to start at the beginning, **Stage 1**, before you can use hidden job market techniques. (By now, I hope you see clearly why you should initiate contact with employers before knowing if they have openings.) Without a job target, you cannot run a proper job search. You might get a job, but it will most likely be an accident.

If you can't find enough companies to apply to, you need to concentrate on **Stage 2**. You need to learn how to research companies and build lead lists. Visit your career center for a lesson in basic business research; Google the industries and types of companies you're interested in; look at www.zapdata.com for ideas, or www.hoovers. com, www.wetfeet.com, and www.vault.com. If you can identify one organization that is interesting to you, you can learn to identify dozens of others just like it. Remember, it takes one hundred to run a job search. Fewer than that and you have a hobby, or something to distract you from your studies, but not a job search. We'll cover this in depth in a few pages.

If you've got a list of companies but don't have contact names, then you need to get on the Web and work your network to resolve deficiencies in **Stage 3**. Google each organization on your list, get as deep as you can into the organization's many web pages, and play the networking game relentlessly: "Who do you know at NASA? Who do you know at the Jet Propulsion Laboratory in Pasadena? Okay, who do you know who lives, or used to live, in Houston or near Cape Canaveral in Florida? Alright, who do you know who now, or in the past, went to school or taught at the rocket research center in Huntsville, Alabama?" You'll get names.

If you're submitting tons of applications but getting no interviews, you've simply got to solve the conundrum of **Stage 4**. If you're sending material to specific people and getting no interviews, then you may be failing to call or email to follow up, or you may be following up three times when seven or eight is what is required. The main difference between successful salespeople and unsuccessful salespeople is that successful ones fail more often. You may simply need to be more persistent and more consistent in following up on your applications. Alternately, your resume may be unimpressive and need some sprucing up.

If you're getting interviews but blowing them, you need more prep for **Stage 5**. You may need to go to the career center and get some interview coaching and practice, or you may need to read a few of the many excellent books that concentrate on interviewing skills. Or you may simply need to keep going to interviews. If you do enough of them, you'll improve automatically!

If you're getting interviews but no callbacks, you need to become more proficient with the unique challenges of **Stage 6**. A great deal of time may pass between an initial interview and a hiring decision. It takes a special kind of patience to stay alive through the repeated delays and frustrating false starts of the placement process. They don't intend to be cruel; it's just that most firms have many priorities, and sometimes hiring simply isn't at the top. **You need to occupy your future employer's mental space** every week to ten days. I recommend rotating media: send an email one week, send a postcard or letter the following week, leave a voice mail message the third week, then start all over again. Change your resume and send in the updated version. Send in your references. Send in a copy of a news article pertaining to their organization or market. Send in a cartoon—funny but tasteful—that might amuse the recruiter, with a note: "Thought you might enjoy this moment of levity while you're making your recruiting decisions." Send a continuing interest letter: "It's been some time since we spoke, but I want to restate that I am very interested in working with your organization and hope to hear positive news from you soon. In case you've misplaced my resume, I've enclosed another."

The sad fact is that most candidates self-select out of the process before the employer dings them! They quit applying for the job before the employer decides not to hire them. Staying alive is critical to getting job offers! And don't be afraid of seemingly stronger candidates!

If you're staying alive and doing everything else right but just not getting offers, if you're always a bridesmaid but never a bride, you need to learn how to close the deal in **Stage 7**. You need to learn how the employer plans to make the decision, how many interviews she expects to conduct, and so forth., so that you can fall into sync with her practices. When it's time to close the deal, say things like this: "Caitlin, you know quite a bit about me now. Is there any reason I wouldn't fit in at _____?" Or "You know, Caitlin, I've learned enough about _____ to know that it's a place I'd very much like to work. I'm ready to make a decision. How about you? What do we need to do to move this discussion to the decision stage, from your point of view?"

Don't worry if an employer tells you that you're a borderline candidate. As long as you're still a candidate at all, you've got a chance at winning an offer. Suppose a recruiter tells you, "You know, Chrys, you're a solid candidate but not a great candidate. In fact, you're our seventh choice at this time." Don't worry, because here's what happens to the other seven:

First Choice: The first-choice candidate is going to get multiple offers. She's nearly perfect, and that's why she's everybody's first-choice candidate. She's statistically unlikely to take this job.

Second Choice: The second-choice candidate fails a second- or third-round interview. He's the type of overprepared flash-in-the-pan who looks great at first but is bound to spill something on the boss's suit or give a dumb interview answer once he gets beyond his prepared answers.

Third Choice: The third-choice candidate's spouse won't relocate. He said he'd go to North Dakota or Los Angeles or whatever, but when it came down to decision time, he chickened out and put the kibosh on the offer.

Fourth Choice: The national average for lying on resumes is 25 percent. Which means that out of any four candidates, one of them is dumb enough to lie on her resume, which means you don't have to worry about the fourth-choice candidate. She's out.

Fifth Choice: It takes a lot of time to get to the offer stage with four candidates, so while the company has been wooing them, the fifth-choice candidate has accepted another offer. He's out.

Sixth Choice: The sixth-choice candidate unwisely smoked some marijuana at a graduation party and failed the drug test. A drug test is a common rite of passage, and an intelligent student will not forgo good long-term employment over a momentary indiscretion. So she's out.

Seventh Choice: That's you, and you get the job offer.

It is important to stay alive, to stay in there trying for the job over an extended period of time. So occupy mental space in the recruiter's mind, and keep trying until they tell you there's no there there.

If a recruiter dings you, be gracious. If you like the company, tell them so and invite them to consider you for anything else that might come up in the future. And hustle them for leads and referrals. An employer who *almost* hires you will feel guilty, and that guilt can be transformed into leads at other companies or other branches and locations within the recruiter's own company. It never hurts to ask!

Traction

How do you know if your job search is going well? This is harder than you might think. You may assume that if you're busy with your job search, it's going well. But that may not be true at all. You can take all your old friends out to lunch forever and never find work. And it's well established that four monkeys in a room are never going to get a job—or write any novels. So being busy doesn't mean much in itself.

Your job search is going well if you're getting traction. If you apply to ten new organizations a week, you're headed in the right direction. If you get four interviews a month for a real job, then you're getting traction. If you get second interviews at least half the time, you're doing it right.

JOB SEARCH TRACTION

- Contacting ten *new* organizations a week, at least
- Obtaining four interviews a month for a real job, at least
- Converting half of those into follow-up interviews, at least

Quantify your search activities every week. How many *new* organizations do you contact per week? Is it always more than ten? How many informational or networking interviews do you set up per week? They don't count toward your minimum ten new organizations to contact per week, but it is important to track them as well. How many first-time interviews for *real, actual jobs* do you get per week? Is it one or more? How many follow-up interviews do you get? How many active leads do you have at any given time? Is it one hundred, or even close?

If you're not hitting these explicitly quantified goals, you have to adjust your search practices.

The Four Dynamic Tensions

If you aren't getting traction, you may need to troubleshoot your target or your effort. This is another diagnostic tool to use in assessing problems with your job search:

- Job
- Salary
- Geography
- Effort

These four priorities will compete for your consideration. If you prioritize one over the rest, you'll have to be more flexible about the others. If you're going after a very specific **type of job**, for example, you'll probably have to be more flexible about the pay, the location, and the amount of effort you're willing to expend on your job search.

If you have to have a certain **salary**, you're going to have to consider being flexible about what kind of work you do, where you do it, and how much effort you will expend on your job search.

If you must stay in a particular **location**, then you are perhaps in the most trouble of all. You will have to be prepared to be very flexible about what kind of job you do, and you may find that it takes considerable effort and time to land a career-track position.

By the way, limiting yourself geographically is unwise. Statistically, you are going to be at your first location less than four years, so why put a geographical restriction on your career before it's even started? Two-earner couples might face geographical constraints, perhaps, but a single person should not put such a constraint on himself. Be adventurous!

Finally, the less you are willing to compromise on the first three issues—job, salary, and geography—the more you're going to have to compromise on **effort**. You need to be willing to search long and hard to find the opportunity you want, if you are uncompromising on the first three.

If you are an enrolled college student, you may think that you don't have enough time to run a proper job search during the academic year, but in fact you do. It is better to look slowly and consistently over a long period of time than to search frantically as you watch your student loans come due. There are 168 hours in a week, and you can surely allocate six of them to looking for work, all year long.

Here's an interesting statistic: Unemployed people who claim to be looking for work "full-time" actually only put about six hours a week into job search activities.[2] Surely you can do better than that, even while studying and running an active social life.

So you *do* have time to look for work.

The Main Source of Failure

For most job seekers, the problem with their job search is overwhelmingly one thing: a failure to get enough interviews. If you get enough interviews, you can do everything else wrong.

Let us imagine the worst job seeker in the world. I can just see this guy: He's late for his appointment with you. He has a sullen demeanor and slumped posture. He won't look you in the eye. His clothes are wrinkled. He's unshaven. He has greasy, slicked back hair. He has an infected piercing and a couple of homemade tattoos. You suddenly notice he's wearing a plastic wristband (like the ones hospitals use); you steal a glance at it and are startled to read "County Jail." Getting close enough to read the wristband caused your nostrils to be assaulted by another problem: personal hygiene seems to be an issue here.

Can this guy get a job? You'd better believe it. If he can get enough interviews, sooner or later someone is going to think, "This guy reminds me of my brother. I'd better save him from himself." Or an employer who has done time himself will say to the candidate, "I made a few mistakes myself when I was younger. I'm going to give you a chance. I won't give you a second chance, but I'll give you one chance." So Mr. Greasy Hair gets a job.

What about you, Mr. or Ms. Privileged College Youth? Can you get enough interviews to get a job faster than Mr. Greasy Hair? Only if you try.

I once watched a man who didn't speak a word of English get a job in less than an hour. I know he didn't speak English because he went into every shop and restaurant in a busy commercial district, walked up to the counter, stuck out his hand, and said, "Excuse me, Mister. Do you have a job?"

Since he said the exact same thing to women, I surmised that he had memorized the words phonetically, without knowing what they meant.

I was so fascinated by this job search demonstration that I followed the guy at a discreet distance. He was walking down Polk Street in San Francisco at two o'clock in the afternoon, pursuing the American dream. It took him exactly six blocks to land a job, even though he didn't speak a word of English. He got a job as a dishwasher, and he started work immediately.

Get enough interviews and you can do everything else wrong. Face time leads to employment. Get out there and get face time. You don't need a perfect resume or a new suit or a new car or better connections. You need to stick out your hand and say, "Excuse me, Mister. Do you have a job?"

More Job Sources

Networking and research are the two best sources of job leads, but there are others. A properly planned job search will involve leads from several sources. The best sources are:

- Networking
- Research

Additional good sources are:

- On-campus recruiting
- Career fairs for undergraduates
- Temporary placement agencies

Possibly useful sources are:

- Career fairs not focused on undergraduates
- Internet-based career sites
- Company employment sites
- Newspapers
- Permanent placement agencies
- Headhunters (executive search consultants)

On-Campus Recruiting

On-campus recruiting has long been the purview of engineering and business majors seeking Fortune 500 employment, but all types of students should participate. No matter what your major or your career goal, on-campus recruiting can benefit you: You can practice interviewing, you can gain knowledge of certain industries, and you can actually get a job.

Although it is true that on-campus recruiting is often designed around the needs of major corporations, many different types of companies recruit on a typical college campus. And even Fortune 500 recruiters need English and zoology majors for some positions.

You probably have to register to participate in on-campus recruiting, so see your career center as soon as you can. You'll need a good resume and a good interview suit, at least. And there are a few critical rules to abide by. For example, never miss appointments. If you miss an appointment with a recruiter, you may be banned from the career center for the rest of your natural life. If you accept a job offer from one employer, you must never, ever renege on that offer, no matter what juicy opportunity crops up for you later.

College relations manager is the correct title for a corporate recruiter. They usually operate in certain regions, so if there is an employer that you are interested in, call or email their corporate human resources department and ask for the name and email address of the college relations manager for your area of the country. She may specialize in certain functional areas (such as engineering) or in certain types of students (M.B.A.'s, for example), but she can explain how her company hires people like you.

College relations managers get tons of email from students. As long as you are friendly and courteous in your message, do not hesitate to email them several times with the same query if at first they don't respond.

Recruiters who interview students at a career center always work from lists. They may meet ten or fifteen students in a single day. A "closed list" is a list of students selected by the recruiter in advance. An "open list" is one that students can sign up on if they are interested in a particular employer. A "restricted list" is limited to certain majors, or to U.S. citizens, or to students with a certain GPA, and so on. Some recruiters will work from a closed list for part of the day, then take a few students from an open list for the rest of the day. Asking a recruiter if you can show up and just hang around in case there is a no-show is not always viewed favorably. Besides, there aren't many no-shows because the penalty is so high.

Some campuses use a bidding system: you have so many points to use throughout the semester with which to bid for interview slots. Someone willing to spend more points than you are can bump you out of your interview slot. So be savvy and learn when the new schedules are posted, usually online, and arrange to sign up before everyone else.

College relations managers tend to return to campuses where they have a high likelihood of finding the students they want to hire, and to avoid campuses where they have not found appropriate candidates in the past. If you are interested in corporate employment but your campus specializes in producing poets or ministers, you may need to meet with a college relations manager on another campus. This is tricky, as you need approval from the recruiter and from the hosting career center. Some students have had success by showing up at the end of the day and offering to help the recruiter carry her materials back to her car. Recruiters often have multiple briefcases, laptops, projectors, and boxes of brochures, so this is a useful service to them.

Getting interview practice is one benefit of participating in the on-campus interview cycle, but *you should never take an interview slot with a company unless you'd actually consider working there.* If you do, you're stealing that slot from another student who might have truly wanted the job! And you're wasting the recruiter's time. If you just want interview practice, sign up for mock interviews. That's what they're for.

College relations managers do often give honest feedback to candidates, which in the career marketplace is actually quite rare and valuable. If your manner of dress or your interview answers are too revealing, they'll usually let you know.

College relations managers are often extroverted people, and even if there is no slot for you at their company, they may be willing to give you career advice about other companies or other industries that would be a match.

By participating in the on-campus cycle, you'll be forced to get your resume and your credentials in order early in the year, facilitating your own self-directed career search activities as well.

You'll have to get along with the career center staff, which can have hidden benefits all year long. Walking into the center in June, saying, "Oops, I graduated without doing anything about that whole job thingy," is not impressive to the career center staff. If you want their help, see them early and often.

The benefits to participating in this cycle are too strong to ignore, and the only challenges will be getting used to dressing professionally and showing up on time for meetings.

Hiring Cycles

In the open job market, a position can be filled anytime the recruiter settles on the right candidate. The open job market runs 365 days a year, and selected candidates are usually expected to begin within a short time of accepting an offer. When you compete on the open market, you are usually competing against people with experience. You can definitely run an open-job-market search while still a student, and the best time to do so is the two or three months before you graduate or need that summer job.

When you're looking for formalized internships and jobs with firms that hire lots of college grads, you are in a different market. Your competition will be other students or grads, which is a good thing. But the most important thing about this market is that it has seasons. If you apply outside of a company's normal hiring season, even if you are perfect, the company is not going to hire you.

So when you contact college relations managers and other recruiting personnel, be sure to ask when and how they select interns or new hires. They'll tell you the rules, and you would be wise to follow them. For example, they often do not accept applications prior to a certain date or after another date. Applying early or late is often useless for clearly defined hiring cycles.

Career Fairs

An on-campus career fair is a great place to learn about many companies quickly, and each company represented will be seeking students from your school. Do not be intimidated by signs you will see in the booths. Recruiters always put up signs for the most difficult or obscure recruiting assignments they have, so when you see a sign begging for paleoichthyologists or nuclear engineering majors to step to the front of the line, don't worry. They need other types of students as well.

If you decide to attend a career fair, be smart: Dress for an interview, even if you think it makes you look dorky for your classes. Carry plenty of resumes with you. Travel light; ditch the backpack, and carry a clean pad of paper in its own case. Don't pick up so many employer freebies that you look like you've gone shopping at the mall. And make yourself some business cards like the one that follows.

Ruby Jewel

B.A. Candidate, French Language and Literature, Minor in Marketing, University of Wisconsin, Madison

Areas of Knowledge

- Fluent in French (read, write, translate)
- International Business
- Intercultural Marketing
- Demographics and Psychographics

39 Elm Street, West Layfayette, IN 47907

rubyjewell@aol.com (765) 494–1234

Work the fair systematically. Quickly survey the entire room; note the companies most likely to hire you and at which you would most like to work. Put your energy into these companies. When you talk to the recruiters, be ready to state clearly what your skills and strengths are and what kind of job you want. If they ask you what kind of job you are seeking, do *not* say, "I dunno. Anything."

At the same time, you need to be flexible. Listen to the recruiter's ideas about where you might fit into the firm. Be ready to consider opportunities you hadn't even thought about.

Most important of all, get a card from each recruiter. Follow up with each and every one who seemed at all interested in you by sending an email with an attached resume. Recruiters meet with dozens of students at events like this, and it's helpful to remind them of the main points of their conversation with you. Here is a sample email you might send with your resume:

"It was great to meet you at the career fair today and to learn more about your company. You were very encouraging and said there might be opportunities for someone like me in your human resources department. I would be very interested in exploring this further. You kindly offered to check who is handling recruiting for that department and get back to me. I'm very much looking forward to hearing from you soon about that. Meanwhile, I have attached an e-version of my resume to remind you of my background. You can respond by email or call me on my cell phone at 310–555–3892. Thank you so much for your help!"

Be enthusiastic! Be positive about your abilities! Act like you want a job! And as long as you are friendly and courteous, it is okay to query a recruiter several times if at first they don't respond. Smart students will linger until the end of the day and help recruiters box up their brochures and walk them back to their cars. The last conversation of the day is usually the one that stays in the recruiter's mind.

Career fairs that are not restricted to students are a bit different. You work the room in the same way, but you may find recruiters are less interested in discussing entry-level jobs. Follow through anyway; try to find out how they do hire people like you, and your time will be well spent, even if you're not a paleoichthyologist or a nuclear engineer.

Temporary Placement Agencies

When you know what kind of career you would like to launch, you now know to build lists of appropriate targets and attack them by networking for personal introductions and by applying directly with enthusiasm and persistence. If you know what you want, you probably have little need for a placement agency of any kind.

Placement agencies are notorious for taking square pegs and pounding them into round holes. If you are pliable and presentable, a placement agency may send you out on dead-end assignments, where you sort junk mail by zip code or work the complaint window at the city towing company. Yikes!

However, if you simply don't know enough about the business world to imagine where you might fit into it, you may benefit from temporary assignments that give you needed experience and exposure while you earn a few dollars as well.

Temporary agencies are subject to local economic conditions, so if the local economy is depressed, they'll have far more candidates than assignments. However, if the economy is moderate to good, they'll be happy to talk to you even if you have little or no prior experience.

Two-thirds of all newly created jobs are contingent on the day they are created, meaning part-time, temporary, or contract assignment. No student can afford to overlook part-time and temporary assignments, whether they are offered through an agency or come directly from an employer.

Finally, any office experience you can get, from any source, will build your clerical skills, which are the basic currency of business. If you have them, you're employable; if you don't, you may find it tougher.

Internet Career Sites

Internet-based career sites do have tons of jobs, but they have even more candidates. There are several types of Internet-based career sites, and they work differently. Resume banks, company career sites, online job clubs, online compilations of help-wanted advertisements, and special interest career sites with everything from career bookstores to real-time career advice are just some of the ways the Internet supports the job market.

The mega-resume banks collect millions of resumes and sell employers access to them. If you are going to post your resume on such sites, you need to protect yourself by using a post office or campus box address, a cell phone number instead of a land line, and perhaps even a pseudonym.

In order to generate hits from resume banks, you have to have unique or at least unusual skills, and it is especially useful to have unique combinations of rare skills. So if you speak Farsi and you know how to do data mining, you might get a hit. But if you just speak Farsi or you only know how to do data mining, so do millions of other people, including hundreds or thousands of them on the same resume bank.

Take a good look at your skills. Are they unusual enough to win you hits in competition with massive numbers of other candidates? If not, don't put too much energy into this direction. Online job clubs, and career sites dedicated to a narrow field, such as www.sciencejobs.com, can be useful.

Company Career Sites

Company career sites usually have three aspects: a public relations component to promote the company as a good corporate citizen and a positive contributor to society, a resume capture system that takes resumes twenty-four hours a day, whether there's any potential for a job match or not, and a posted openings section that advertises those positions the company is right now trying to fill.

The stunning truth is that these components are all virtually useless to a young job seeker. You will be told many, many times during a job search, "Just go to our website and fill out an application." There is nothing wrong with doing so, but it has a low success rate, especially for inexperienced young people. Many open jobs that the company has no trouble finding candidates for will not be listed. Being dumped into the resume database will only result in a hit if you have unusual combinations of skills (as mentioned above).

And of course no company is going to put negative information about itself on its own website! However, before you go to any interviews or networking meetings, you do need to familiarize yourself with a company's web presence.

Newspapers

Most students consider newspapers to be low-tech or old-tech—so last century. Newspapers suffer from many of the same problems as Internet job sites: advertised positions draw dozens if not hundreds of applicants, about half of jobs are never advertised anyway, and some unscrupulous scammers use newspapers to troll for victims.

The right way to use the newspaper in a job search is to read the articles for information about organizations that might want to hire you. The *news* in a *news*paper is the part that should interest you. If you read about an arts organization doing interesting things, and you are seeking a position like that, then you can:

- Add the organization to your lead list.

- Look up information about it on the Internet, including both its own web presence and whatever you can find by running a general search on its name.

- Ask everyone you know if they know anyone who works at or is otherwise involved in the organization.

- Apply for any appropriate jobs you find on the company's website.

- Call the organization and ask who hires interns or new grads.

- Write a letter or email message to anyone listed in the article, asking them the same question. (Do not be afraid to write to top officers!)

- Go to the organization, walk into the human resources department, and ask to speak to someone about career opportunities.

- Stand at of the organization's location and hand out resumes to people entering the building.

- All of the above.

In other words, discovering an interesting organization in the newspaper should initiate a sophisticated, multifaceted, job search response, not just a resume and cover letter sent in response to an advertisement.

When you look at them in this way, newspapers can be great idea generators for a job search. The help-wanted ads are often the least useful part of the paper for job seekers. It's the rest of the paper that's valuable.

If you do look at the help-wanted ads, caveat emptor: many of the "jobs" in this section are really thinly disguised multilevel marketing opportunities. If someone invites you to buy hundreds of dollars of their products to sell to your friends and family, or offers you the exciting opportunity of paying for your own training, maybe you should keep looking for a more appropriate, career-launching job.

Some companies do use the newspaper to look for entry-level candidates, so it's not impossible to get a job this way. It's just unlikely.

Turning One Lead into Many

One of the seductive features of job postings is the idea that there is a job "behind" the announcement. There may be a job behind the announcement, but dozens if not hundreds of other candidates are trying to get that same job.

If you see a job posting, you should view it as a research opportunity. If a job you see listed is attractive, you should conclude that if one company hires someone to do this, every other company in the same industry is also likely to hire someone to do this.

So research all the other companies like the one that's hiring, and approach each of them about the same position. You now have the skills to do this, based on the techniques in this book. You know how to seek a personal introduction, contact an organization through multiple channels, and apply whether they are advertising or not. And applying to the other, nonadvertising companies is more likely to result in less competition for your application. Let me repeat this: **You are more likely to find an opportunity at a company before they have a chance to post an announcement and create all that competition for you.** Just keep reminding yourself that half of all jobs change hands without being advertised, and you need to find one of those opportunities.

Use advertised jobs and posted announcements as idea generators. Follow up with research. Turn one idea into many, and you'll have a successful job search that capitalizes on the hidden job market.

Headhunters and Permanent Placement Agencies

More properly called executive search consultants, headhunters tend to concentrate on executive and professional positions, while permanent placement agencies are open to any placement from receptionist on up. But there really is no clear line between the two. To complicate matters, almost all temporary agencies also place candidates permanently, and most permanent agencies are happy to fill a temporary assignment for a favorite client.

The thing to remember about all of these services is that you are not the client; the employer is. You are the product. To understand this thoroughly, read the following sentence many times: **Headhunters and permanent placement agencies find people for jobs, not jobs for people.**

Few headhunters will be interested in recent grads. If you want to learn more about the executive placement industry, read John Lucht's *Rites of Passage* and look at www.kennedyinfo.com.

If you want to know whether a placement agency would be interested in you, call them up and ask. Say something like this:

"I am a recent college graduate with a major in political science and a minor in psychology. I understand statistics and can both understand and design social science research. I like people and have been successful at working on teams. I'm looking for a career-launching position, not just some fast cash. Would your agency ever have a need for someone like me, or do you only represent candidates with more experience?"

Write out your own script describing yourself as briefly and as concisely as possible, and give them a pitch. If they agree to interview you, go for it. If not, then you haven't wasted very much of your—or their—time.

Be careful not to get yourself railroaded into a job that doesn't match your interests and needs, however. Agencies want to make placements, whether the person placed is happy or not. Your agency associate is going to have a strong personality, so don't leave your personality under the doormat as you go in.

Fake Employment Agencies

"We have direct access to thousands of unadvertised jobs!"

"Looking for work? Look no further!"

"New in town? Stop beating your head against the wall! Let us market you to 1,000 employers."

And so on. These are typical come-ons from "executive marketing consultants." This is a shadowy industry that preys upon discouraged, depressed, and cash-challenged people all over the country. They frequently disguise themselves as headhunters or employment agencies or employment websites, and run ads that imply that they are conducting hiring operations when in fact they are trolling for victims. They may ask you to fill out extensive employment applications, extracting personal information such as social security number, date of birth, mother's maiden name, current and prior addresses—basically everything they need to run a wholesale identity theft operation. They may call you in for a "job interview" and then reveal that they want you to pay them thousands of dollars to help you find employment.

Worst of all, they frequently change their names, so that if you do your due diligence and call the Better Business Bureau, you may not find the trail of complaints they have just "washed."

If you are hussled by any of these cons, run for the door! Their "secrets" are common knowledge in the employment business; you can do for yourself what they purport to do for you, and you can do it at a fraction of the cost. Their contracts never guarantee anything, except that you won't get your money back.

If it feels like a scam, it probably is. If it sounds too good to be true, it definitely is.

Straightforward resume-writing services do not fall into the above category, however, and in some cases it can be a good idea to contract for their services.

Resume-Writing Services

Perhaps you are a nursing major or a math major, and writing isn't your strongest skill. You might consider hiring a qualified resume writer to help you craft a good document. Look in the Yellow Pages and online, and follow this prudent buying strategy:

- Research more than one service.

- Read the provided samples carefully.

- Look for a good, clean presentation of content, not vacuous fluff.

- Inquire about who will be doing the actual writing.

- Call the Better Business Bureau and inquire about complaints.

Before you seek outside help, however, you should give it your best college try. Writing a resume is a critical skill you will need over and over again, so don't assume you can avoid it. Writing a check for a good resume doesn't solve the whole problem. Resume-writing services are expensive, and they typically produce only one model. You'll need to do extensive customization during your job search anyway, so you can't really avoid writing altogether. Also, your career center may be able to help you craft a good resume, even if you graduated years ago. See the Skills Inventory at www.donaldasher.com/careers for resume writing ideas and a tutorial.

CASE STUDY Cassie L.

"It took me three months to get a job. I didn't really start looking until July after graduation. I was an art major, and I had a lease on my studio until August 1. I was finishing an installation of boxes and screens, using animal metaphors for human childhood. It was a rich piece and I had a lot on my mind, so I didn't think once about a job. I should have, I realize now, but I didn't. Well, actually, I was avoiding the whole issue.

"I worked on my piece and ignored this impending doom. In the back of my mind, I could hear the clock ticking, but the alarm didn't go off until I had to close down my studio. Then, in the same week, I lost my studio and my mom called and reminded me that she wasn't going to pay my rent anymore. That's really when the alarm went off. Time to wake up.

"So I applied for AmeriCorps positions in Puerto Rico, to do community work for a year and learn a foreign language. I filled out the apps and kept emailing the coordinator in San Juan. But she disappeared for a while and didn't respond, so that fell apart. I speak Spanish, and I'm proficient enough in the language to have done that work. For a year, I'd been studying one-on-one in a language exchange agreement with a recent immigrant from Mexico. We spoke Spanish for an hour and then English for an hour. He wanted to go to college in the United States, and I wanted to help him. I was pretty disappointed that this AmeriCorps assignment didn't come through. I thought it was a sure thing.

"So then I just started applying for all the jobs I could find on the Internet. I didn't really pursue it beyond that, and I didn't make personal connections. I just sent out my resume, and that was pretty fruitless. I'd fill out these online forms, submit my resume, and then nothing would happen. I never got any responses. Sometimes I'd get a form letter saying they were not interested. It's perverse, but I kind of liked getting those emails. It let me know that something, even a database, was acknowledging my existence. Job search is really intimidating, and I didn't have any experience, so it was easy to hide behind the Internet.

"Then I went to a resume workshop at my career center, and I learned to count a lot of my student experiences as professional experiences, to talk about them in more businesslike terms. I took my volunteer experience, my service on a public affairs committee, and one office job, and really amped up my resume.

"When I first transferred to [the university] from community college, I worked in the news and publications office. I was a paid intern on the alumni magazine and a volunteer editor on *Nervy Grrrl*, an artsy community rag. Also, I was secretary for the student senate, and in that role I was liaison to the Wisconsin statewide student association. So I rewrote my resume featuring these experiences. These seemingly random connections did, in fact, get me my current job.

"It's amazing how tenuous my experience was. I got the job with the alumni magazine because of a paper I wrote in community college: 'Diversity Initiatives at a Rural Community College in Wisconsin.' That was my writing sample, and they liked it.

"*Nervy Grrrl* was equally chancy. I saw them on a newsstand, then called them up and said, 'Hey! I want to do some volunteer work for you.' I just called the volunteer coordinator, who was listed in the publication, and we talked. Very informal. I had made a list of ideas for the magazine, and she liked them. I called them last July, and I started working for them in the beginning of September. It took a little time to explore all this and get the relationship defined, but I did it through my senior year. I was the only college student on the staff.

"I thought I was really interested in publications, but in this internship I discovered I didn't really enjoy the work. I prefer to do community work and to serve people directly. It looked great on my resume, though.

"When I went to the resume workshop, I noticed a flier for a program sponsored by the Wisconsin Student Association. I had worked with them when I was in student government, and somehow I just forgot about them. It occurred to me to see if they had any jobs, so the next day I called their office. They had a position for a full-time campus organizer, working with student leadership programs and developing advocacy for student-related political issues. Wow! I thought. This is ideal.

"I knew they typically hired recent graduates who had been involved in statewide activism and student government, and in the past I had briefly worked with the executive director of the organization. I called her up, reminded her of who I was, and asked for the job. She said I had to go through the formal channels, but she'd help me out if I had any questions. They had an unbelievable amount of supplemental application materials. I had to write three essays and respond to over twenty position statements. I spent the whole weekend in the library getting this together. I customized my resume for the job, and I wrote a personal cover letter detailing my experiences with them. I heard that 114 people had applied, and I was the one they hired.

"One of my assignments now is to teach student leadership seminars. I tell students to line up some kind of internship. If you can't do it before you graduate, set something up for the summer after you graduate. Even if you don't like your internship, it can be critical to getting a job. You have to have something to put on that resume besides your GPA."

Will work part-time for millions.

—*Clyde Watkins, capitalist*

16

The Job Interview

A job interview is different from an informational interview. As you know, in an informational interview, your goal is to pursue a career idea, learn more about a job or an industry, perhaps get referrals to those who may be able to hire you, and get tips on specific employers. Because you are seeking information, you are really relying on the largesse of your contact. Their benevolence is a gift.

When you apply for a known opening, or interview with an employer who is considering hiring you, the rules of the interview are slightly different. The interviewer is self-interested. They are taking time to meet with you in the hope that you will make a good addition to their organization. So they approach the meeting with a very different agenda than the intent to help a young person or spread goodwill. They want to obtain certain information from you and about you, and to assess your potential as an employee.

And in a job interview, your status is different as well. You're not a novice seeking information, but a potential contributor offering skills and abilities. You want to present yourself in the best possible light, minimizing focus on your deficiencies and highlighting your talents.

It is your job to present yourself well in a job interview. This is no place for false modesty, or even sincere modesty. An interviewer will *want* to know what you can do for her. In fact, I have written before that interviewers have a sentence tattooed on the inside of their eyelids: What can this candidate do for me, my department, and my organization? So be ready to answer that question throughout the interview.

The Interview Begins Before You Arrive

An interview cannot be won before you arrive, but it certainly can be lost. You have several tasks to manage before the interview begins:

- Research the organization.

- Prepare the points you want to make and the examples you want to use.

- Confirm the appointment the day before.

- Suss out the right clothing.

- Be sure you know where you're going.

Research the Organization

Whether you're interviewing with a Fortune 500 company or a local nonprofit, research the organization in advance. Use the library or the Internet. Be sure you know the answers to the following questions before you walk into the interview: When were they founded? What is their principal line of business? Where do they have locations? Who are their competitors? What competitive or economic or technological challenges do they face? And what's been written about them in any media outlet over the last few years?

Failure to research a company before an interview reveals poor judgment or a serious lack of interest. In these days of instant access to information, it is simply inexcusable to walk into an organization and ask, "Hey, what is it you guys do around here?"

At a minimum:

- Visit the organization's own website to see what it says about itself.

- Google the company and its main product lines to see what others say about it.

- If it is a major corporation, look up company profiles on Hoover's or www.wetfeet.com or www.vault.com.

- Go to your university library's home page, find the online service covering the business and popular press, and see what journalists have been saying about the organization.

- Find someone who uses the company's products or has interacted with the company in some capacity, and interview them.

Get Ready to Talk about Yourself

Trained interviewers will ask you a lot of questions about your past behavior, hoping to elicit specific examples from you. So you need to prepare a pool of ten to twenty examples from your past that illustrate your talents, your ethics, and your ability to solve problems. The ideal examples are short vignettes in which you are the hero—in which you demonstrate leadership, mediate disputes, advance a team project, or pursue virtue when faced with an ethical temptation, and so on. Examples from student activities and in-class experiences are fine, but be ready to deliver specific stories, not generalities.

Prepare examples in advance for categories like these:

- Tell me about a time when you had to organize a team, how you did it, and how it worked out.

- Give me an example of a time when you had to work with someone who didn't carry his or her weight, and how you dealt with the situation.

- Tell me about a time when you witnessed a colleague or fellow student cheating or stealing.

- Tell me about a time when you had to complete an assignment but didn't have the resources—time or money or reference materials or whatever—and how the project turned out.

- Is there a time in the past when you didn't get along with a boss or a professor? Can you tell me about that?

- Give me an example of a major challenge that you faced, how you went about addressing the problem, and how it turned out.

- Think of the greatest disappointment you've faced as a student. Can you tell me about that?

- When in the past have you had to solve interpersonal differences between others, perhaps friends or colleagues who were not getting along? What did you do?

- Tell me about a time when you had to work really hard. Can you tell me what the situation was and what you did? Was there a deadline? Did you miss it by much?

- It says here on your resume that you speak (Spanish/German/Portuguese/ etc.). Tell me about the last time you had to speak that language in a non-classroom setting.

- Can you think of the biggest writing project you've attempted in college? Tell me how you organized that and how it went. What grade did you get?

- What was the last computer program you learned? How did you learn it?

Again, develop hero stories that make you look good! Do not tell disaster stories that don't end well. Keep those to yourself. A standard technique for preparing hero stories is **P.A.A.R.L.A.**:

Problem

Analysis

Action

Result

Learned

Applied

For example, "I faced a specific problem (define the problem). I analyzed the situation (give the analysis). I took action based on my analysis (specify the action), achieving this result (tell the result). From this, I learned the following (report what you learned), which I applied in the following ways (thereby leveraging the experience as a lesson)."

Here's how an example might look, prepared in advance: Evidence of leadership: I noticed there was no career planning function for the biology department. **(Problem)** I knew from talking to faculty and other students that most biology majors didn't actually get jobs in biology; they thought most of the career center activities were for business majors. **(Analysis)** So I organized a meeting with a few biology majors, the career center director, and two biology professors I knew were interested in this topic. We set up some career programs just for biology majors—a resume workshop, an alumni panel, and a survey of recent biology grads to see just what kind of jobs they were getting. **(Action)** Within a year, biology majors had access to career planning services as good as anyone else at the university. **(Result)** From this, I learned that if you see a need or an opportunity to help others, you should discover who you want to be involved, and get them involved. You can't wait for others to fix a problem! **(Learned)** Now I am much more confident of my ability to make a difference; I've organized a biology softball club and I've gotten the biology computer lab to stay open twenty-four hours a day during finals week. **(Applied)**

In addition to these examples, have in mind five points you want to leave with any interviewer. They might be "I am honest," "I am creative at overcoming challenges," or "I can learn new computer skills without being trained." Whatever they are, know them in advance and be ready to establish them with evidence, that is, be sure your examples show you exhibiting these traits or skills. Prepare a list:

Five Points I Want to Make in This Meeting.

Finally, practice answering this question: Why should we hire you? The answer should include your five points. If *you* can't explain why you should be hired, how can you expect them to figure it out? Be ready to answer the question:

Why should I hire you?

Confirm the Day Before

The day before your interview, confirm the appointment. You don't need to reach a human, and you can use email or voice mail to deliver your message. In fact, an argument can be made that it is probably better to use voice mail because it reduces the chances that your contact will try to reschedule or cancel the interview. Say something like this: "Hello, this is Alexandra Student, and I am confirming my appointment with Mr. Biggs at 3:15 P.M. to discuss a marketing analyst position. If you should need to reach me tomorrow for any reason, my cell phone number is 301–555–8901. I'm looking forward to the meeting, and to learning more about your organization and your marketing function."

CASE STUDY Stan R.

Stan R. rented an apartment with several roommates, but spent most of his time at his girlfriend's place. He'd been trying for months to get an interview with Apple Computer, where he hoped to work translating technical documents into and out of modern Romance languages. (Stan was fluent in French, Spanish, Italian, and Portuguese.) He finally arranged a screening interview by phone, which he passed with flying colors. The in-house recruiter set up an appointment for Stan to meet with five department heads who needed technical translation support. Stan was ecstatic, and bragged to everybody he knew that he was "one step away from a job at Apple!"

On Friday morning, the week before the big interview, the recruiter called and left a message at Stan's apartment. She wanted him to call and confirm, as she had arranged for five managers to meet Stan on Monday morning at nine o'clock. She didn't say it in so many words, but she implied that it would be very embarrassing for her if Stan was a no-show on Monday. Stan spent the weekend at his girlfriend's, never got the message, and did not confirm.

Monday morning, Stan arrived at Apple at five minutes to nine, right on time—or so he thought. The recruiter was in a nasty mood, and the five managers were hostile.

Stan flunked the interview, mostly because everybody he met that day was mad at him before they even met him. Stan's chances at Apple ended on Friday afternoon before five, when he did not call and confirm his interview.

CASE STUDY Kahlin W.

Kahlin W. had several interviews for internships in Washington, D.C., in the spring of her senior year. She was a finalist several times, but no one had offered her an assignment by graduation day. Undeterred, she decided to just move to Washington, D.C., and continue looking for a job in government. She decided to celebrate her graduation with a road trip in the new car her parents had just given her. She and her boyfriend had a great time visiting national parks, friends, and relatives in a meandering path across the country. Before leaving, Kahlin had cancelled her college email account and turned off her phone. She put a forwarding message on her disconnected phone that gave out her parents' number, but she never called her parents during her adventure. "I just didn't feel like checking in like a little kid, I guess," she told me when I interviewed her about it later.

As you've probably guessed, when she got to Washington, D.C., she discovered that one of the places she had applied to had tried to reach her for a whole week but finally gave up. Her disappearing act cost her a plum assignment.

Dress for Success

What should you wear to a job interview? The wrong outfit will sink your chances, and your brilliant performance in the interview will come to naught. **You want to look like you already work at the company.** Wear what an employee at your level would wear on a day when a VIP was visiting your work area. Obviously, this is not necessarily a suit. In some departments or companies, a suit would make you look completely out of place.

When an interviewer looks at you, they are forming an immediate impression of you based on your appearance. This first impression is very hard to shake. If your clothing and grooming choices make you look like you do not belong in the organization, then nothing that comes out of your mouth will matter.

Your career center can give you some direction about the best way to dress if they know anything about the company. You can also drive by the location and see what people are wearing. You want to dress one or two notches better than whatever employees are wearing on any given Monday. And if your appointment is for a Friday, casual-Friday dress certainly does not apply to you as a candidate. It's not wrong to call a lower-level person at the company and ask them for advice. However, avoid your actual interviewer; contact a secretary or salesperson or receptionist and ask, "I have an appointment with Mr. Biggs on Monday for a position as sales assistant. What do you think would be most appropriate for me to wear? A suit, a dress, or business casual? Considering what you know about Mr. Biggs, what's your advice for me?"

Once you select your main outfit, it's time to consider the details. Do you have the right shoes, belt, scarf, tie, watch, pen, coat, umbrella? These things matter, so please take the time to assemble the complete outfit, including the appropriate accessories.

Consider covering tattoos and removing piercings. Times change, and many employers are not as stodgy as they used to be, but why not get the job first, before sporting potentially controversial style choices? Most appearance consultants recommend minimizing jewelry and scents, as they can be distracting, at best.

If you don't own the right clothes for your interviews, it's time to borrow some or spend the money to acquire them. Your appearance is that important.

Know Where You're Going

Being late is considered an unforgivable sin for a candidate. Never, never, never be late. To ensure that this never happens to you, know your route and allow plenty of time for error or the unexpected, such as bad weather or heavy traffic. Your goal is to arrive at the location of the interview exactly five minutes early. In case you've never heard this before: If you're five minutes early, you're on time; and if you're on time, you're late.

Arriving five minutes early, however, may be complicated. There may be a security gate before you can even park, for example, or you may be going to a sprawling corporate campus with a long walk from the parking lot to the right building. So be sure to factor that in as well. Allow for bad weather or a wrong turn. And you certainly want to allow a couple of minutes to make sure your hair is just right before walking into a waiting room. You may be asked to fill out forms or sign some kind of security or nondisclosure agreement, which can take precious time as well. Your goal is to arrive at the interview location exactly four minutes and sixty seconds before your appointment. Arriving too early is rude and potentially disruptive. Arriving less than five minutes early is stressful to those you are going to meet. If you're unsure of how much time will be taken up at the front door or security desk, don't hesitate to ask!

In the highly unlikely event that you are going to be late, call the employer and say, "I'm so sorry, but I've been unavoidably detained at a prior interview (or by an inexplicable and horrific traffic jam or failure of public transportation). I wonder if you would prefer to reschedule, or can we meet later than originally scheduled?" You've probably blown your chances with that employer, but at least give them a chance to forgive you.

The Parking Lot and the Waiting Room

When does the interview begin? When you meet Ms. or Mr. Biggs? Or sooner? You are on show from the moment anyone in the company can see you. Your behavior in the parking lot, and even what kind of car you drive, can influence the decision to hire you.

I was once hiring a new career counselor who had all the right skills. He passed a telephone screening interview in which he had been both charming and impressive. We had several things in common, which predisposed me to like him. When we set up an appointment for a job interview, I expected it to be a mere formality. I was confident that my placement project was over, and we would have a new staff member within days.

During our conversation, it transpired that we were both motorcycle enthusiasts. On the day of his interview, I saw someone drive a motorcycle into our parking lot, then stretch out on the bike and take a nap. I said to myself right then, "If he's the guy we're interviewing, I'm not hiring him." He was, and I didn't. If he thought it was okay to nap on his bike in our parking lot, he was unlikely to portray the image I had in mind for my company.

What image do you project when you think no one is watching you? Think about it, and prepare accordingly.

Once you announce yourself to the receptionist or security officer, what do you do while you wait? This is not a trivial question. I know a consulting group that is fond of placing the *National Enquirer,* the *Weekly World News,* the *Star* and *People* on a coffee table in their waiting room. If you pick up one of these, you're very unlikely to be hired.

Support staff, from the security guard to the receptionist to those you pass in the hall, are all serving as the eyes and ears of the manager who makes the hiring decision. Be extra charming to everybody. If you are anything other than gracious, friendly, and courteous to anyone, they will be sure to tell the interviewer about it as soon as they can!

If you are offered coffee or a soft drink, decline! You are here as an applicant, not a guest. If you're parched to the level that you won't be comfortable in the interview, ask for a glass of water if you must, but decline other goods and services.

While waiting for your interview to begin, sit up straight, go over your notes, and mentally rehearse the examples you want to weave into the conversation.

Travel light. Leave your book pack at home, and carry only a small leather or vinyl folder with extra resumes, a pen, and a pad of paper inside. You can tape a small list of points you want to make inside the folder, to prompt your memory.

Waiting

How long should you wait to meet with someone when you have an appointment for a certain time? There is more than one right answer to this question. I've interviewed students who waited as long as four hours for an interview and thought it was definitely worth it. In my opinion, in most cases, you should not wait more than an hour past your appointed time for an interview to begin—unless there is an extraordinary reason for the delay. You are a valuable person. If you have to, wait about half an hour, maybe a little more, and then reannounce yourself. Walk up to the receptionist and say, "Hi. I'm Donald Asher, and I'm waiting for an appointment with Dr. Wilson. My appointment was for 9 A.M., and it's now 9:40. Is everything okay? I don't mind waiting, but I just want to make sure there isn't a problem with the appointment." If Dr. Wilson doesn't appear, after an hour I'd get up and say, "Hi. I'm Donald Asher. I had an appointment with Dr. Wilson for 9 A.M., and it's now ten o'clock. I have some other obligations today, so I'm going to leave now. If Dr. Wilson is interested in resetting this appointment, please ask her to give me a call." Then walk out. You have ninety-nine other possible employers to meet with, and one of them is bound to treat you better. You'll feel fantastic for asserting yourself, and Dr. Wilson will learn that if she wants to hire valuable people, she'll have to start treating them as if they're valuable.

Of course, in Hollywood, in Washington, D.C., and on Wall Street, waiting hours to meet with Big Shots is a long-standing tradition.

The Greeting and the Handshake

When you finally meet your interviewer, look them in the eye, give them a firm business handshake, and repeat their name when you say it is a pleasure to meet with them. The handshake is critical! In a recent poll, employers reported that they would be more forgiving of piercings and tattoos than a wimpy handshake. Foreign students, in particular, need to learn to have a confident, firm, businesslike handshake. If you are uncertain of yours, go to the career center and get it tested!

In the first few seconds of the meeting, the interviewer will decide if he does not want to hire you. It may take longer to convince an employer to hire you, but convincing an employer not to hire you takes only seconds. The wrong clothes, the wrong attitude, the wrong posture, and you're in a hole that is very difficult to dig yourself out of. First impressions are powerful, and difficult to reverse.

Small Talk

The interviewer will set the tone for the interview. Usually, he will begin with small talk about the weather, or mention something you have in common, or ask you how you're doing.

Or he may ask, "Did you have any trouble finding this place?" Even if you spent an hour driving around lost before arriving, say, "No. No problem at all."

Be in a good mood, whether you feel like it or not. You're having a good day. You're going to enjoy this meeting. You're glad to be here.

Small talk builds a bond between people who are meeting for the first time, and creates a foundation of trust for more challenging communication later in the interview. The interviewer is simply trying to put you at ease.

Here is the wrong way to converse:

BOSS: How are you?
YOU: Fine.
BOSS: It sure is nice weather out today.
YOU: Yeah.
BOSS: Do you have plans for the weekend?
YOU: No.
BOSS: What do you usually do on weekends?
YOU: Sleep.

Monosyllabic answers will create the impression that you are a dullard. Give answers that invite further discourse. Here is the right way to converse:

BOSS: Did you go to the game last weekend?
YOU: No, Mark. I did see the highlights on the news, though. Wow, what an exciting finish! I spend most weekends with a hiking club, so I was up on Mount Wilson during the game.

Responses like this will support several different directions for continuing conversation. Within a few minutes, the interviewer will start asking more substantive questions.

"So, Can You Tell Me a Little about Yourself?"

This is the most classic interview question of all time. Although this sounds like an open-ended, anything-goes type of inquiry, it is not. This is a business question that requires a business answer.

In short, you want to provide evidence that you have skills and are prepared to contribute to this employer's endeavors. By now, because you've done so much life planning and worked so hard to get relevant information in your resume, you're ready to represent yourself well in an interview and to respond to these classic questions:

- What are your strengths?
- What are your weaknesses?
- What has been your biggest failure?
- Where do you see yourself in five years?
- What would others say about you?
- What would you like to change about yourself?
- What other types of jobs are you applying for?
- Why should we hire you?

Behavioral Interview Questions

Behavioral interview questions begin with some version of "Tell me about a time when . . ." or "Describe a situation when you. . ." So when you hear this language, it is your cue to provide an example, a specific story to demonstrate that you have the skills, character traits, ethics, and judgment that the employer wants.

You cannot prepare for every form of behavioral interview question, but with the collection of examples you prepared before the interview, you should be able to adjust one or more of them to fit most queries.

Be as specific as you can when asked to provide an example. If they say, "Tell me about a time when you had to work on a team with someone who let you down," this would not be a good response: "I think it is important for everyone on a team to have clearly defined responsibilities." A policy statement is not what was requested. The interviewer wants to hear a story about a time when you faced a slacker for a teammate, what you did about it, and what you learned. Remember your P.A.A.R.L.A. technique for fielding behavioral questions: **Problem, Analysis, Action, Result, Learned, Applied**.

If you cannot come up with a good example, you can say, "I've never faced that before. But here's how I think I'd deal with the situation . . ."

Don't panic when asked an unexpectedly challenging question. Use your conversational skills and ask them to rephrase the question, or further define the question yourself by saying, "Let me be sure I understand what you're asking. Do you mean . . .?"

In any interview, you can say "I don't know" once, maybe twice, but interviewers really do expect you to field the questions.

Case Questions and Problems

Case questions are common for consulting jobs and Wall Street opportunities. And you never know when you're going to run into an M.B.A. who loves to use case questions just to see how you will deal with them.

Here are some examples:

- How many golf balls would fit in a Boeing 747?

- How many gas stations are there in the United States?

- If a family business in Kansas City has been making pizza boxes for twenty years, and their biggest client is about to merge with a company that uses a different supplier, what business survival measures would you recommend, and what would be your plan to help this business?

With case questions, the goal is not to actually solve the problem, but to demonstrate the thought processes you would use to solve the problem. Grab a piece of scratch paper if you need to, and don't be afraid to think out loud. For example, concerning gas stations, you might say, "Well, there are about 300 million Americans right now, and probably three-fourths of them are old enough but not too old to drive, so that's about 250 million Americans. I read somewhere that there are just slightly more cars than drivers now, so that means there are maybe 260 million cars. Each car needs to fill up once a week, for normal commuting. Whenever I go to a gas station, there are about 2 to 4 other cars at the gas station, so let's say 3. It takes me about five minutes to fill up, so at 12 cars per hour and 3 at a time, a gas station could serve 36 cars per hour. A gas station that is open from 6 A.M. to 10 P.M. would serve about 575 cars per day, or about 4,000 cars per week. With 260 million cars and one fill-up per week, that's maybe 65,000 gas stations in the United States, as a ballpark figure."

It doesn't matter how many actual gas stations there are; it's the logical, quantifying, problem-solving techniques that you need to demonstrate. That's what they're after.

No-Right-Answer Queries

Some questions don't have right or wrong answers; the interviewer is simply trying to get you to reveal more about your values and personality. They are trying to stretch you beyond your prepared interview answers. Here are some examples of no-right-answer questions:

- If you were a breakfast cereal, what would you be and why?
- If you were an animal, what animal would you be?
- What kind of car most perfectly expresses your personality?
- What's your favorite color? What do you like about it?
- Let's say you won a really big lottery tomorrow, $100 million; what would you do in the first ninety days?

Look again at the question that Andrew H. answered on page 160. That's a perfect example of a question with no single right answer.

One warning: Take these questions seriously, and do your best to answer them. They are not jokes. If you joke about them, you will be considered immature.

By the way, here's my own favorite stress interview question: I probably should have been a cop. One of my hobbies is investigating people. Let's just say I'm really good at it. I'm going to be doing a background check on you. It doesn't matter who you give as references; I'm going to be developing my own contacts from your past, as well as checking databases most people don't even know about. Is there anything you want to tell me right now, rather than have me find out about it later?

You would simply not believe all the things that candidates have dumped on the table when faced with this question.

Illegal Questions

It is rare to get asked an illegal question by a human resources professional, but a manager from another part of the organization may ask you one without even knowing it. Illegal questions include queries concerning race, religion, national origin, nonemployment-related health conditions, and information with a high potential for use in discrimination.

Here are some classic illegal questions:

- Did you grow up speaking English at home?
- Do you plan to start a family soon?
- Are you gay?

- What church do you attend?
- How much do you weigh?

I think the best strategy when facing an illegal question is this: **Answer the concern, not the question.** Instead of literally answering the question, answer the concern that is unstated behind the question. For example, with the question "Do you plan to start a family soon?", you needn't answer the literal question, but you could address the concern behind the question by saying, "I would never let my family responsibilities interfere with my ability to do my job."

As much as you might desire to blurt out, "Hey! That's an illegal question!", that's probably not going to advance your candidacy.

CASE STUDY Interview with a Supervisor—Brendan L.

"If I were to complain about the new college grads we hire, I'd say the main problems are rooted in a poor attitude. The problem may appear to be work habits, tardiness, a sense of entitlement, or an inability to make a firm commitment, but all of these are just outward manifestations of worker attitude.

"Let me give you three examples. I had a guy who came in at all different hours. He'd come slinking past my cubicle at random times, like 9:30 one day, 10 the next, 9:15 another. I didn't see any pattern to it. So I said to him, 'What's the matter with you? You're coming in at all different times of the morning.' And he said to me, 'What? That's a problem?' I actually had to tell him, 'Hey. You're the new guy. You work 8 to 5. You're supposed to be at your desk before 8 A.M., not hanging up your coat and hunting for a cup of coffee. At your desk working at 8.' He claimed he didn't know that.

"Then I had a guy who carried around a copy of his job description. If he didn't like an assignment, he'd literally pull out the J.D. and ask, 'Where exactly would this task fit into my job description?' I had to explain to him that we were all on a team here, and that we sometimes did things because that's what needed to be done. I finally had to write up an incident report and file it with HR. After that, he got more cooperative.

"And I was on an account team with a young lady who just couldn't guarantee anything. No matter what I wanted, she'd say, 'I'll try,' or 'I'll do my best.' I said, 'I don't want to know that you're going to try. I need to know you'll get it done without my having to think about it again.' I could ask her for something brutally simple, like, 'Do you think you'll be at work tomorrow?' and she'd say, 'I'll do my best.'

·Why couldn't she just say, 'Yes. You can count on me. I'll take care of it. I guarantee that this assignment will be done on time'? Her work was good, but it was stressful working with her. I never really knew if she'd deliver or not.

"Most of the young people we hire are great. They work hard and they're creative and they're fun to be around. But a bad attitude is something that spoils the job for everyone in a work area."

Questions to Ask Them

At some point in the interview, usually toward the end, the interviewer will ask you if you have any questions. This is a great opportunity. You want to ask two types of questions: those that help you learn more about the employer and the job, and those that help you learn more about the selection process.

Here are some questions to help you learn more about the employer and the job:

- Can you tell me how you got started with the company and how things have gone for you?

- Can you tell me a little more about the position and what you're looking for? (Ask only if that has not already been covered.)

- What resources will I have to complete my assignments? Will I have access to the [boss, tools, budgets, specialists, tech support, etc.]?

And you might structure your questions to reveal you've done research:

- I talked to my family doctor, and he indicated that your sales force seemed to have more technical product knowledge than your competitors. Is that because you hire people with more scientific backgrounds, or is that a result of your training?

- I visited the local Saturn dealer and spoke with the sales manager and the maintenance center about their relationship with Saturn corporate offices. They expressed a great deal of satisfaction with the corporate-dealer relationships, but could you tell me more about how corporate supports the dealers, and how cars are allocated to particular dealers and regions of the country?

Ask questions about competitors, market position, and the company's plans for and commitment to your department, division, branch office, or product line.

Always ask this question:

- What happened to the last person who held this job?

And ask questions about the selection process:

- How many interviews do you anticipate having before you will be able to make an offer?
- How many candidates will you be interviewing for this position?
- How am I stacking up against the competition? Do I have the skill set you're seeking?
- When do you think you'll be able to make a decision?

Follow-Up Questions

How do you know if you're doing well in an interview? If your interviewer is sitting up, looking at you, and nodding, you know you've got his attention. You're making good points. But if he starts to lean back, clasps his hands behind his head and stares into the corner, or crosses his arms and frowns, you know you've either lost him or somehow blown an answer.

So how do you get back on track? You ask a follow-up question:

- Did I answer your question?
- Is that what you had in mind?
- What approach does your company use to address this issue/problem?
- Would that work at your company?

This allows the interviewer to bring you back from some error, as in this exchange:

YOU: Did I answer your question?
BOSS: No, actually. I asked a finance question, and you gave an accounting answer. Can you reframe your answer in light of that?

By the way, a trained interviewer will not let you know when you make a mistake. He may, in fact, invite you to compound the mistake by asking you leading questions or by simply repeating the last word or phrase you gave, as in this example:

YOU: Blah, blah, blah.

BOSS: Lost in Wyoming. . . ?

YOU: Blah, blah, blah.

BOSS: Police lights in your mirror. . . ?

YOU: Blah, blah, blah.

BOSS: Felony probation. . . ?

A particularly crafty interviewer can let you dig a hole and then hand you a shovel to help you keep going deeper.

Whenever you've given a particularly long answer, or any time you're unsure of an answer, you can ask a follow-up question. Don't overuse this technique, however, or you will appear to lack confidence.

Great questions to close an interview:

- Is there anything I failed to address to your satisfaction?

- Is there anything you want me to provide you before we meet again?

And finally, before you leave, get an answer to this question:

- When, if I haven't heard from you by then, should I give you a call or send an email?

Then you have explicit permission to call them, even if they have already said, "Don't call us, we'll call you."

Questions Never to Ask in a First Interview

Never ask about salary or vacation or education benefits or retirement plans or holidays. Just don't do it.

Follow-Up Notes and Thank-You Cards

As your interview progresses, get business cards from everyone you meet, and if you have a card of your own (see example on page 194), give them one. Exchanging business cards is a standard business practice, so no one will find your request odd. If they ask you why you need their cards, just tell them the truth: "I'm going to be sending you a thank-you card, and I certainly don't want to get your name or email wrong."

Immediately upon leaving the interview, take a few minutes and write up your notes to remind you later of everything that happened and everything that you learned. Whom did you meet? What did they say? What seems to be the hiring criteria for this company? What are the specific concerns of the different managers you met? What did you promise to do to follow up? When should you expect a next contact? And so on.

Then, the same day if possible, send a thank-you note to everyone you met. I am a big fan of sending duplicate thank-you notes: one by email and another by snail mail. Email has immediate impact, and snail mail is the height of good manners. Email is too informal, but snail mail can miss recruiters who travel often. So send both. They can be identical, or they can be different.

A thank-you note can be very short:

> Dear Paul:
>
> Thank you so much for your time today. I was very interested in your company before I arrived, but I must say that I am more interested in it now. I look forward to the next steps in the selection process. Let me know if you need references or other information from me before our next meeting.
>
> Sincerely,
>
> Iwana Job

Some thank-you notes will be longer than this and may go into different aspects of the interview, but a short note like this is sufficient.

Thank-you notes can be used to recover from a gaffe or omission in the interview. Upon reflection, you can add information or further explain a point that didn't go well in the interview. Here's an example of this technique:

> Dear Jennifer:
>
> Thank you so much for your time yesterday. I was very impressed by everyone I met, and I look forward to the next steps in the selection process.
>
> Something has been on my mind since we met, however. You asked me if I had taken accounting, and when I said I had not, you seemed disappointed. I didn't think of it at the time, but in fact I have been keeping the books for a summer work crew that my brother and I have been running for years. As I mentioned, we paint houses in the Connecticut suburbs, and that's how I've paid part of my college expenses. I provide written estimates to clients, calculate break-even points for jobs based on projected time and materials, and I even set up the company as a Connecticut employer so we could go after larger jobs and legally employ other painters. I've done payroll manually, which few accountants can say these days.
>
> I realize I still have a lot to learn about accounting, but I didn't want to leave you with the impression that I didn't know anything about it! I think I have some talent for quantitative business functions, and I'm sure I could quickly master the skills

required for the position we discussed. If you have any questions about this, please just pick up the phone and give me a call.

Again, it was a pleasure to meet your team and learn about your department. I look forward to speaking with you again soon.

Sincerely,

Your Name Here

Do not be overly familiar with recruiters just because you've met them, or just because they're about your age, or just because they have an informal demeanor. "Be friendly but not familiar" is the advice of one of my recruiter acquaintances. She recruits for a famous high-tech company, and she has complained to me in the past that candidates sometimes treat her like a pal rather than a professional, which turns her off. Keep your communications, both in person and in writing, on a professional level throughout the selection process.

Screening Interviews

Your first contact from an employer is most likely to be an email. A common second contact is some form of screening interview, most often by telephone. Screening interviews have a different dynamic than job interviews. The employer is trying to find a reason to throw you out of the applicant pool. In other words, your goal is not to convince the employer to hire you but simply to survive the interview. Screening interviews ostensibly last ten to twenty minutes, but in reality, they last only until you are disqualified.

With this in mind, be careful never to say no to an employer in a screening interview. You cannot recover from any kind of negative answer. If they ask if you want to move to the middle of nowhere and catch snakes for a living, you answer, "I'd be delighted to start with your company in an assignment like this. Please tell me more."

You can decide later that snakes are not for you, but at the screening interview stage you cannot ask a lot of questions of your own. The employer is in charge, and he'll be asking probing questions. Don't hesitate and lose an opportunity. Maybe they want someone to star in a new television show about a snake handler, and all the snakes are handled by stunt professionals, and the job will pay more than the gross domestic product of a small country. But if you hesitate, you're going to be thrown out of the applicant pool, and someone else will become rich and famous.

Never say no to an employer in a screening interview. It's just a preliminary interview, and there will be plenty of chances to back out later, once you know more about the opportunity.

Prepare for a screening interview exactly the same way as you'd prepare for an in-person interview: Know the company, know what points you want to make, and dress in interview clothes. Stand up for the interview and you'll be able to convey more energy, and you can read the notes you'll have taped to the wall behind your phone. Put a smile on your face, and a smile will come through in your voice.

Finally, if an employer calls you and catches you totally unprepared and off guard, it is okay to say something like this: "I'm so sorry, but this is not a good time for me to speak on the phone. Can we make an appointment for this interview? I'd really appreciate it. I'm available anytime you want after my next class lets out at 2 P.M."

Restaurant Interviews

Interviews in restaurants provide myriad opportunities for a candidate to make mistakes. Even if you eat out often, remember, this is not a social engagement. You are being evaluated, and no matter what your hosts may do, you should not relax. Unfortunately, you will probably have to order first. A good way to get some guidance is to say to your hosts, "This place looks great. What's good here?" They'll drop a few hints at how you should order.

Here are a few tips for the restaurant interview:

- Order something simple and easy to eat. For example, avoid spaghetti and finger foods.

- Order off the middle to the bottom of the price range. Don't even think about ordering something expensive or difficult to prepare or eat.

- Forgo alcohol. If it is overwhelmingly obvious that everybody at the table is going to order alcohol, you may select a moderately priced glass of wine and sip it all night, *no matter how much your hosts may consume.*

- Pace yourself so that you finish your meal at the same time as the most important person sitting at the table.

If your career center offers an etiquette dinner, be sure to go to it! I have been to dozens of these, and I learn something new every single time.

CASE STUDY A Disaster

In spite of the fact that N.A.C.E. (National Association of Colleges and Employers) rules specifically prohibit alcohol at a college recruiting function, a leading consulting company held a "finalists' reception" in a bar for a carefully selected group of students. The students were told they were "very likely" to be hired—and that the event was purely social—just a chance to get to know them better, and for them to meet some of the firm's consultants.

Some of the candidates tried to impress the company representatives by buying them shots and getting themselves more than a little toasted in the process. Unfortunately, they were operating under the woefully misguided idea that they needed to prove they were "just regular guys" who would be fun to have on the team. The recruiter considered the event a disaster: he had no choice but to drop several candidates that he had really liked up to that point, and he was reprimanded by his boss for poor judgment. So the candidates' behavior harmed themselves and the firm, and they hadn't even been hired yet!

No event is "purely social" until you are hired and begin working.

Staying Alive through a Protracted Hiring Process

The hiring process can take months, even at the entry level. You're eager to have a job now, but the company has a different agenda. It takes a strategy to survive this process with grace. Here are the two most critical rules for staying alive:

- Never self-select out.

- Occupy mental space every week or two.

When an employer dings you, you know that the selection process is over. You'll get a letter or email that says, "Thank you for your time. Although your skills and abilities are impressive, we had an unusually large and well-qualified applicant pool, and other candidates that were simply a closer match to our requirements. We will certainly keep your materials in our database, and should positions open up in the next six months, we will automatically consider you for those opportunities."

Okay, that's a ding, and you're out of contention. But most students are not dinged. They drop out themselves before the employer has made a selection. Keep tickling an employer until you get a job or you get a ding. Don't just disappear because the employer doesn't get back to you! Don't self-select out of the process!

Which means you need a plan to stay on the employer's radar screen every week or two, sometimes for months. I recommend that you rotate contact methodologies: Send an email tickle one week, leave a voice message ten days after that, then send a card or note in the mail, then start over with an email tickle, then leave a message, then send a newspaper article about their business or markets, then email, then voice message, then send a new reference or an updated resume, ad infinitum.

Rotate contact media:

- Send an email.

- Leave a voice mail.

- Send a card, letter, article, revised resume, or new reference in the mail.

- Repeat until hired.

This is a polite way to occupy mental space while you wait for the selection process to work its way out.

One warning: Employers will do mean things to you. They're like a bad date. They swear they're going to call, and then they don't. They tell you they love you, but then you see them out with someone else. Don't worry about it. Don't take it personally. As emotionally stressing as this behavior is, the employers don't usually wish you any harm. They are just busy, or they may even have the best of intentions and may not want to disappoint you.

Don't try to guess what's going on with an employer during this process. They may be out of town, or they may have stumbled onto an especially promising late candidate who needs to be interviewed, or a big boss may need to interview you next but she's too busy, or they may have other hiring assignments that get bumped up in priority, or the position you were being considered for is back-burnered or gets frozen. My point is this: You can't tell what's going on unless they tell you, and even then you can't be sure. Just don't self-select out. Keep occupying mental space every week or two. Stay on their radar screen until (a) you get dinged or (b) you get hired. Be nice. Be polite. Be persistent. But don't allow any outcome other than (a) dinged or (b) hired.

It is not the best candidate who gets the job. **It's the best candidate who is still around at decision time.** Other candidates will come and go, but you'll still be there, like the weather. Look again at the candidate on page 187 who was told he was "seventh choice" for a position. Seventh-choice candidates are routinely hired. If they're still around.

If you can't think of anything else to send the company, send them a continuing interest letter:

Dear Moishe:

I haven't heard from you in the last month about the cost accounting position we discussed. I've left you a couple of emails and messages, but I understand you are very busy. Please know that I remain very interested in the position, and in your company. When you are ready to continue the selection process, I am eager to be considered further. My email is don@donaldasher.com, and my cell phone is 415–555–2146. Thank you so much for your consideration, and I hope to hear from you at your convenience.

    Sincerely,

    Still Looking

Then, one week later, send an email, and so on. Remember the only two outcomes you are interested in: (a) dinged or (b) hired.

I know a college grad who made a list of two hundred movers and shakers in commercial real estate in her region of the country. Then she emailed them all a copy of her resume every two weeks with this note: "Here's an updated copy of my resume. Please let me know if any openings have come up that might match my skill set, since the last time we connected." Here's how she updated her resume: she'd either put her middle initial in her name at the top of the resume or take it out. It gave her a reason to contact her target employers every two weeks, and not one of them ever commented on it!

Salary Negotiations

As mentioned earlier, you should not bring up the topic of salary or inquire about the particulars of benefits in a first interview. But sooner or later it's going to come up. One of your tasks as a candidate is to try to get some idea of pay for entry-level jobs in the field you're trying to enter. As you do your informational interviewing, remember to ask about typical salaries industry wide, but not about salaries in your host's particular organization. Also, there are several websites on salaries, although they are notoriously inaccurate for new hires.

Everyone should ask for more money. Part of adult career management is to ask for more money as part of the hiring process. A recent study discovered that women negotiate for salary at a lower rate than men, thus creating part of the gender-based wage gap, right from their very first post-college job. So women, especially, need to learn to ask for more salary.

Here is an exchange to show how you might avoid naming an exact figure:

BOSS: What kind of salary would it take to get you on board?

YOU: Salary is not my first concern. I'm much more interested in the job, the people I'll be working with, and the opportunity to advance within the company. I'm sure this won't be a problem for us. Can we come back to it later?

Later,

BOSS: What kind of salary is it going to take to get you on board?

YOU: Are you offering me the position?

BOSS: Not exactly.

YOU: "Then it seems a little premature to be negotiating the terms of employment. Really, I'm sure this won't be a problem for us. Can we come back to it later?

Or it may go like this:

BOSS: What kind of salary is it going to take to get you on board?

YOU: Are you offering me the position?

BOSS: Yes.

YOU: On what terms?

BOSS: (Whatever she says.)

YOU: I had in mind more than that, but we're in the same ballpark. How much room is there in the range?

And so on. As negotiations continue, remember to be gracious and positive. A win-win negotiation means that at the close of the deal, both parties are happy.

For more on this, see the M.B.A. handouts on www.donaldasher.com.

NOTES

1. This letter has been floating around the Internet for years. I'd used it in workshops for six or seven years, and then I heard one day on NPR that a student was representing it as his own, and actually using it with employers! I like that kind of gumption. Many thanks to the original author, but alas, this is only a joke, folks.

2. In 1999, the California Employment Development Department had research showing that job seekers spend an average of twelve to fifteen hours a week on job search activities, but my own surveys show that the real number is closer to six. It is unclear to me why there would be such a big discrepancy in our numbers, except that I run my surveys in workshops that have nothing to do with retaining unemployment benefits. Finally, on this issue, even my surveys do not count the efforts of people who do not go to workshops and are, one could argue, more likely to be discouraged, depressed, and inactive.

In Conclusion

I find that the harder I work, the more luck I seem to have.

—*Thomas Jefferson*

Good Luck!

By now you've learned how the hidden job market works, how the overwhelming majority of all jobs that change hands are never advertised, why it's no conspiracy that this is true, and how the greatest competition arrives only at the point when a job is posted on the Internet, placed with a headhunter, or advertised in a newspaper.

You also know that you cannot go out and look for any job on the hidden job market without a clear picture of that job in mind before you even start. You know that people will only be able to help you if you can ask specific questions like this: "Do you know anybody who would know anybody in the field of _____?"

You also understand that networking—the real secret to job search—is about information, not power, and that anybody and everybody you meet, or can meet, has the potential to give you the tip, advice, or introduction that will result in your next career move. You also know not to ask your networking contacts for a job directly, but for a tip, a piece of advice, or an introduction that could lead you to a job.

You also know that you will be fired at some unexpected and probably inconvenient point in your career, and that taking care of your credentials and your own career development is the responsibility of every thinking careerist. You know you will keep learning about careers, developing your skill set, preparing and planning and strategizing so that when opportunity knocks, you will be ready.

You will be ready because you know that every time you have a job change you have a magnificent new opportunity to find something that will make you even more excited about your work, and to achieve greater alignment between your employment and your personal goals and values.

I'm proud of your work. My best wishes for your continued success,

Donald Asher

Index

A

Absolutely certain students, 11
Accounting major, 29
Actors, income for, 143
Admirable people, listing, 34–35
Advanced degrees, benefits of,
    140–142
Advertising industry, 100
Aggressiveness, 179–181
Air Force service, 80–81
Alcohol at recruiting function,
    222–223
Aligning jobs and happiness,
    68–73
Alternatives to the Peace Corps: A
    Directory of Third World
    and U.S. Volunteer Oppor-
    tunities (Powell), 77
Alumni
    employment information
        from, 96
    information networking and
        alumni offices, 95–96
    "no" answers from, 181
American Red Cross National
    Headquarters, 78
American work ethic, 55
AmeriCorps, 74–75
Annual conferences, 135–136
Appearance for interviews,
    208–209
Aptitude testing, 48–52
Army service, 80
Art majors, 8
    entrepreneurship case study,
        153–155
Asher Career & Life Values
    Survey, 42
Aspect vs. whole dichotomy,
    64–66
Assaf, Saleem, 111
Athletes, income for, 143–144

Authentic Happiness (Seligman), 57
Authority and responsibility, 56
Avocations, 62–64

B

Baby boomer generation, 46
The Back Door Guide to Short-Term
    Job Adventures (Landes),
    77, 112, 127
Baker, Russell, 26
Ball, Victoria, 12–13
Ballet dancers, 147
Behavioral questions at inter-
    views, 213–214
Beliefs. *See* Values
The Best 109 Internships, 111
Better Business Bureau, 199
Bidding systems for recruiting,
    192
Birkman Method, 51
Blood, Sweat and Tears (Donkin), 55
Boys and Girls Clubs of America
    (BGCA), 78

C

Calendar for job exploration,
    121–127
Call of the Wild (London), 62
Campbell Interest and Skill
    Survey (CISS), 51
Campus activities, 90–91
Capstone projects, 88–90
Career centers, 95
Career counseling, 87–88
    job exploration and, 86
Career education model, 12
Career fairs, 193–195
Career notebooks, 24–25
Careers. *See also* Overseas jobs
    college majors and, 6–7
    defined, 5

Careers for Travel Buffs and Other
    Restless Types (Plawin),
    77
Career testing, 48–52
Career websites
    company career sites, 196
    Internet career sites, 195–196
Case questions at interviews, 214
Case studies
    advanced education, 139
    alcohol at recruiting func-
        tion, 222–223
    aligning jobs and happiness,
        71–73
    aspect vs. whole dichotomies,
        64–66
    confirming interviews,
        207–208
    continuing education, 136
    entrepreneurship, 151–155
    entry-level exploratory jobs,
        131–133
    first career job, obtaining,
        160–162
    getting a job, 14–16
    good vs. bad internships,
        115–116
    high-risk jobs, 145–149,
        147–150
    internships, 108–109, 110,
        117–118
    job exploration ideas, 94
    more than one way
        approach, 21–23
    networking, 98–99
    post-baccalaureate intern-
        ships, 127–130
    right job, finding, 16–17
    supervisor, interview with,
        216–217
    taking no for answers,
        181–183

Case studies, *continued*
troubleshooting job search,
200–202
values in workplace, 37–39
vocation *vs.* avocation
dichotomies, 63–64
Catholic Charities, 78
Celebrities, contacting, 98
Chance, 20–21
Change, reasons for, 5–6
Class projects, 88–90
Clueless students, 11–13
Coast Guard service, 80–81
The College Majors Handbook
(Fogg, Harrington &
Harrington), 6, 29
College relations managers,
191–192
Collegiate Entrepreneur's Organi-
zation, 153
Community activities, 90–91
Company receptions, 91
Competition, analyzing, 166–170
Compromises and jobs, 69–70
Computer industry, 44, 45
Conferences, professional, 135–136
Confirming interviews, 207–208
Contact media, rotating, 224–225
Contentment. *See* Happiness
Continuing education, 134–142
CPAs, education for, 138
Credentials, 136–137
Csikszentmihalyi, Mihaly, 58, 59

D
Dcinternships.org, 112
Democratic National Commit-
tee, 78
Demographic trends, 46–48
Disengagement, 13
Distributed computing, 45
DNA, 45
Doctoral studies, 137, 138
Donaldasher.com/careers, 113
Donkin, Richard, 55
Dressing for interviews, 208–209

E
Early job ideas, 26–28
Economics major, 29
Education. *See also* Graduate
education
advanced degrees, benefits of,
140–142

as competitive issue in hiring,
142
continuing education,
134–142
for credentials, 136–137
interviews, asking about
benefits at, 219
Educational hiring, 170
Effort and job search, 189
Elevator speech, 174–175
Email
to employers, 173–174
gatekeepers, getting past,
175–177
interviews via, 221
networking with, 101
rotating contact media,
224–225
screening interviews, 221
thank yous for interviews,
220
Emerging industries, 43–46
Employers
career websites, 196
hiring and, 168–169
identification with, 40–41
internships, looking for,
113–114
new hire skills and, 9
telephoning employers,
172–181
Employment agencies
fake employment agencies,
199
permanent placement agen-
cies, 198–199
temporary placement agen-
cies, 195
Encyclopedia of Associations, 136
Engineering majors, 8
English majors, 7
English teaching overseas, 77
The Enneagram, 51
Entrepreneurship, 150–155
resources for, 153
Entry-level jobs, 72
exploratory entry-level jobs,
130–133
Environmental Careers Organization, 112
Envisioning the future, 68–73
Etiquette of networking, 101–103
Event planning, 15
Executive placement agencies, 198

Experience and internships,
109–111

F
Faculty and networking, 97
Failure
to launch, 18
sources of, 189–190
Fake employment agencies, 199
Familiarity with interviewers, 221
Family and parents
advice from, 11, 17–19
career notebook including,
24–25
industries of, 28
networking and, 97
Fantasies about careers, 26–27
First impressions and interviews,
208–209
Five issues list, 31–33
jobs relating to interests,
selecting, 33–34
Flow (Csikszentmihalyi), 59
Flow periods, 58–59
Fogg, Neeta, 6, 29
Follow-up calls, 174
Follow-up notes for interviews,
219–221
Follow-up questions at interviews,
218–219
Foreign languages, studying,
88–89
Friends
happiness and, 56
networking and, 97
post-college plans of, 28–29
Future
envisioning, 68–73
and job hunting, 4–5

G
Gatekeepers, getting past, 175–177
Gates, Bill, 45, 62
Genentech, 45
Generation gap, 18
Gene-splicing, 45
Geographic location and job
search, 189
Getting started, 23–30
The Global Citizen (Kruempel-
mann), 77
Golf, 87
Good at *vs.* enjoy dichotomy,
61–62
Google internship searches, 113

Government hiring, 170
Graduate Admissions Essays (Asher), 137
Graduate education, 74, 134–142
    benefits of, 140–142
The Green Party internships, 78
Greetings at interviews, 211–212
Growing Up (Baker), 26
Growth pattern for emerging
    markets, 44

H
Habitat for Humanity, 78
Handshake at interviews, 211–212
Happiness
    flow periods and, 58–59
    and job search, 54–61
    Mood-O-Meter, 59–60
    peak moments and, 57–58
    studies, 55–56
Harvard Business School, 140
Headhunters, 198–199
Help-wanted ads, 197
Hero stories for interviews, 206
Hidden job market, 165–166
High-risk jobs, 72, 143–156
    entrepreneurship, 150–155
High school career fantasies,
    26–27
*High-Tech Careers for Low-Tech
    People* (Schaffer), 7
Hiring cycles, 193
Hiring process, length of, 223–226
Hispanic demographics, 46
Holidays, asking about, 219
Holistic assessment, 66–68
Hot jobs lists, 47–48

I
IBM, 45
Idealist.org internships, 113
Illegal questions at interviews,
    215–216
Income. *See also* Salary
    for actors, 143
    and advanced degrees,
        140–142
Independent study, 88–90
Industries
    emerging industries, 43–46
    experiences with, 28
Informational interviews, 93–95
Information networking, 93–96
Information Theory and Evolution
    (Avery), 140

INROADS internships, 112
Interests
    listing, 31–33
    testing to determine, 48–52
Internal, informal recruiting,
    167–168
International careers. *See* Overseas
    jobs
Internet
    career sites on, 195–196
    as industry, 44
    internships, searching for, 113
    job search on, 163
The Internship Bible 2003 (Oldman
    & Hamadeh), 111
Internships, 107–108. *See also*
    Summer jobs
    benefits of, 114
    defined, 107
    good *vs.* bad internships,
        114–118
    great internships, features
        of, 117
    Internet searches, 113
    paid internships, 109
    post-baccalaureate intern-
        ships, 77–79, 121,
        127–130
Internships 2003, 111
Interviews, 203–226
    arriving for, 209–210
    behavioral questions at,
        213–214
    case questions and problems,
        214
    confirming day before,
        207–208
    directions for, 209–210
    dressing for, 208–209
    face time and, 190
    follow-up notes, 219–221
    follow-up questions, 218–219
    frequency of, 162
    greetings at, 211–212
    handshake at, 211–212
    illegal questions, 215–216
    informational interviews,
        93–95
    mock interviews, 192
    no-right-answer questions
        at, 215
    P.A.A.R.L.A. technique,
        206, 213
    parking lots, behavior in, 210
    preparation for, 204–207

researching organization,
        204–205
    restaurant interviews, 222
    screening interviews, 221–222
    small talk at, 212
    stress interview questions, 215
    talking about yourself,
        205–207
    thank-you notes, 219–221
    waiting, etiquette of, 211
    waiting rooms, behavior in,
        210–211
    your questions, asking,
        217–218
Introductions, value of, 169
Introspection, 87

J
JAG (Judge Advocate General), 80
Jesuit Volunteer Corps, 78
Job exploration, 85–87
Job search
    seven stages of, 185–187
    troubleshooting, 184–202
Job targets, 161–170
Journalism major, 29

K
Kalamazoo College externships,
        77
Kick Start Your Dream Business
    (Wolter), 151
Kiersey Temperament Sorter, 51
The Kolbe Assessment, 52
Kruempelmann, Elizabeth, 77

L
Landes, Michael, 77, 112, 127
Law school, education for, 138
Leads
    developing, 164
    as sources for jobs, 197–198
Learned Optimism (Seligman), 57
Liberal arts majors, 7
Lifelong learning, 134
Life planning, 3–4
Life planning errors
    aspect *vs.* whole dichotomy,
        64–66
    good *vs.* enjoy dichotomy,
        61–62
    vocation *vs.* avocation
        dichotomy, 62–64
Life plan notebooks, 24–25
Life values survey, 42

Location and job search, 189
London, Jack, 62
Lottery, 39
    happiness and winning
        the, 56
Luck, 21

M
Majors, 6–10
    obvious career choices and,
        29–30
Marine Corps service, 80
Marketing communications
    departments, 100
Marketing major, 9
Marriage and happiness, 56–57
Master's degrees, 137
Meaning and happiness, 56
Medical College Admission Test
    (MCAT), 11
Medical school, education for, 138
Microsoft, 45, 62
Military service, 74
    as post-college choice, 80–81
Mistakes, 5. *See also* Life planning
    errors
Mock interviews, 192
Mohamad, Jeff, 77
Money, Meaning, and Choices
    Institute, 56
Mood-O-Meter, 59–60
More Than a Native Speaker: An
    Introduction for Volunteers
    Teaching English Abroad
    (Snow), 77
MOS (military occupational
    specialty), 80
Music major, 7
Myers-Briggs Type Indicator
    (MBTI), 51

N
Nassembly.org, 112
National Assembly, 112
National Association of Col-
    leges and Employers
    (N.A.C.E.), 9, 12
    on alcohol at recruiting
        functions, 222
National Directory of Arts Intern-
    ships, 112
Navy service, 80
Needs, envisioning, 68–73
Networking, 93–106
    creating networking list,
        104–106

etiquette of, 101–103
    important channels for, 97
    information networking,
        93–96
    initial networking contacts
        lists, 103–104
    permission to apply, asking
        for, 102
    planning and, 101
    questions, asking, 99–101
Networking Game, 96–97
Neuromancer (Gibson), 45
New hires, skills of, 9
Newspapers as job source,
    196–197
"No" answers, 181
No-right-answer questions at
    interviews, 215

O
Objects, anticipating and
    overcoming, 177–179
On-campus recruiting, 91, 191–193
Online education, 137
Openness to careers, 13–14
Optimism and happiness, 56–57
Overseas jobs, 77
    English teaching overseas, 77
    foreign languages, studying,
        88–89

P
P.A.A.R.L.A. technique, 206, 213
Parents. *See* Family and parents
Parking lots, behavior in, 210
Paying to learn, 39–40
Peace Corps, 74, 75–76
Peak moments, 57–58
People you admire, listing, 34–35
Permanent placement agencies,
    198–199
Personal best qualities, listing,
    35–36
Personal introductions, value
    of, 169
Pets and happiness, 56
PhD.s, education for, 137, 138
Philosophy majors, 7
Placement model, 12
Poe, Edgar Allan, 133
Portfolio employment, 4–5
Possible career choices list,
    66–68
Post-baccalaureate internships,
    77–79, 121, 127–130
Post-college jobs, 27–28

Powell, Joan, 77
Prescriptive interest tests, 49–50
Presley, Elvis, 133
Prestige, importance of, 39
Pride in choices, 37
Priorities in job search, 188–189
Professional conferences, 135–136
Professionals, contacting, 98
Proust, Marcel, 19
Publishing industry, 93–94

R
Rapid-growth companies, 43–44
Recruiting
    alcohol at recruiting func-
        tion, 222–223
    at career fairs, 193–195
    internal, informal recruiting,
        167–168
    on-campus recruiting, 91,
        191–193
Republican National Commit-
    tee, 78
Researching
    contacts, 173
    for interviews, 204–205
    Resources. *See also* Sources
        for jobs
    for entrepreneurship, 153
    for international careers, 77
    for internships, 111–113
    for post-baccalaureate intern-
        ships, 77
    for teaching English
        overseas, 77
Responsibility and authority, 56
Restaurant interviews, 222
Resume banks, 195–196
Resumes, 162
    writing services, 200
Retirement industry, 46
Retirement plans, asking about,
    219
Rites of Passage (Lucht), 198
The Road to Success Is Paved with
    Failure (Green), 133
Road trips, 81
Rotating contact media, 224–225

S
Salary
    interviews, asking about
        salary at, 219
    and job search, 189
    negotiating, 225–226
Sales, peak moments in, 58

Save the Children, 78
SBA (Small Business Administration), 152
Scams, 199
Screen Actors Guild (SAG), 143
Screening interviews, 221–222
Secrets of job search, 163–165
Self, opinion about, 35–36
Self-discovery, 20
   interest tests and, 50
Self-employment, 4
Self-selecting out, 223–224
Selling with passion, 40
Seminars, 135
Senior projects, 88–90
Seven stages of job search, 185–187
Sex as peak moment, 58
Shadowing, 92
Sheldon, Kenneth, 55–56
Shyness, dealing with, 181
SIC code, 164
Sierra Club San Francisco, 78
Sierra Club Washington, D.C., 78
Signature strengths, 57
Small businesses, 152
Small talk at interviews, 212
Social integration, 74
   internships and, 116
Sources for jobs, 190–200. *See also* Career websites
   career fairs, 193–195
   headhunters, 198–199
   hiring cycles, 193
   Internet career sites, 195–196
   leads as, 197–198
   newspapers, 196–197
   on-campus recruiting, 191–193
   permanent placement agencies, 198–199
   temporary placement agencies, 195
Speech-pathology major, 29
Stages of job search, 185–187
Stanford Business School, 140
Starting the job search, 23–30
Strangers, calling, 177
Strategy for job search, 162–165
StrengthsQuest, 51
Stress interview questions, 215
Strong Interest Inventory (SII), 51
Structure of Intellect (SOI/SI), 51–52
Student debt loads, 18–19

The Student Success Manifesto, 153
Sudden wealth syndrome, 56
Summer jobs. *See also* Internships
   calendar for, 121–127
   job-related experience, obtaining, 120–121
System for Interactive Guidance and Information (SIGI), 52

T

Teachers, education for, 138–139
Teach For America, 76–77
Teaching
   English overseas, 77
   volunteer opportunities, 74–77
Teaching English Abroad (Griffith), 77
Teaching English Overseas: A Job Guide for Americans and Canadians (Mohamad), 77
Telephoning
   follow-up calls, 174
   job possibilities, 172–181
   strangers, 177
Temporary placement agencies, 195
Testing for career interests, 48–52
Thank yous
   for interviews, 219–221
   to networking contacts, 102
   Thirty-six hour rule, 174
Threshold needs, envisioning, 68–73
A Time to Kill (Grisham), 133
Top Five Issues in the World list, 31
Touring after college, 81
Traction in job search, 188
Troubleshooting job search, 184–202
Tvjobs.com/intern, 112
Twain, Mark, 19, 142, 153
Twc.org, 112
Types of jobs, looking for, 165

U

Uncertainty, 10–13
The Undecided College Student (Gordon), 6
U.S. Census Bureau, 140–142

V

Vacation benefits, asking about, 219
Values
   alignment, 40–42
   identification exercise, 37
   life values survey, 42
Visualizing jobs, 171–183
Vocation *vs.* avocation dichotomy, 62–64
Voice mail, getting past, 176–177
Volunteering, 74–77, 107–108
   paid volunteering, 109

W

Waiting, etiquette of, 211
Waiting rooms, behavior in, 210–211
Wal-Mart, 44–45, 62
Walton, Sam, 62
Washington, D.C. internships, 112
Washingtoninternship.com, 112
Watkins, Arthur, 56
Watkins, Clyde, 202
Watson, James, 45
Wealth and happiness, 56
Websites. Visualizing jobs, 171–183
   Vocation *See also* Career websites; Resources
   donaldasher.com/careers, 113
   on internships, 112
The WetFeet Insider Guide to Getting Your Ideal Internship (Assaf & Lurie), 111
What Color Is Your Parachute (Bolles), 167
Work college and work, 6–10
Writing
   apprenticeship for writers, 147
   resume writing services, 200

Y

Young Entrepreneur, 153
Young Entrepreneur's Guide to Starting and Running a Business, 153
Young Entrepreneur's Organization, 153

About the Author

Donald Asher is a nationally known speaker and writer specializing in careers and higher education. He gives over two hundred lectures a year from coast to coast.

Here are some of the sponsors of Asher's events in recent years:

East: Brown, University of Pennsylvania, Penn State, NYU, Oberlin, Babson, Carnegie Mellon, Swarthmore, Case Western Reserve, University of Maryland, Middlebury, Haverford, Bryn Mawr, University of Pittsburgh, Indiana University of Pennsylvania, Hillsdale, Villanova, Ithaca, New England College, Wells, Cedar Crest, Muhlenberg, Dickinson, Rutgers, Gettysburg, Franklin & Marshall, Washington & Jefferson, SUNY Institute of Technology, SUNY Geneseo, SUNY Fredonia, SUNY Stony Brook, SUNY Pottsdam, SUNY Purchase, Post, Providence College, Buffalo State, University at Buffalo, CUNY-Hunter College, Mercy College (New York), Niagara, Ursinus, Skidmore, Lafayette, Moravian, Baldwin-Wallace, Ohio University, University of Dayton, St. John's (Annapolis), Michigan State, University of Tennessee, Davidson, University of North Carolina, Piedmont Virginia Community College, University of Puerto Rico-San Juan, and more.

West: Stanford, Reed, Caltech, Harvey Mudd, Scripps, U.C. Berkeley, U.C. Irvine, U.C. San Diego, U.C. Santa Cruz, U.C. Merced, Cal State-Dominguez Hills, San Jose State, Lewis & Clark, Linfield, University of Santa Clara, Claremont Graduate University, Academy of Art (San Francisco), Azusa Pacific, University of Arizona, University of New Mexico, Portland State, University of Portland, Occidental, University of Colorado, University of Denver, Colorado School of Mines, Central Washington University, University of Alaska-Fairbanks, University of Alaska-Anchorage, University of Texas-Austin, University of Texas-Arlington, Texas A&M University-Kingsville, Texas Tech, Baylor, Abilene Christian University, Texas Christian University, University of San Francisco, San Francisco State, Mills, University of Oregon, Oregon State, Willamette, Whitman, University of Nevada, Brigham Young University-Hawaii, and more.

Midwest/South: University of Chicago, Tulane, Purdue, Indiana University, Washington University in St. Louis, Virginia Tech, Rose-Hulman Institute of Technology, Marquette, University of Wisconsin-Madison, Beloit, Creighton, IUPUI, Concordia (Minnesota), North Dakota State, University of Missouri, University of South Carolina, Babcock, Rhodes, Hendrix, University of Arkansas, Henderson State, Oglethorpe, Earlham, DePauw, DePaul, Wabash, Truman State, Kansas State, Principia, Knox, Albion, Hanover, University of Oklahoma, Harding, Emory, S.M.U., Centre, Transylvania, Murray State, Berea, University of Indianapolis, New College, Florida International University, University of Central Florida, Rockford, Franklin, East Central University (Oklahoma), Jacksonville University, University of Alabama, University of the South (Sewanee), and more.

India: India Institute of Foreign Trade, Birla Institute of Management Technology, Rai Institute, Rayat-Bahra Technology Centre of Excellence-Chandigarh, IESC, IIMT, and more.